STUDYING EARLY AND SILENT CINEMA

STUDYING EARLY AND SILENT CINEMA
BY
KEITH WITHALL

auteur

First published in 2009 as *Early and Silent Cinema: A Teacher's Guide*.
This revised edition published in 2014 by
Auteur, 24 Hartwell Crescent, Leighton Buzzard LU7 1NP
www.auteur.co.uk

Copyright © Auteur Publishing 2009; 2014

Designed and set by Nikki Hamlett at Cassels Design www.casselsdesign.co.uk

Printed and bound by Printondemand-worldwide, Peterboroough, UK

Cover: *Our Hospitality* (1923)

British Library Cataloguing-in-Publication Data
A catalogue record for this book is available from the British Library

ISBN 978-1-906733-69-8 paperback
ISBN 978-1-906733-70-4 cloth
ISBN 978-1-906733-87-2 e-book

CONTENTS

KEITH WITHALL has taught in adult education, FE and HE, and delivered both the pre- and post-2000 A level Film Studies syllabuses, for over twenty years. He developed a particular interest in early and archive film from attending Le Giornate del Cinema Muto and Il Cinema Ritrovato Festivals, starting at Pordenone in 1993. He has a blog dedicated to Early and Silent cinema at hhtp://cinetext.wordpress.com.

Dedication, thanks and acknowledgement

I want to thank the organisers, staff, supporters and participants at Il Giornate del Cinema Muto – Pordenone and Sacile – and also of Il Cinema Ritrovato – Bologna. These are the events at which I have seen most of the silent films I have enjoyed, along with the music, the translations and the film notes and the after-screening discussions.

STILLS INFORMATION

All illustrations courtesy of the Joel Finler Archive, except: *Oliver Twist* (p. 5), *the Lumière brothers* (p. 12), *Le Voyage à travers l'impossible* (p. 17), *The Great Train Robbery* (p. 19), *Our Hospitality* (p. 90), *The Man with a Movie Camera* (p. 110), on the set of *Blackmail* (p. 131), *A Cottage on Dartmoor* (p. 145), BFI Stills; portrait of Oscar Micheaux (p. 124), Barton County Arts Council; *An Unseen Enemy* (pg. 36), *Mad Love* (pg. 61), author's own.

PROLOGUE: WHAT WAS SILENT CINEMA?

Our sense of cinema as a site of commercial entertainment can be traced back to the Lumière brothers. In December 1895 they attracted a fee-paying public in Paris to sit and watch flickering images on an illuminated screen. The commercial Pandora's Box they opened was to blossom in a few years into a world cinema industry and, at its peak, the fantastical Hollywood. Yet in the 30 years in which this miraculous construction was accomplished, audiences rarely had to listen to films, only watch them. Hence, the early decades of cinema were characterised by the title 'silent'. In fact, there was a lot of noise, machinery, audiences, musicians and commentators. Even so, the absence of the human voice and dialogue make the films seem rather strange when viewed by a modern audience.

Equally unfamiliar now are the frequent appearances of title cards imparting dialogue and plot. The screen image was different, commonly in black and white rather than colour. And it was projected in a square frame rather than a letterbox. Yet despite these important differences the mature silent films had many common features with those produced today. The majority related stories, frequently melodramatic and commonly constructed around action. Some of those stories are actually recycled in modern versions. The silent period had epics like *The Fall of Troy*; its own versions of classics like *Romeo and Juliet*[1] or *Oliver Twist*,[2] and any number of documentaries or actualités about the everyday lives of ordinary people. The fictional stories were peopled with heroes, heroines and villains; the most successful portrayed by larger than life icons known as stars. And these stories were constructed around conventions that were learnt by audiences without having to pay particular attention to them – conventions that, to a degree, can still be found in contemporary films.[3]

Oliver Twist (1922)

They still, today, offer unexpected pleasures. Silent film historian Kevin Brownlow, speaking on BBC Radio 4, commented: '*The silent film, actually it's a misnomer, silent sounds as if you're missing something, in fact when you see a silent film, you don't miss the dialogue, and you do not miss the effects. You supply all these. It's rather like watching ballet. You become a creative contributor to it in a way that you don't with a sound film because everything's done for you. That's why I think that people who remember the silent film were so deeply in love with it.*' Most silent films were accompanied by music, frequently a piano, but sometimes a small ensemble or orchestra. The emotional links between the musical themes and the film stories can add immeasurably to their power. The images also come in a number of forms, not just black and white, but with tints, tones and colour. Various techniques were used to achieve colour on early film, including hand-painting the image. And while they lack the audio impact of the sound film, the photographic quality of many silents is superb. Not only had the film-makers mastered the main techniques of photography, but as the industry developed they also added a whole range of techniques for editing and movement. By the 1920s the best films had sophisticated construction and filming which still provide pleasures in their own right.

Our sense of early film owes much to a process of rediscovery that took a qualitative leap in the 1980s. A series of festivals, notably Le Giornate del Cinema Muto in Italy, have provided forums for archivists, collectors and historians which aim to restore the full gamut of silent film viewing. The sadly now defunct Thames Screenings at London Film Festivals and on Channel 4 in the UK provided examples of this in the 1980s and early 1990s. Increasingly, quality silent films can be found in the DVD and Blu-Ray market.

It is not that difficult to make sense of or to enjoy silent films. They offer moments of excitement, suspense and emotional catharsis on a par with modern cinema; and they offer a storehouse where we can study and understand the development of cinema as it is today. There are, however, important points to be made about the presentation of silent film history in this volume. Only about a third of silent film production survives. Much is lost and our knowledge of this scanty. In addition, the keeping of records and commentaries evolved slowly in the early industry, so there is much that scholars do not know or are uncertain about. There is often a lack of consensus about how and where the industry developed. This is particularly true of the earliest periods, where fresh research is continually uncovering more information.

Even allowing that only a partial record and archive survives, silent cinema is a vast area. Because the US-based Hollywood became the dominant sector of the industry, this is treated in greater detail. A large amount of space has been devoted to our own British films. Other countries have been included because of their importance, for example, the French pioneers or the Italian film-makers of epics. And certain countries and films have been included because they are accessible on DVD and Blu-Ray. Early Russian cinema is an example of this. Some countries are missing because there is little opportunity to see them. There is to date very little material from Latin America and, while there were Egyptian silent films in the 1920s, unfortunately I have yet to see one of these.

Affluent, white men from North America and Europe dominate this history. This reflects the class, gender and geographical dominance in the industry from its earliest days. There are a few important female directors in this period: Alice Guy in France, Lois Weber in the USA, Esfir Shubb (also known as 'Esther') in Soviet cinema and Germaine Dulac with the French avant-garde.[4] In the western industries there is only one black director who achieved note, Oscar Micheaux. The situation is better in the craft areas. Women were often prominent as editors and writers: the successful sound film director Dorothy

Arzner started out in editing; and Frances Marion was one of a number of important women writers for Hollywood in the teens and twenties. Women do stand out in the world of stars, both in the USA and Europe. And successful stars were powerful: Lillian Gish had control over her scripts and her-co-stars in the 1920s, while Mary Pickford actually ran the company producing her films. But black actors had little opportunity, even so charismatic a performer as Paul Robeson could only achieved worthwhile roles outside the mainstream industry.

The working class members of the commercial film world were always overshadowed by the affluent and powerful figures that headed the industry. Many of these came from working class backgrounds; Charlie Chaplin's poverty stricken childhood is a constant reference in his films. But, at the top of the industry, they soon became rich and, if not bourgeois, then at least petit bourgeois. The working class viewpoint is only to be found outside the mainstream, usually in oppositional films like those made in the Soviet Union or in the films made by Labour organisations.

The same difficulty confronts our image of film-makers in the world beyond the North-Atlantic states. Other countries had moving images before Europe and North America. Shadow puppets in Asia are one example. But commercial moving images were tied to the industrialised processes dominated by the west. So it was exported to other regions along with other manifestations of western dominance like the railway. It was then taken up and developed indigenously in many places. There were a rich variety of films all round the world. Many of these have not survived. Both then and now they rarely have the distribution or attention provided for Hollywood or European films. This is still true today in terms of access to screenings, and to DVD and Blu-Ray. One of the virtues of the silent film festivals is that they have opened a limited access to these movies.

The chronology followed is similar to that followed by recognised textbooks. Especially in the earliest decades there were developments taking place simultaneously in a number of countries and at a great pace. Any division is artificial, but at least has the merit of relating to the materials and readings that are available on the subject.

FOOTNOTES

1. There are numerous silent versions of this Shakespeare play: they include the earliest in 1900 in France: three more made in 1908 alone, in the UK, USA and Italy; and as a star vehicle with Theda Bara in 1916.

2. There was a short film featuring Mr Bumble in 1898. There were at least eight more adaptations before the 1922 Hollywood version, which starred the young Jackie Coogan as Oliver and Lon Chaney as Fagin. This film is featured on the BFI *Dickens Before Sound* DVD.

3. Early film usually had an aspect ratio (the ratio of the horizontal to vertical dimensions) of 1.33:1. With sound film, in accommodating the optical track, the ratio changed slightly to 1.37:1. Modern ratios are usually widescreen, 1.85:1 or anamorphic, 2.35:1.

4. The *More Treasures from American Film Archives* DVD set includes *Falling Leaves* (12 min., 1912) by Alice Guy Blaché. Guy was the leading director for the French Gaumont Studio and later worked in the USA for the Solax Company. Overall, Blaché made almost one thousand films, a staggering number by any standard.

I. THE BIRTH OF CINEMA

The Praxinoscope Theatre, a moving picture device of 1880.

INTRODUCTION

This section deals with the technical and inventive basis for cinema, and briefly describes the important pioneers. It covers the developments prior to the invention of cinema and the first decade of its development, 1895 to 1905, approximately. This is a distinct period in film, sometimes characterised by the term 'primitives and pioneers'. Not all scholars are happy with the term primitive. The films seem simple compared with the complexities of late silent features, but they are also sophisticated in their own way. The screening of a good quality copy of a Méliès' film would emphasise this point of view.

The films of this period operate on a different basis from the feature story film that has dominated most of cinema history. Tom Gunning (1995), the US scholar, calls it a 'cinema of attractions'. It had as much in common with a visit to the fair or the music hall as to the story telling Victorian theatre. The latter was a prime influence for the later narrative developments in cinema.

There are three clear avenues for study: firstly, the technology itself. Some of the heavily illustrated histories are helpful here. Even better a visit to a venue like the UK's National Media Museum, based in Bradford, Yorkshire (there is film material in several of the galleries, and there are also the Special Collections, which hold early cinematic material). Another possible resource would be a local or regional film archive.

A second area is technique and language. A number of the recommended textbooks discuss film form and style in considerable detail. Equally important would be access to a variety of the films. There are now a number of good collections on Blu-Ray and DVD.

In some ways the most interesting area of study is the idea of the 'cinema of attractions'.

Gunning's ideas are stimulating, and a number of other writers have developed this approach. There is scope for a cross-medium and cross-cultural approach, including photography, the fair ground, the music hall and other popular entertainment mediums. It should be clear that even though these early films are not strictly narratives in the accustomed sense, they are full of opportunities for the study of representations and value systems. For example, the different versions of *The Kiss in the Tunnel,* raise issues around gender, sexuality and moral codes of behaviour. There are also issues of 'race' as one Edison version has the man mistakenly kissing the lady's black maid in the darkness. Both women see this as funny but also shaming.[1] This sort of 'joke' has a long life in popular cinema, lasting well beyond the silent era.

I. THE DEVELOPMENT OF THE TECHNOLOGY OF SILENT CINEMA

Cinema grew out of a number of nineteenth century developments and inventions. Foremost among these was photography. This technological and artistic innovation appeared in the 1840s. By the 1890s it was widespread, and its uses included both scientific and commercial activities. It offered a way of producing life-like images of the world around us and of people's activities within it. In 1888 George Eastman started marketing the new Kodak camera, a simple device for producing still images from a paper roll. Quickly a flexible celluloid film replaced the paper roll. This was a key development in mass photography.

Cinema was to add movement and projection to these. The illusion of motion for the human eye, produced by a rapid succession of still images, was explored and researched in the nineteenth century. A succession of still images created the appearance of movement. The lower limit to this perception was about 14 images or frames per second. There were a variety of toys and scientific devices that produced such phenomena.

An exhibition system had developed for the Magic Lantern shows. Glass slides were optically projected and displayed on a large screen.[2] They could be fantastical, both in content and style. And voice narration and/or music frequently accompanied them. There was even a sophisticated system, the Praxinoscope, built by the Frenchman Émile Reynaud, which produced movement on the screen.

Some of the key inventors in cinematic development were:

- Eadweard Muybridge (1878). He used 12 cameras to record the movement of a running horse. He later projected copies using a type of Magic Lantern combined with a rotation device to create the illusion of movement.

- Étienne Jules Marey (1882). He used a photographic gun to record bird flight. In 1888 he used paper film to record motion. He developed an intermittent mechanism that was necessary to produce the series of still images that could mimic movement.

- Augustin Le Prince (1888). He used Kodak paper rolls to record very short films. One was of the bridge in Leeds City Centre.

2. THE PIONEERS OF THE NEW MEDIUM

In the 1880s and 90s there were a number of experimenters and inventors working towards some type of moving photographic images. But two names are key in the successful delivery of such an apparatus. In the United States, Thomas Edison was a noted inventor. He had already produced the light bulb and the phonograph. However, Edison's importance was really as an entrepreneur, exploiting the inventions developed by his paid technicians. His assistant W. K. L. Dickson was the key person in the actual developments. He used Kodak celluloid film, produced in 35mm filmstrips, to develop a camera that could record a series of images. Crucially though, Edison exploited this on a commercial basis in the form of a peep show, the Kinetoscope. Only one person at a time could view the moving images.

A Kinetoscope 'parlor' was opened in New York in April 1894. The 'parlor' had 10 machines costing $250 apiece. A ticket at 25 cents entitled the customer to view five machines in a row, each containing a filmstrip of between 30 and 40 feet in length. Many of these were shot in the Black Maria film studio built in 1893. The 10 debut films, including well-known performers and topical interests, were: *Sandow, Horse Shoeing, Barber Shop, Bertholdi (Mouth Support), Wrestling, Bertholdi (Table Contortions), Blacksmiths, Highland Dance, Trapeze* and *Roosters*.

Edison set up a syndicate to exploit the invention and in their first years the 'parlors' were very successful. They were also marketed abroad where they provided technological inspiration for other inventors. But they were to be overtaken and rendered redundant by just such technological developments.

The Lumière brothers, Louis and Auguste, brought the idea of the cinematic projection to fruition. They used Magic Lantern technology to produce a projection from a film camera. And on a key date in cinema history, 28 December 1895, in a Paris cafe, they charged patrons one franc to view a 25 minute selection of short films with musical accompaniment. Thus, cinema arrived, both as a projected display and a commercial entertainment. It is worth noting that the Lumière's had already given displays earlier in the year to scientific and commercial groups. Also, two brothers, Max and Emil Skladanowsky, had given a public screening of film in Berlin in November 1895. Their system was called the Bioskop.[3] However, it was cumbersome and much less efficient than the Cinématographe of the Lumière Brothers.[4] There was also a screening of *Boxing Films* by the Latham Brothers in New York in May 1895 using a system called the Eidoloscope.

The Lumière brothers

Both Edison and the Lumières were successful entrepreneurs, with established businesses, access to capital and the power to expropriate others' labour power. Dickson, however, is the actual inventor of the key element of the cinematic machine. He is the person who set the frame at 35mm, a size that has lasted over a century. But Edison owned the copyright. When Dickson moved to the rival Biograph firm he had to develop a camera that was clearly of different design from that which he had produced for Edison. Equally, the smiling workers we see in the early Lumière film *La Sortie des usines* (1895) actually produced the equipment that made that film. But its ownership and control were vested in the Lumières.

The new invention spread and developed rapidly. The Lumières themselves recruited a team of operators who toured France and abroad, filming and then exhibiting in rented theatres and cafes. The expanding nineteenth century transport industry (immortalised in Jules Verne's *Around the World in 80 Days*) enabled them to trek far afield. In 1896 Lumière cameramen screened moving film for first-time audiences in (among others) Australia, Belgium, Brazil, Britain, China, Czechoslovakia, Egypt, India, Mexico, Russia and Spain. Predominantly the Lumières produced what became known as actualités, records of actual places and events.

Another French director, Georges Méliès, was a key person in developing cinema as a site for tricks, spectacle and stories. Méliès worked as a magician in his own Théâtre Robert-Houdin. He soon incorporated many of the tricks and effects from his theatrical work in his short films. He perfected the simple technique of stop motion to create fantastic moments on film, making people appear and disappear, change shape and transporting them to strange locations. He used his theatre as a small studio, and generated places and settings through flats and props. His visually richest films were often in hand-tinted colour, like *Le Voyage à travers l'impossible* (1904).[5]

Cinema developed initially in Europe. Film-makers in France and Britain were among the important pioneers. Two key film-makers in the UK were R. W. Paul and Bert Acres.[6] They built their own cameras, copied from the Edison model. Acres commenced shooting film in 1895, including a record of the Derby (only rediscovered a few years ago). There were also two film-makers in Brighton, G. A. Smith and James Williamson. One of Smith's films was *The Miller and the Sweep* (1898), a simple joke performed by an established music hall artist; another was *Mary Jane's Mishap* (1903), a sardonic piece with quite sophisticated editing.

The most famous name in the UK was to be that of Cecil Hepworth. He first worked with Magic Lantern shows; then, from 1896, he produced and toured his own films. He also published the first technical manual on film-making in 1897. Two of his early films feature motor car accidents, a popular gag in these early years. His later *Rescued by Rover* (1905)[7] is a seminal film in which the family dog is key to the rescue of a kidnapped baby.

One popular type of film was the 'supposedly factual record'. Méliès produced a film about the notorious Dreyfus Affair in France, using stock footage. A British film-maker, J. Williamson, produced *Attack on a Chinese Mission* (1900)[8]. This showed western Christian missionaries under attack by armed (and stereotypical) Chinese during the Boxer rebellion. It was actually filmed in Williamson's own garden starring his family members. *A Révolution en Russie* (*Revolution in Odessa*, 1905) appears to be a Pathé newsreel about the events in Odessa in 1905. These events were later to be dramatised in the Soviet *The Battleship Potemkin* (1925). The Pathé newsreel is obviously a recreation, though it is not clear whether contemporary audiences were fooled by these reconstructions. And increasingly cameramen did venture far afield for actual footage. The Boer War in southern Africa was recorded on both photographic and cinematographic film.

3. THE EARLY FILM AND FILM SHOW

These first primitive films were only strips of celluloid running for less than a minute.[9] Gradually the strips became longer, finally settling at the length of a reel or 1000 feet. The running time depended on the speed of projection. Early machines were hand-cranked. The consensus is that early films were cranked at around 14 to 16 frames per second. A reel would last approximately 15 minutes or less. The film-makers sold these completed films to the distributors, or exchanges, by the foot. This enabled exhibitors to fit the films to their programmes, and the films were often pruned, edited or even combined for exhibition. It would seem that exhibitors had as much or even a greater influence on what audiences saw in this period than the actual filmmakers. Certainly the programme context was of their making. Prints were also frequently re-used by competitors in copies and remakes. Thus, the lack of copyright enforcement was a major problem for the copyright holders in early cinema.

Exhibitors often had someone adding narrative information from alongside the screen. In fairgrounds and similar venues they were known as 'Barkers'.[10] Very soon film-makers developed the technique of inserting cards that bore information about the plot and captions indicating dialogue. Such title cards (Intertitles) enabled more complex information to be provided for audiences. However, many audiences were virtually illiterate and the cards had to be read out for them by other members of the audience. One revealing remark by an early audience member was that 'you could not take your eyes off the screen' or you missed important information (recalled in the *People's Century* BBC TV programme).

Early projection had a pronounced 'flicker', one popular name for the movies. The flicker stemmed from the technology of projection. This included a mechanism that 'interrupted' illumination between each frame of film. An early improvement was the four-bladed Maltese Cross that increased the shut-off to three for each frame. This virtually eliminated the flicker. A US invention, the Latham Loop, relieved the tension on film rolls, enabling films longer than three minutes to be screened uninterruptedly. The Latham Loop was a key patent in the struggles in the US film industry around 1910–12.

The early film stock was nitrate celluloid, which was combustible, as indeed were some of the components used in the projectors, such as ether. In 1897 in Paris a fire broke out at a screening, killing about 125 people. Although this one of the worst, similar incidents were not infrequent in the early days of exhibition and tended to discourage more affluent audiences from patronising the new medium.

Early film shows were frequently part of a combined entertainment in music halls, fairs and side shows. Their main audience was the working classes, especially in the urban environments. Early films are a combination of spectacle, jokes, shocks and very simple stories. Audiences did not pay to see a feature film story, they paid to see entertainment. Rather than seeing the movie, they visited the Biograph, the Cinematograph, the nickelodeon, moving pictures and any number of names for a variable experience. These appealed to the novelty and wonder the medium inspired, which many entrepreneurs thought would quickly lose its appeal.

STUDY FILM: THE FIRST LUMIÈRE PUBLIC SCREENING

This is probably the definitive moment for cinema in the sense that we have come to understand it. The two brothers hired a room at the Grand Café on the Boulevard des Capucines in Paris where approximately 35 customers paid to watch a programme of 10 films, lasting about 25 minutes in total.

The programme of films, each 50 feet in length, was as follows (as presented in a recreation of the first Lumière show at the 1995 Il Cinema Ritrovato): *La Sortie des usines Lumière a Lyon* (*Workers Leaving the Lumière Factory*); *La Voltige* (*Horseback*

Jumping); *La Pêche aux poissons rouges* (Fishing for Goldfish); *Le Débarquement du Congrès de Photography à Lyon* (*Arrivée des Congressistes à Neuville-sur-Saône / Debarkation of Photographic Congress Members at Lyon*); *Les Forgerons* (The Blacksmiths); *Le Jardinier* (*L'Arroseur arrosé / A Little Trick on the Gardener*); *Le Repas* (*Repas de bébé / Feeding the Baby*); *Le Saut à la couverture* (Blanket Toss); *La Place des Cordeliers à Lyon* (The Place des Cordeliers at Lyon); *La Mer* (The Sea).[11]

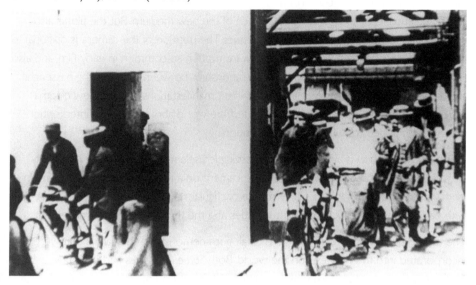

La Sortie des usines Lumiere a Lyon

Films and film programmes were re-arranged and reused, often produced in new and slightly different versions, as the Lumières developed their business and catalogue. Hence, titles, and dates, of films can vary in the literature.

The Lumière brothers owned and ran a photographic company, making them well equipped for the new technology. There is clear evidence of the influence of photographic techniques in early cinema in the way the camera is positioned as if for still portraits and scenes. It took a considerable period before film-makers developed techniques for moving the camera, both between and within shots. This does appear rather surprising in retrospect, but possibly stems from this photographic influence.

Film-makers and audiences were intensely aware of the novelty of movement from the various pre-cinematic devices discussed earlier. However, film offered a consistent, fairly convincing and finely detailed record of all sorts of movements. Salt remarks (BFI *Early Cinema* DVD) how audiences were fascinated, not just by the movement of characters, but also by little details like the moving leaves in *Le Repas*.

While the early films appear as mere records of events, they are more complex than that. *La Sortie des usines* includes not just the factory workers responding to the presence of the camera but a narrative structure as the sequence's opening and closure are signalled

STUDYING EARLY AND SILENT CINEMA

through the use of the factory gates. *Le Jardinier* is the first exhibition of a fictional film. The staging is carefully organised so that the action is clear and central for the viewer.

The BFI disc also includes later films, some of which were attributed to the first screening. The most famous is *Arrivée d'un train en gare à La Ciotat*. The shot of an approaching train gave rise to stories of audiences jumping up in fear of the expected crash. Whether this actually occurred is uncertain, but it certainly fed into contemporary tales and films about audience fears and gullibility in the face of the new medium. But the film is also interesting in terms of its staging and techniques. The position of the camera is diagonal to the oncoming locomotive, enabling the forward motion so common in early film, and also allowing a crossing of space and changing relationships between train, waiting passenger and audience. Thus, it is apparent from its earliest manifestations that the new cinema provided not an innocent and realist record of the world about us, but an intervention presented to audiences with deliberate positioning.

This play with motion is also apparent in *Leaving Jerusalem by Railway*. Here is an early technique for illustrating motion: placing the camera on a moving platform. A similar film from Venice used a gondola as platform. The particular format was extremely popular with early audiences, leading to phantom rides and the thrills of excessive movement.

The other titles from the early Lumière catalogues demonstrate the values that were incorporated into this new eye on the world. Both *Sortie des usines* and *Le Repas* replicate a class structured view of the world, with bourgeois relationships dominant. *Le Jardinier* demonstrates the paternalism of the period.

The Lumière camera, the Cinématographe (writing in movement), operated as both camera and projector. This simplicity of design aided the brothers in developing their business. Cameramen were employed at home and abroad, and were able to film on the spot and then project to paying audiences. The growing Lumière catalogue constituted over 2000 titles by 1903. An important factor in the Lumière success was their position as established businessmen with ready access to capital. Thus, they were able to carry the costs of research and development as they established their new venture. The bulk of the catalogue were actualités, which were records of real-life events as they happened. The Lumières are often seen as the founders of what we call realism: moving images of a world that we recognise and assume is more or less accurately recorded.

STUDY FILM: LE VOYAGE À TRAVERS L'IMPOSSIBLE

France 1904. Running time 24 minutes.

Directed by Georges Méliès.

The BFI *Early Cinema* disc has an extract of 157 feet from a film made in 1904 that apparently ran in full for 20 minutes; about three times the length of the extract. It is

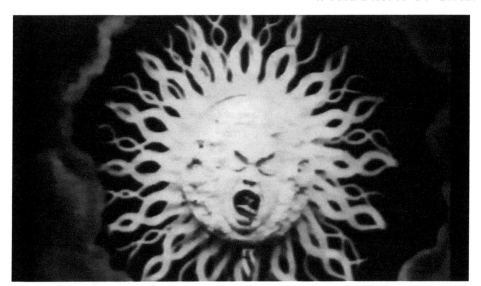

typical of Méliès' films in its combination of cinematic tricks and fantastical narrative. The colour was added by hand-painting the film frame by frame. This was relatively expensive but the exotic effects were popular with audiences.

Méliès brought theatrical experience to the new medium rather as the Lumières brought photographic experience to it. After a fairly varied employment career Méliès used an inheritance to buy the Théâtre Robert-Houdin and develop it as a venue for stage magic and illusion. When the Lumière screenings started Méliès was immediately excited at their potential. He purchased a camera from the UK inventor R. S. Paul and commenced making short (20 metre) films. He soon graduated from actualités to the type of illusion and fantasy represented by *Voyage…. Impossible*. The story is told how his camera jammed whilst filming a street scene; when restarted, the film included an unwitting edit. One version tells how a horse and a cart magically disappeared. In fact, Edison had already used edits in one of his films and Méliès may have learnt of the technique from viewing this. However, it provided the basis for his successful specialisation. He set up Star Films to sell his productions and in 1896 constructed Europe's first specialised film studio. His films became immensely popular, both in France and abroad. Film-makers elsewhere clearly learnt from and copied his techniques. Pirated copies became a particular problem, and in 1903 he opened a New York Office to protect his copyright and distribute the films. His output fell off around 1907. This was the point at which large scale film companies like Pathé and Gaumont were developing and expanding. The style of films was developing and the costs were increasing. Méliès did not have the capital to compete with the new large companies. In 1911 he was forced to take loans from Pathé and a few years later they acquired his business. Méliès is considered the father of fantasy film, and one view argues that this provided a separate strand in cinema from the Lumière actualité approach.

Méliès does share some techniques with the Lumière brothers. The film is basically a series of long shots, with the action more or less centred in the frame. But he develops a quite sophisticated narrative through the sequencing of the action. A key technique is the editing together of separate shots to construct this narrative: Méliès cuts from one shot to another to develop temporal and spatial changes; he cuts between shots to produce trick effects that defy realism; and, in a couple of places, Méliès uses a dissolve between shots, i.e. one frame fades into another, for a more subtle transformation.

The most important element in the film is the *mise-en-scène*, that is, the staging. Most of Méliès' effects stem from his theatrical background. So we get the use of flats, including moving fields, mattes and masks, and the superimposition on backgrounds. These were all effects that Méliès had been able to produce in the theatre prior to taking up film-making. His ability to cut between these differing effects produces both the surprise and fantasy of the film.

FOOTNOTES

1. The use of black faces for 'comic effect' was widespread and long lasting. A 1925 German film, *When A Filmcutter Blunders*, includes an edit where instead of the star Lil Dagover, the audience sees a black African woman breast feeding her baby. The extract features in the *Cinema Europe* series (see resources).

2. There is an example of a fairly sophisticated lantern slide show with a narration on *Dickens Before Sound*. Additionally, the *Screening the Poor 1888–1914* DVDs contain several Magic Latern shows with music and commentaries.

3. 'Bioscope' was an alternative title for film for a period and graced the masthead of an important British trade paper.

4. Lumière titles from the first exhibition are featured on the BFI *Early Cinema Primitives and Pioneers* DVD.

5. This film was a version of his earlier *Voyage dans la lune*. An extract, of 157 feet, showing both the effects and the fine colour tinting of the film is included on the BFI DVD *Early Cinema*. Lobster Films recently discovered and have restored the 1902 hand-coloured *Le Voyage dans la lune* and at the time of writing is planning to release a digital print and DVD/Blu-Ray.

6. There is a BFI DVD collection of films by R. W. Paul, including a booklet and accompanying audio commentary. Both *The Miller and The Sweep* and *Mary Jane's Mishap* are included on the BFI DVD *Early Cinema*, with other examples of their early films.

7. A number of the films of Hepworth, including a version of *Rescued by Rover* are included on the *Early Cinema* DVD.

8. *Attack on a Chinese Mission* and *Revolution in Odessa* are on *Early Cinema volume II*.

9. For well into the 1920s cameras and projectors were handcranked. Brownlow notes how the film speed would vary for both comic effect and dramatic moments (1968, p. 243). In the first two decades of the twentieth century handcranking was usually at 16 frames per second (fps), in the 1920s it gradually increased to 20, 22 then 24 or even 26. The spread of motorised projectors helped standardise speeds.

10. Recent research, including by Graham Petrie for his articles on the DVD Silent Dickens, suggest that narrators were still quite common at screenings up until the teens.

11. Three of these films feature on the BFI Early Cinema DVD, with comment from the film historian Barry Salt. Salt has conducted detailed studies of the techniques found in early film. His books are the most detailed studies of technique in early cinema.

2. THE GROWTH OF AN INDUSTRY

The Great Train Robbery

INTRODUCTION

The second decade of cinema runs approximately from 1905 to the start of World War
I in 1914. This period sees the establishment of an industrial organisation for film, both in
Europe and the USA. The development of the industry involves two key concepts in film
studies: vertical and horizontal integration. Essentially, as the industry developed and firms
grew larger they attempted to exert ever greater control on the market. The key was
exhibition, which is where the actual money from admissions was made.

Both France and the USA are interesting models for study in this development, and each
has distinctive features. The study should include as many of the key factors that enabled
this growth in monopoly. These include the development of the dedicated film theatre,
the introduction of a rental system and the developments in programming and film form.
Also, there is the rich area of stardom.

Film theatres have their own scholars. There are several well-produced and richly
illustrated volumes on cinemas. Distribution and rental systems are trickier. This involves
not only the carriage and hire of the film, but also questions of enforcing copyright. If
students examine the frames of early film they can often identify the company logo (e.g.
'B' for Biograph). Also, as noted in the text, changes in distribution affected exhibition. One
key development was the increased standardisation of product as films and programmes
were provided complete to the exhibitors. This development could be studied with that
of the producer's involvement in exhibition and vertical integration. Horizontal integration
is another important issue. If you can obtain the material (Low, 1948, or Dickinson, 1985,
for example), British cinema is an interesting topic.

This is an instructive period for studying the development of film form. The key focus would be narrative style, as the cinema developed its grasp and presentation of the story film. It is possible to make comparisons between the way that different films handle narrative. Early films like *Rescued by Rover* or *The Great Train Robbery* are really useful. D. W. Griffith is a key film-maker in these developments and many of his films are accessible on DVD. Between 1908 and 1914 it is possible to study his development and innovations as the films increase in sophistication.

There is real scope for students to explore technique and style in this period. Close study of the films offers examples of different techniques and it is possible to compare and contrast films across the period. There is also scope for judging the meanings and values exemplified in such films. Griffith's films includes stereotypes and representations across whole classes and peoples.

There is also the potential to examine the development of genre in films of this period. Several examples mentioned above are clearly embryonic genre movies. Griffith's vast output includes early examples of nearly all of the successful Hollywood genres of later periods. In addition, there is the study of the emergence of the star system in both the USA and Europe. Included in the recommended books is information about particularly successful individuals, such as Mary Pickford.

Finally, this is the period that sees the establishment of the film centre Hollywood. Several of the books discuss this in detail. Finler's *The Hollywood Story* (revised 2003) has a mass of dates, names and places that are important in this period, offering scope for a study that can be pursued beyond the silent era.

I. THE EARLY EUROPEAN FILM INDUSTRY

Despite fears that it would be a short-lived attraction the new film medium developed and thrived. From about 1905 entrepreneurs were confident enough to develop dedicated film theatres. These were most frequently converted shops or similar. In Britain they were known as the penny-gaff and in the USA as the nickelodeon. Early theatres were cheap and crowded, emphasising the medium's working class appeal and frightening off more affluent patrons. Later the building of more grandiose theatres provided venues that did attract a middle class audience. The dedicated theatres enabled the repetition of film programmes. This was one factor in the increasing length of films.

The early production, distribution and exhibition sectors were cottage industries. However, the complexities of film production led quickly to the development of larger units. As we have seen, the Lumière brothers owned and ran a large photographic company. In Britain, Bamforth and Company, an established lantern slide and picture post card firm, took up film-making in 1899, as did the Sheffield Photographic Company.[1]

Bamforth's films were clearly successful and they developed their film techniques and created popular characters. Their *The Kiss in the Tunnel* (1899) is an early example of editing being used to cross space on screen. Bamforth's was a family business, and its production work was fairly dependent on the family and the local population. Their later films did use a professional troupe of players rather than the earlier semi-professional approach. The firm dropped out of film production in 1910, restarted this in 1912 and then finally gave up to concentrate on picture post cards in 1915. The reasons for these decisions are not completely clear, but a small family firm with limited capital was less able to compete in the developing industry of the teens. And Hollywood films, with more developed continuity and productions values, were beginning to dominate the UK market.

It was in France that the first development of a proper industrial organisation occurred. Pathé Frères was formed in 1895 to exploit both phonographs and film. In 1902 the firm constructed a glass-sided studio for film-making. The business expanded and opened offices for overseas sales: one of its key markets was in Russia where it dominated cinema for some years. This broad reach across the world industry gave it horizontal (or geographic)[2] integration and made it a key international company. Pathé was also the first firm to effectively achieve vertical integration. This describes control across the industry in production, distribution and exhibition. Pathé not only produced films but also film cameras and film stock. Then, in 1906, it began buying up film theatres. In 1907 it set up a rental distribution network to replace the earlier sales system. This development quickly spread. It increased the control of producers and renters over the product, and also gave greater copyright protection. For a time Pathé was the largest film company in the world, marketing not only its own films but those of other companies. Pathé's main French rival was Gaumont, which followed a similar path of development and expansion.

A key contributor to the rise of the Gaumont Company was Alice Guy. She started as a secretary at the Company in 1894 and became the key person as it developed its new cinematic arm:

> A truly transnational figure, pioneer Alice Guy was at the forefront of international, technological, industrial and cultural changes that defined cinema as the new popular form of mass-media entertainment in the twentieth-century. Her long impressive career comprises the novelty period through to the single-reel film and the nickelodeon era – to the multi-reel feature and photoplay of the mid to late teens. Not only was Guy the first woman to direct films, she also wrote, produced, supervised and distributed films. (Kim Tomadjoglou, writing in the 2011 *Il Cinema Ritrovato* catalogue)

Guy was head of production at Gaumont until 1907. Then she moved to the USA, where she married (becoming Alice Guy Blaché). There she operated her own studio Solax, and directed one and two-reel features.

Her earliest films are the typical short 100 metre actualités. A panorama of the Seine in Paris: *Exposition Universelle* (1900); a military manoeuvre in *Charge À La Baïonette d'un Regiment de Ligne* (1899); *La Marâtre* (*The Stepmother*, 1906, 8 minutes) is a short drama with a focus on children, a recurring theme in Guy's films. Her US films are generally longer: *Falling Leaves*, (1912, tinted, 13 minutes at 16fps) presents another child story; a young girl tries to save her sister from dying 'before the last leaf falls' by tying leaves back on to a tree. *Dick Whittington and His Cat* (1913, 37 minutes) recounts the classic tale of the young man who makes good.

Other European countries were developing their film-making industries. But the market in film was international. To circulate in other countries all that was required was the substitution of intertitles in the host language. Different language versions could be made merely by changing title cards and other shots with printed or written information. As the technique developed prints were exported without full intertitles, often only including 'flash titles', which indicated the place and the information necessary for new cards. There was an added economic benefit here, as import duties were charged per foot, and the deleted titles cut down costs. Thus, the French strength was based on capturing a large part of other markets: in Russia it was estimated to control 50 per cent by 1910.

2. THE RISE OF THE US FILM INDUSTRY

Thomas Edison built the first film studio in New Jersey (Black Maria) for the filming of his Kinetoscope reels. And when projected film arrived he both engaged with the new technology and tried to control it through the patents and the law courts. There were already significant profits to be made. Very early on the United States emerged as the largest market in world cinema. It had a large population, and urban areas were expanding rapidly with the influx of migrants from overseas. It soon had more film theatres per head of population that any other country.

In 1902 the first US film exchange opened in San Francisco. Prior to this, exhibitors ordered from the producer's catalogue by mail, buying films at so much per foot. The exchange bought the film from the producers and then rented it out to exhibitors. The San Francisco Miles Exchange charged one fourth of the purchase cost for a rental. This was extremely profitable for the exchanges but also much more businesslike for exhibitors. By about 1907 there were around 150 exchanges serving the whole country.

The exchanges and the introduction of a rental system were important factors in a new style exhibitor. In 1905 a Pittsburgh storeroom was turned into a purposely-furnished film theatre. It offered seating for a hundred, and an admission price of five cents (a nickel). The price inspired its name: the nickelodeon. After two weeks capacity houses were producing profits of a $1,000 a week.

From here the nickelodeon developed as a dedicated theatre for film shows. It appears these usually seated up to a maximum of 200 patrons. This avoided the theatre tax charged on larger venues. They ran all day and up to midnight. They spread rapidly in urban areas and by 1910 it is estimated there were 10,000 of these theatres across

Edison's Black Maria Studio

the United States. Their spread generated intense competition, both from indigenous entrepreneurs and from overseas companies. The more productive European companies soon established New York offices to protect and market their films.

The issues surrounding patents and copyright were extremely important in the developing US industry. Thomas Edison tried to make different companies pay him royalties on the grounds that his ownership of the original invention meant all models were derived from his patent. He used the courts again and again to chase down competitors. Two of his key competitors were American Mutoscope & Biograph, and Vitagraph. Biograph won their lawsuit with Edison, whilst Vitagraph made a deal with him. However, in 1907 Edison, on appeal, won a further victory. The ruling declared that all manufacturers of cameras, with the exception of Biograph, had to pay Edison royalties. There followed a chaotic period of rivalry between these two major firms and their many smaller competitors. In 1908 a truce led to the creation of the Motion Picture Patents Company (The Trust), including Edison, Biograph, Vitagraph, Essanay and Lubin, whose founder, Sigmund Lubin, had been an early competitor of Edison (his company was founded in 1897) supplying material for the peep-show arcades (Finler, 1992, p. 67). The MPPC also took steps towards vertical integration by obtaining an agreement with Eastman Kodak to only sell its film stock to members. This enabled them to charge a weekly fee to theatres for the right to exhibit member's films. They also addressed horizontal integration by setting limits on the import of foreign films, which at this point still dominated the US market.

This oligopoly was soon confronted by new entrants to the industry. These independents objected to or avoided paying fees to the MPPC. Theatres that declined to join the fee-paying system of the MPPC provided outlets for their products. This cat and mouse battle between the MPPC and independents carried on for a number of years. Edison famously used the Pinkerton Detective Agency, featured in many US film dramas, to hunt down those not in compliance. In 1915 the MPPC suffered a setback under US Anti-Trust legislation (the equivalent of Britain's anti-monopoly laws). By then, however, another oligopoly was developing in Hollywood.

3. EARLY FILM NARRATIVE AND STYLE

As already discussed, the first film shows offered a spectacle to audiences, Gunning's 'cinema of attractions'. The idea of movement before their eyes was a new and exciting novelty for audiences. Some exhibitors opened the show with a projected still frame and then commenced moving pictures in order to increase the impact. There are stories told of audiences reacting with horror and fear at the onward rush of a locomotive in L'Arrivée d'un train en gare à La Ciotat (1985)[3]. An early skit on watching films used this tale as the basis for The Countryman and the Cinematograph (1901). The onscreen approaching train frightens the rustic. The way that such innovations were copied (duped) and spread can be seen with the remake made by the US film-maker Edwin Porter, Uncle Josh at the Moving Picture Show (1902).

Another incident common in early films was The Kiss in the Tunnel (1899) played to a voyeuristic appeal. The British example by George Albert Smith (there were French and US versions) was distributed by The Warwick Trading Company who suggested in their catalogue that the sequence be joined to what was known as a 'phantom ride'.[4] The latter was a moving shot, with the camera usually placed on the front of the engine, offering audiences both the excitement of strange panoramas and the sensation of movement.

Along with movement colour was an important part of the 'cinema of attractions'. Early films were often hand coloured or hand painted. Although a complex and relatively expensive process, the results were inspiring. The Georges Méliès' film, Le Voyage à travers l'impossible (1904), demonstrates the added attraction that appealed so much to audiences.

As the industry developed two particular sets of techniques became conventional: tinting and toning. In the former, the whole frame was coloured; in the latter, lighter parts of the frame remain transparent. The colours used had conventional meanings for audiences: sepia for daytime, blue for night, green for rural scenes, amber for interior lighting, and red for fires and passion. Quite often important information was imparted through the colour scheme. For example, in a blue coloured scene the action was at night, which meant characters could not see objects which might still be visible to the audience. There is a famous scene in a US film, The Lonedale Operator (1911),[5] where the heroine wards off the villains with a wrench. Clearly visible as such, in the original version the blue tinting signalled to the audience the darkness that blinded the villains. One historian reckons that up to 90 per cent of US films were tinted or toned by 1910.

Both Gaumont and Pathé developed colour systems based on the use of stencils. Kevin Brownlow described the latter:

> Pathécolor, as the best process was called, was introduced in the early nineteen hundreds and was used on special sequences of dramatic film, in trick films and for Pathé's regular fashion reports. It was a costly and elaborate process … At Vincennes… Pathé employed about three hundred women. Each worker sat at a bench…. One woman would work on the blue, another on the red, another on the yellow. (1968, p. 331)

In Britain Charles Urban financed Kinemacolor. This handled only two of the three primary colours effectively and required specialist projection equipment. None of these systems were successfully marketed on a mass basis. Kinemacolor was noted in the 1920s for a series of fashion films, which relied on its visual brilliance.[6]

A particular attraction for audiences was to see their own locales and their selves, friends and neighbours. There was a whole stratum of entrepreneurs who profited by filming in the locale and then screening the films in local venues.[7]

However, spectacle and novelty were gradually to be replaced as the cinema industry developed and expanded. *Rescued by Rover* is a rather different British film from 1905. The film tells a simple story, as the family pet Rover follows the kidnappers of a middle class baby, and then returns to lead the father to her rescue. The popularity of the film was such that three successive versions were made to cope with demand.

A key early US film was *The Great Train Robbery* (1903), directed by Edwin S. Porter for the Edison Company. The film follows the process of a robbery, and the pursuit and capture of the gang of robbers. The story was rather similar to some of the earlier British films that circulated in the USA. But Porter's film was incredibly popular, and its iconography looked forward to the development of the western genre.[8]

Both these films are indicative of an important development after the first decade of cinema: the growing dominance of film narratives. As films grew longer and became part of set programmes in specialised theatres stories offered a format that enabled audiences to focus on a complex series of events. Attractions remained, but sited and explained within the larger structure.

The most important technique for giving the audience a clear sense of action and events on screen was the introduction of the intertitle or title card. As noted before, early shows often had narrators or 'barkers' who explained the action and provided background for the audience. The renter's catalogue, like the Warwick, provided basic information for the exhibitors. But the information card provided a consistent source for audiences. George Smith's *Mary Jane's Mishap* (1903) depended on onscreen printed information read by the audience. And Edwin Porter used text on cards in his 1903 version of *Uncle Tom's Cabin*. Their early examples were increasingly followed as the cards provided basic plot information, commentary and character dialogue. Later cards offered more sophisticated visuals, with artwork, decoration and (for a major film-maker like Griffith) the director's name.

As films grew longer and the stories developed in complexity film-makers also needed to evolve a set of techniques that audiences could follow: a film language, or 'grammar', they could recognise and understand. The earliest films were composed of single shots. Though shots multiplied the camera technique remained very similar – a long shot that took in the whole set with the main character near the centre of the screen; succeeding shots either reproducing the same set or proffering a clearly related one. Thus, in *Rescued by Rover*, the camera follows the heroic dog from place to place in a linear fashion. The direction of onscreen action from one shot to another is also consistent so that audiences could easily identify the successive scenes and their interrelationship.

Gradually these basic techniques were built upon and developed. Film-makers started to vary camera shots, introducing what we now recognise as mid-shots and close-ups. However, such changes depended on audiences being able to understand the relationships between shots. How did the greater detail relate to the larger image? In *Life of an American Fireman* directed by Edwin Porter in 1903, two shots show the climactic rescue of a child. One is an interior shot; the other an exterior, but they show the same action: they offer the audience different views from different vantage points of the same moment in time (later Porter produced a re-edited version where the shots of the action followed their sequence). Such alternate viewpoints were not uncommon in early films. As films alternated different shots showing different action, different characters and different places, there was the risk of confusing the audience. Crucial to an audience's understanding of the progression of shots was the development of a set of conventions which standardised the relationships between shots allowing them to be read consistently. Scenes tended to start with a long or establishing shot, in which audiences could see the overall relationships in the scenes and then identify the detail when shown in a larger image (i.e. a mid-shot or close-up).

Such continuity was even more important when films started using successive shots which were spatially or temporally separate: for example, cutting from the departure for a journey to mid-way or even near the end of this journey; cutting from the house of one character to another travelling to or from the house. Increasingly, films intercut shots of different scenes, in order to introduce complexity and drama in stories. Such developments took place in a number of countries and over several years. However, one film-maker was especially noticeable in these developments. This was David Wark Griffith, a US film-maker, who between 1908 and 1914 made over 400 one and two reel films. Griffith constantly experimented and developed ways of using camera and editing techniques in a more sophisticated fashion. He was popular with audiences and influenced other film-makers.

Griffith made particular use of dramatic chases and a rescue, using intercutting to show audiences the victim, the threat and the rescuers in a sequence of changing camera shots. In *The Country Doctor* (14 min., 1909) the story concerns the doctor who is faced with the dilemma – treating a sick neighbour or his own daughter who is ill. The film cuts between shots of the doctor treating the neighbour and his own house where the mother tends his daughter. The film builds a suspenseful climax and resolution. And it requires the audiences to fill in the ellipsis (gaps) in the chain of events and place the two distinct settings to the overall story.[9] Cutting between places or events in the same time frame became known as parallel editing.

Audiences were helped in this because Griffith tended to use the store of popular stories from literature and theatre. He had worked in repertory theatre before entering films and the majority of his one reelers recycle the melodramas popular in nineteenth century theatre. Historians have also drawn a comparison with the stories of Charles Dickens. Like Dickens, Griffith utilised a store of popular and sentimental tales. A story he returned to more than once is *Enoch Arden*, a character in a poem by Tennyson (Griffith made a version in 1910, and then a two-part version in 1911). A sailor is shipwrecked; meanwhile, at home, his beloved, believing Enoch dead, marries a family friend. Later Enoch is rescued and returns to find his beloved married with a husband and children. The film's climax has Enoch peering at the family through a window and then stealing away, later to die alone.

Griffith also started to lay out the parameters of what became some of the popular genres of Hollywood cinema. *A Corner in Wheat* (1909) tells the story of a speculator who drives up the price of bread but pays a penalty for his exploitation. It is a sort of protest melodrama combined with a social problem angle. *The Musketeers of Pig Alley* (1912) is a proto-gangster film that depicts the corruption found in the ghetto. And *The Mothering Heart* (1913) is a family melodrama where tragedy strikes newlyweds. Finally, there is the *House with Closed Shutters* (1910). This film stands out because of the production values and the sophistication of the melodrama. It is a civil war story where a sister pays the penalty of her brother's cowardice. The civil war and the south were to become central themes in Griffith's later career.[10]

4. THE RISE OF THE STAR SYSTEM

Griffith developed a team of collaborators who contributed to the conventions and techniques found in his films, and developed their own skills in them. A key member was the cinematographer Billy Bitzer, who worked with Griffith right through a 16-year period. Bitzer had been a cameraman cum director before working with Griffith, turning out about 400 short films. As the films developed in sophistication he and Griffith were able to produce the required one reeler on a regular basis. New films went out every week to meet the demand of the nickelodeons. The parent company, now American Biograph, prospered on the basis of the growing demand and popularity of these films.

The popularity also impacted on Griffith's stock company of actors. For the first 10 years of cinema the performers remained more or less anonymous. For example, both Hepworth and Méliès used their family members in their productions. But as the Biograph films in particular played week in and out to entertained audiences the performers became both familiar and popular.

A star system already existed in the theatre and vaudeville industries. It gradually developed in cinema. In the USA films were commonly identified by the brand name of the production company. Initially, audiences identified their favourites by that brand name. Two early stars were Florence Lawrence as the 'Biograph Girl' and Florence Turner as the 'Vitagraph Girl'. Around 1910 there is the first appearance of comments on particular actors by critics, and in 1911 the appearance of fan magazines. Companies responded by using favoured actors for publicity purposes. The star system was under way.

Norma Talmadge, a film star in the 1920s, was herself a fan in her teens. 'Florence Turner was my idol. I never missed a single picture in which she appeared and I would rather have touched the hem of her skirt that to have shaken hands with St Peter. Leaning forward in my hard chair, I was as much a part of Florence Turner as her own reflection on the silver sheet. I laughed when she laughed, suffered when she suffered, wept when she wept. A veritable orgy of emotions for five copper pennies!' (*Saturday Evening Post* article from 1927, quoted in Balio, 1976).

The popularity of the films by Griffith was clearly key in the development of the US star system. Apart from Florence Lawrence, Griffith also launched the careers of both Dorothy and Lillian Gish, major stars in the 1920s, and of Mary Pickford, who was to become the most popular female star of the silent era. It is interesting that whilst a male star system also evolved, the first popular faces were female. This presumably relates to the centrality of melodrama in early cinema. In most of these films, as in nineteenth century theatre, the peak of emotion and catharsis is rendered round the plight of the female victim.

5. FURTHER DEVELOPMENTS IN EUROPE

Parallel developments to those in the USA took place in Europe but Britain appears to have lagged behind the US film industry. The purpose-built film theatre developed more slowly in the UK. Around 1906 exhibitors were still relying on fairs, the music hall and the penny-gaff. There were experiments: Bioscope teas 'with animated displays' between shopping exhibitions. One company screened a version of the *Ride of Valkyries* at Convent Garden; and there were also travelling showmen who took films from town to town using hired venues or even tents for screenings.

The first dedicated film theatre seems to have been Balham Empire (1907), revealingly programmed by the French company Pathé Frères. Gradually more cinemas were opened across London and in the provinces. There was also a mushrooming of companies involved in exhibition, from 3 to 500 between 1908 and 1912. There was some development in horizontal and vertical integration among larger companies. The most successful at this time, Provincial Cinematograph Theatres Ltd, formed in 1909, developed a chain of film theatres and then moved into film production. However, increasingly the market was dominated by French film production. In 1909 only the Hepworth Manufacturing Company was among the six largest releasing firms in the UK. It was last on the list comprising Pathé, Gaumont, Vitagraph, Lux and Edison. Hepworth's production was only about a quarter of that of Pathé.

A large proportion of films were factual, what we would most likely now term news or documentary. Several of these focused on the topical Antarctic exploration. In 1911 there was the first film footage, shot by Herbert Ponting, of the ill-fated expedition led by Captain Scott. A three reel version was exhibited in 1911, and a second instalment in 1912. The tragic events were only fully known later. Ponting produced a feature length version, *The Great White Silence*, in 1924.

Comedy was a popular genre, though the British variant failed to develop stars in the way that French and US companies did. Bamforth's Winky series featured a popular comic character with distinctive regional characteristics. Winky appeared in about 50 films between 1912 and 1914, though most are now lost. They offer quite bizarre mixtures of apparent real-life and fantasy, not uncommon in early film. There were also a plethora of films adapting English literary classics, versions of *Romeo and Juliet, Julius Caesar, Macbeth* and *Richard III*. Novels adapted included *Heart of Midlothian, Old St Paul's* and *David Copperfield*. This was, however, a competitive area. There were numerous versions of famous novels from both US and French companies, and even Danish Nordisk.

The industry was developing in a number of countries across Europe. In this second decade of cinema France was dominant with Pathé and Gaumont. One aspect of story films was the attempt to widen audiences. In 1908 a new French company, Film d'Art, produced *L'Assassinat du Duc de Guise* (*The Assassination of the Duc de Guise*). This depicted a famous incident from French history. There were stars from the theatre, a script and even a composed score to accompany the film. Such a work was clearly intended to appeal to a more sophisticated audience. There were a number of films that attempted to build their success on theatrical status. From 1908 such films also appeared in the British and US markets. One of the famed actresses who appeared in several films of this period, including for Film d'Art *La Dame aux Camélias* (1911), was Sarah Bernhardt, the famous theatre actress. In fact, Bernhardt was over 60, with little time to develop a career in the new medium. In Britain, two Drury Lane stars Johnston Forbes-Robertson and Gertrude Elliott appeared in a film version of *Hamlet* (1913) for the Hepworth Company.

The French industry was important in several aspects of development: Using adaptations from theatre, producing longer features of sometimes up to eight or ten reels running close to two hours, and in utilising settings that were both dramatic and aesthetically pleasing. A key film-maker was Albert Capellani, who moved into film from the theatre and made many of his films for the newly formed Société Cinématographique des Auteurs et Gens de Lettres (S.C.A.G.L.). Much of his output was adaptations from stage and literature. His first was a one-reeler, *The Vagabonde* (*Le Chemineau*, 1905, five minutes at 18fps), a version of a particular sequence in Victor Hugo's great novel *Les Misérables*. A tramp is given hospitality by a kindly priest, but repays his kindness by stealing silverware. When apprehended the priest pretends the tramp's innocence by claiming that the silverware was a gift.

Hugo remained an important source for Capellani who in 1912 made a full version of the novel, released in four parts running to a total of 166 minutes. Later Capellani also directed a striking adaptation of Hugo's *1793* (*Quatre-Vingt-Treize*, 1914). The most impressive of his adaptations is his 1913 version of Émile Zola's *Germinal*. Running for 147 minutes, the film had extensive tinting, using nine different shades, which have only recently been restored. The film captures both the deprivation of the mining community, and the heroic resistance waged by the workers against exploitation.

Capellani's early films tend to be dominated by the front-on long shot, and frequently include fairly long takes. What is most noticeable is his use of settings, with the mise-en-scène both striking and important in the dramatic developments. The *Il Cinema Ritrovato* catalogue notes:

> Capellani's speciality as a director is the broad scope of his narratives, connecting different locations and characters, which invest even short films with grandeur and space ....The filmic quality is not only to be found in the fluidity of the narrative and the dramatically effective montages, but also in the sheer photographic beauty of exterior shots. (Marian Lewinsky, 2011)

Capellani worked in film into the 1920s, including several features made in Hollywood.

The development of a star system in Europe occurred slightly earlier than in the USA. In France there was Max Linder, noted for his regular role as a dapper dandy caught up in slapstick comedies. From 1905 he juggled parallel stage and screen careers. But his growing popularity persuaded him to concentrate on film for Pathé. He not only starred in the films but became involved in scripting his films and then progressed to directing them. In this sense he was an early example of an *auteur* in the manner that the term is used today. He enjoyed immense popularity both in Europe and the USA, and was extremely influential on later comics, including Chaplin.

Another early star was Asta Nielsen, from Denmark. The Danish film industry was developing fast. It offered films with a distinctive style in the use of light and shadow and an unusually wide range of camera angles for the period. An established stage actress, Nielsen made her first film in 1910. She moved to Germany in 1911 and became one of the earliest divas of European cinema. The idea of the 'diva' was a complex one. It was partly tragic, as in *The Lady of Camellias*, but it also offered the allure of the femme fatale. Nielsen herself played powerful characters, often suffering from wrongs by men, but also tempting men to their doom. Her screen character embodied the qualities found in her 1920 features: as Mata Hari (1920), Lulu in *Earth Spirit* (*Erdgeist*, 1922), *Miss Julie* (*Fräulein Julie*) (1922) and *Hedda Gabler* (1925). Despite the melodrama she was noted for a restrained acting style. Early film performance was rather like mime, and gestures and facial expressions were emphasised in order to sign emotion and motivation to audiences. But as the close-up became common there was a need for greater restraint.[11]

Linder appeared in comedies, already one of the most popular staples of the industry. Nielsen appeared mainly in melodramas, the developing centre of the expanding industry. The Film d'Art titles were frequently historical dramas. A variant of this in Italy laid the basis for the historical epic. One of the principal companies, Ambrosio, based in Turin, adapted the historical novel *The Last Days of Pompeii* (1908). The final destruction of the city provided the opportunity for grandiose spectacle. In 1910 another historical epic *The Fall of Troy*, ran for three reels, a screening time of about 45 minutes. This was part of an important development. In the period up to World War I the length of films increased rapidly to four and even eight reels.

STUDY FILM: RESCUED BY ROVER

Hepworth Manufacturing Company. UK 1905. 382 feet in length, original length 425, running time of about seven minutes.

Directed by Lewin Fitzhamon and (possibly) C. M Hepworth.

Cecil Hepworth's father was a lecturer with Magic Lantern shows. Cecil provided the British film pioneer R. S. Paul with specially designed arc clamps. In 1897 he toured with a cinematography show and then published possibly the first handbook on film, *Animated Photography: The ABC of the Cinematograph* (1897). In 1898 he moved into film printing and in 1899 film production. By 1900 he was producing about a 100 short films each year. The quality of his early films made him one of the pre-eminent producers in Britain in that period. He had a film studio at Walton-on-Thames built about 1903. The studio had glass walls to admit and diffuse sunlight, supplemented by internal arc lamps.

Rachel Low (1948) remarks that *Rescued by Rover*, like a number of contemporary British productions, relies heavily on exterior filming. A variety of chase films, often very innovative in terms of techniques, were a staple of the period. With the interiors, as in the gypsy woman's garret, it is possible to note that the lighting is provided by arc lighting rather than natural daylight.

The cast included Hepworth himself as the father; his wife and Hepworth's 8-month-old daughter as the kidnapped baby; and the family dog, Blair, played Rover. Two professional actors, a Mr and Mrs Sebastian, appeared as a soldier and a gypsy woman. Their fee was 10s 6p each. The entire production cost of the film was recorded as £7 13s 9d. Hepworth produced 400 prints for distribution from the original negative; these sold at £10 12s 6d. Because of the heavy use of the negative Hepworth had to make two further (slightly different) versions of the film.[12]

The plot shows the theft of a child from the nurse of a middle class family. The family dog, Rover, tracks down the Gypsy woman who has stolen the baby, then returns home to lead the grieving father to the lost child. The film ends with the reunited family. The BFI version consists of 21 shots, in a straightforward chronological sequence. The camera mainly uses long shots and mid-shots, and the framing is not always central. For example, when the nurse brings news of the lost child the intent is clearly to focus on the dog as well as the mother: 'and the dog, which is listening intently, licks her face for a moment by way of comforting her'. Rover is positioned on the edge of the frame so that his actions and responses are not clearly presented to the audience. However, in the final return home the last shot moves from a long shot to (effectively) a mid-shot, which focuses on Rover's actions, allowing a sort of close-up effect.

Much of the film is taken up with Rover's pursuit and tracking of the lost child. In these shots the movement is towards the camera providing a consistent movement forwards, and then reversed when he returns to his home. In three sequences – the tracking of the child; the return home; leading his master to the garret – the shot sequence is almost identical, providing a clear continuity of space for the audience. Much of the film is exterior daylight; however, in the garret scenes, it is possible to discern the shadows created by the use of interior arc lighting.

The representation in the film clearly accords with the hierarchy of Edwardian middle class values. The child is stolen because of the inattention of the nurse, who has a romantic tryst with a soldier. This is a staple plot device of such stories. However, the villainy in the film resides in the gypsy. Her initial kidnapping is motivated by the nurse's refusal to give her money. Her object in kidnapping the child appears to be the value of her clothing. She is also shown as addicted to alcohol, swigging from a bottle several times. The demon drink was a staple of early cinema just as it had been in moralistic lantern slides in the nineteenth century. However, the gypsy woman does not appear to be punished for her crimes. When the father rescues the child he leaves behind her valuable clothes, and we see the gypsy gloating over these.

Rover, the hero of the film, is a rough collie. This is not dissimilar to one of the greatest canine protagonists, Lassie. In an interesting description in the catalogue Hepworth describes, 'a little baby, an only child, is lying peacefully asleep, guarded by a faithful collie dog three times her size. The dog appears to be fully sensible to his privilege as guardian of his master's choicest treasure, and the child seems safe enough in his care.' Revealingly, the child is lost whilst under the care of the nurse, a lower class employee. Canine members appear to be higher up the social scale than working class servants, probably because they uncritically accept their position in the hierarchy. This might be considered symptomatic in a period when working class militancy was on the increase.

STUDY FILM: A CORNER IN WHEAT

Biograph. USA 1909. Filmed in New York Studio. 953 feet in length. Directed by D. W. Griffith.

Source: novels and story by Frank Norris: *The Octopus, The Pit and A Deal in Wheat* (not all credited).

The film includes actors later to be famous with Griffith: Henry B. Walthall and Blanche Sweet; and an extra who became famous elsewhere in the industry, Mack Sennett. To modern eyes it offers a seemingly simple story: a speculator 'corners' the wheat market, driving up prices, and causes hardship to ordinary working people and the farmer who grows the wheat. Providence, or God, strikes down the speculator in a grimly appropriate accident; he 'drowns' in a wheat store. Scott Simmon suggests that 'nature itself is opposed to urban speculation and so takes its revenge' (1993: 38–39). But the ruin induced by his speculation remains. The manner in which Griffith, and his collaborators, especially Billy Bitzer, presented this story made it an unusually complex experience for the contemporary audiences. Historians and critics have extensively discussed the film (see *The Griffith Project*, Volume 3 – article by Tom Gunning and a detailed shot analysis in *Griffithiana* 59).

This is a one reel film, consisting of 24 shots, seven intertitles and one insert (a letter). The intertitles preface a scene and offer a succinct account of what is to follow. The staging and editing offer important innovations for cinema. An early shot is a type of tableaux or 'realisation', showing the farmer sowing his fields. The inspiration for this is a famous painting by Jean François Millet, *The Sowers*. The first two shots, at the farm, are long takes of 67 and 76 seconds (at a projection speed of 16 fps). This emphasises the symbolic and ritualistic nature of the scenes.

The use of visual 'quotations' was a common technique in early cinema, playing to an audience's knowledge of other art and entertainment media. In the 1920s whole feature films had their design constructed from particular artists or period looks, a technique still utilised in modern cinema. However, not only the staging but also the lighting shows the influence of Millet. Besides the framing, which 'raises the horizon line … rooting them in the earth' (Färber in *Griffithiana* 59) a shot of the farm homestead uses 'natural back and edge lighting'. Bitzer was developing more sophisticated approaches to lighting and camera, which fed into the increasing excellence in US film.

Most significant in the film is the way that shots of different people and places, in varying time and space, are interlinked. One of the important developments pioneered by Griffith was intercutting between different events, notably in the chase sequence. *A Corner in Wheat* draws connections and parallels between separate characters and places (parallel cutting). Thus, the film commences with the farmer sowing wheat; we then meet the speculator; and, as the narrative develops, we see the speculator at the exchange, and also socialising and celebrating his fortune. But cut into these scenes are others of poor people forced to pay more for their staple diet; and even poorer people who depend on the Bread Fund (charity) which is cut off by rising prices. By this stage the relatively long takes have been replaced by shots from 5 to 30 seconds in length. And, when it comes to the nemesis of the speculator, we get the sole use of close-ups in the film. Griffith is asking the audience to draw connections and make judgements on events that are connected not by action but by social relations. His was a sophisticated use of a basic film technique, which was a key influence on the later Soviet montage school.

Just as Millet offered an influence which Bitzer could translate onto film, there was a literary inspiration for Griffith's editing. These were the writings of Frank Norris, the source for the later Hollywood masterpiece, *Greed* (1924). Norris's novels dealt extensively with the problems of speculation in agriculture. This was a reflection of a populist movement against speculation in the USA in the late nineteenth century. Many of the narrative events in the film come from the Norris writings. In *The Octopus*, Norris describes the rise and fall of a wheat magnate, alternating descriptions of his excesses with those of the poverty of dispossessed farmers. This is the presentation of social relations in a fairly abstract sense that Griffith is able to visualise in *A Corner in Wheat*.

The values that Griffith embeds in the story of theft and comeuppance seem less directly radical than that of Norris. The judgement on the speculator appears to be neither social nor divine: he is the victim of an accident, but coming at the moment when he has triumphed does suggest poetic justice. The film does not appear to envisage any social solution to the exploitation: the farmers and workers remain victims of capital.

Certainly one would not expect a commercial company like Biograph to actively ferment opposition to capital and profits. However, they do appear to have recognised the commercial potential of the film: 'No subject has ever been produced more timely than this powerful story of the wheat gambler, coming as it does when agitation is rife against that terrible practice of cornering commodities that are the necessities of life' (*Biograph Bulletin*, 13 December 1909).

For many in the audience the film dramatised their feelings of exploitation in relation to a basic need. Apparently Griffith was given more time on this particular production than on other contemporary Biograph films, usually completed in two or three days. And the film was released for the Christmas market, already in 1909 a lucrative season for exhibitors. The season was presumably also appropriate because of the strong parallels between Griffith's and Charles Dickens' melodrama.

STUDY FILM: AN UNSEEN ENEMY

Biograph. USA 1912. 999 feet. Filmed on location on the East Coast.

Directed by D. W. Griffith. Authored by Edward Hacker.

The film is notable for being the screen debut of Lillian and Dorothy Gish. It also features Robert Harron, a staple lead in Griffith's later films until his untimely death in 1919. In other ways *An Unseen Enemy* is less innovative than *A Corner in Wheat*, but it represents the distinctive and recurring approach used by Griffith. This is what is now called 'parallel editing', cutting between two different spaces in the same time frame, as in the cutting between shots of the trapped sisters and the brother and friends racing to the rescue.

While it is almost the same length as *A Corner in Wheat* there are five times as many shots in the production. Eight of these are intertitles. The early titles are fairly wordy as they struggle to set out the complexities of the plot: 'Their brother, having disposed of a portion of the small estate and it being after banking hours, places the money in the safe.'

The shot length nowhere equals the early shots of *A Corner in Wheat*. Partly this is because it does not use the tableaux shots found in the earlier film. But the main reason is the fast intercutting used as the excitement of the plot develops. At the start of the film two orphaned daughters and their brother receive the inheritance monies. The money is placed in the safe. Whilst the brother is out the maid and accomplice attempt a robbery. The sisters are terrorised with a revolver. But, warned by phone, the brother races to the rescue, whilst the younger sister's boyfriend helps them escape through a window. The plotting is rather schematic, and the main interest and excitement are in the race to the rescue. There is constant intercutting between the trapped sisters and the burglars, and between these and the brother as he races home in a commandeered car.

The two sisters are trapped in a room whilst the maid's accomplice attempts to open the safe. Meanwhile the maid terrorises them by pointing a gun through a stovepipe hole in the wall. There is an interesting distinction between the two sisters; whilst both display fear, at two points the younger sister (Dorothy Gish) braves the gun to use the telephone. This does seem to have made an impact on contemporary audiences, and Lillian Gish, for a considerable period, came to represent the heroine in danger. In a number of Griffith's films, notably *Broken Blossoms* (1919) and *Way Down East* (1929), she is the victimised young maiden rescued by the hero, whereas Dorothy is frequently more active. In *Hearts of the World* (1918), while Lillian and Robert Harron consider suicide in the face of the German threat, Dorothy throws the hand grenade that kills the enemy soldier.

The camera shots are almost uniformly head-on. There are a number of close-ups in the dramatic section of the film, most of them of one or both of the trapped sisters. There is an extreme close-up of the gun and the hand when the maid terrorises the sisters. And there is an interesting scene where the car has to cross a swing bridge. There are two shots that appear to have pans in them, but the swinging of the bridge itself exaggerates this movement.

The use of melodramatic characters and actions is typical of the bulk of Griffith's films for Biograph. Whilst his work was pioneering the command of continuity editing that came to characterise Hollywood films, Griffith was not overly concerned with such matters. (In the article in *The Griffith Project*, Volume 6, Lea Jacobs lists a series of 'continuity errors' in the film.) But Griffith was concerned with the emotional responses of audiences, and they, presumably, did not pay great attention to such errors either.

STUDY FILM: *L'ARLÉSIENNE*

France 1908, black and white, 17 minutes at 16fps. 335 metres.

Rediscovered by Lobster films and restored at Il laboratorio L'immagine Ritrovato della Cineteca di Bologna.

Direction and scenario: Albert Capellani. From the short story and play by Alphonse Daudet.

The original exhibition used music by Georges Bizet composed to accompany the earlier stage version.

The film was one of the *scènes dramatique* that was the main film genre followed by Capellani in his early years. These were part of the tendency to increased length and expanded narratives in this period: earlier films rarely exceed 400 metres in length. But later examples by Capellani, for instance his adaptation of Emile Zola's *L'assommoir*, ran for twice this length (740 metres).

The *scènes dramatique* dramas offer not just action or comic effects, but placed the characters in evocative settings and developed psychological states. *The Bioscope* commented thus after an English screening:

L'Arlésienne was (…) a distinct success – a story of earnest human passion in peasant life spoilt by duplicity. There was no delay in production of the film, the scenes following each other so quickly that the interest of a critical audience was not only maintained but deepened. The rural scenery forming the background is singularly beautiful, and the warm glow of sunshine upon it took [us] in a fancy to a fairyland of sunshine. (Quoted in the film notes on the Albert Capellani DVD)

One immediately notices the use of actual landscapes in the film and it becomes apparent that these comment quite subtly on the characters and their emotions, developing the conflict between town and country so common in the early stories.

It is a simple story. Frederic lives with his family in a village in Arles. He has a relationship with fellow villager, Yvette. However, at the local town he meets 'the Girl from Arles'. He is immediately smitten, but unaware that she already has a relationship with Milifio. Fredric takes the girl home, presumably to announce his intention to marry her. The jealous Milifio gives Frederic's father a note of love sent him by the girl and she is forced to leave. After a period of despondency, Frederic becomes engaged to Yvette. However, his passion for the Girl continues to haunt him and, in a fit of despair, he falls to his death.

The Bioscope's comments about 'no delay' are certainly accurate. The audience is plunged straight into the drama without establishing scenes. The opening scene shows Frederic, his father and Yvette at the entrance to the village, but the context has to be worked out subsequently by the audience. In fact we only learn the names of the characters later, in the film's title cards, excepting the femme fatale who remains 'the Girl from Arles'. Such sparse contextual information is fairly typical of such dramas in this period, the emphasis being on narrative drive, presumably in part to hold the audience's attention for what then must have seen quite a long drama. But it probably also relies on audiences familiarity with the basic story from other versions. The acting is still that fairly emphatic style found in early film. There is no mistaking the emotions of, say, Fredric, riven by jealousy and loss. Equally the tempestuous quarrel between the Girl and Milifio may now seem over-dramatic.

The film relies extensively on locations: there are a number of interiors, which are obviously constructed sets, but the majority of the film is in the rural settings praised by *The Bioscope*. The use of particular settings is carefully selected to add to the audience's sense of characters. Thus Frederic's meeting with the Girl takes place at the local bullring: shades of fiery passion and *Carmen*. A slow pan introduces the amphitheatre across the tiers of seats and later, as Fredric and the Girl walk together, another slow pan shows us the skyline of the town. This scene is followed by a meeting between the Girl and the now jealous Milifio. He follows the Girl to her house, and as they turn into the street Capellani uses a reverse angle shot, a rare technique at this period.

The film is shot using long shots, mainly head on to the action. There is a continuous line of intertitles explaining the action prior to the actual visualisation. Thus after the opening shot the intertitle prepares us as 'Frederic meets the Girl from Arles'.

Frederic and the Girl's second meeting takes place away from the urban setting amongst grass and trees. Here the passionate relationship develops, leading to Frederic taking the Girl home to his family and setting in motion the cycle of jealousy and tragedy. Later in the film Capellani makes effective use of superimposition. Distraught after losing the Girl Frederic wanders past their earlier meeting places. As he remembers these occasions the Girl fades into the scene briefly and then fades out again, so we get a real sense of Frederic's mental state. Later, having locked himself in the attic, another superimposition conjures up an obsessed Frederic's vision: this time of Milifio together with the Girl. The anguished Frederic dashes towards the vision and falls to his death.

What is most notable about *L'Arlésienne* in terms of film grammar is the developing narrative techniques. But the strongest impression is the sense of landscape and its importance. This would seem to presage and later feed into the fine realistic dramas of French cinema in the 1920s and 1930s.

FOOTNOTES

1. Both have films featured on the *Early Cinema* DVD and Bamforth and Company was the subject of a documentary, *Holmfirth Hollywood*, shown on BBC4 in 2006.

2. A term less commonly used than vertical integration, 'geographic' is a companion approach, referring to a company's dominance in a number of contiguous film markets. Thus Pathé was the leading producer and distributor in a number of European countries.

3. Both *Arivée d'un train en gare à La Ciotat* and *The Countryman and the Cinematograph* are on the BFI *Early Cinema* disc, as is *The Kiss in the Tunnel*.

4. *More Treasures from the American Film Archives* features a phantom ride, *From Leadville to Aspern* (1906).

5. *The Lonedale Operator* is included on the *Treasures of the American Archives* DVD.

6. *More Treasures from the American Film Archives* includes examples of tinted and toned films and early colour formats. The BFI *Early Cinema* DVD includes examples of tinting and stencil colouring. And *Silent Shakespeare* includes films with stencil colour. There is also the film *The Open Road* (1925) made in Kinemacolor, the subject of a series on BBC 2006, now available on DVD.

7. *The Lost World of Mitchell & Kenyon* (available on BFI DVD) has a range of actualities films of northern British towns and resorts between 1901 and 1910. They offer a whole sweep of life, events and personalities from the period.

8. Versions of both *Rescued by Rover* and *The Great Train Robbery* are included on *Early Cinema*. Another Porter film, *Life of an American Fireman* (1903) is on *More Treasures from American Film Archives*.

9. *The Country Doctor* is on *More Treasures from the American Film Archives*.

10. *The House with Closed Shutters* is included on *The Unseen Cinema* DVD collection.

11. The Danish Film Institute has issued a DVD with four early Neilsen films, including *The Abyss* (1910), a film that launched her career.

12. The version on the BFI *Early Cinema* disc is 43 feet shorter than the original Hepworth version. Hepworth produced a synopsis of the film for their distribution catalogue (reprinted in Rachel Low, 1948). There are apparently no missing scenes on the disc, but the opening of the film may be slightly truncated.

3. THE TEEN YEARS OF CINEMA

D.W. Griffith (pointing) on the set of Death's Marathon *(1913)*

INTRODUCTION

This period roughly corresponds to World War I, 1914–18. However, many of the changes were under way before the war and only reached full development afterwards. Thus, the Hollywood studio system had its roots at the start of the teens, and it is only considered fully developed with the arrival of M-G-M in 1924. It was in these years that Hollywood first became synonymous with 'the movies' for the large majority of film-goers, at home and abroad.

The development and increasing sophistication of Hollywood film-making are clear subjects of study. One can take a broad view and look at the overall system or one can focus on a particular example, like Famous-Players Lasky (or Paramount).

In terms of film-makers, D. W. Griffith is once more a key example. Just one of his films from this period, *The Birth of a Nation*, is a seminal production for Hollywood. The production and marketing of the film are important topics. But any study will have to grapple with the film's racist values. Paul Gilroy balanced the competing aspects of the film when for a UK television screening he argued that the film is both a masterpiece and clearly racist (Channel 4, September 9 1993). These contradictory qualities need to be teased out: both its immense popularity and success, and the shock and abhorrence it generated even on its release. If it were at all possible to study the film together with some of the alternative Afro-American films, I would recommend this.

Cecil B. De Mille would make a good alternative study. He is also a very influential Hollywood film-maker, with his work differing both in terms of style and content from Griffith; and a number of his films are readily accessible.

Both directors can be studied in order to understand the development of Hollywood's narrative and continuity system. While this was not fully developed until the end of the teens, the conventions on which it is built can be clearly identified in the work of both directors. I would suggest that the 180-degree rule, shot / reverse shot, on- and offscreen matching and three-point lighting are key conventions, which can be identified and studied. Since these are conventions designed to plot narratives, this is best studied with the idea of the Hollywood narrative and some attention to screenwriting.

Outside the USA there are many interesting developments and changes. However, it is quite difficult to access copies of the films from this period. The one exception is the BFI *Early Russian* collection. This has the advantage of following some conventions in common with Hollywood, but also having distinct aspects of narrative and style.

I. WORLD WAR I AND THE RISE TO DOMINANCE OF THE US INDUSTRY

At the start of the 1910s the international film market was still fairly open, with no individual industry dominant. The French industry enjoyed the largest share, with the Italian industry developing fast. The US industry was still mainly directed towards its expanding home market, with US films taking an increasing share of domestic consumption. From 1914 the war in Europe, considered a world conflict even though vast stretches of the globe were not involved, dominated political and social life. When the war ended, late in 1918, the international film industry had changed fundamentally. It was now dominated by the US industry, a situation that has continued to this day. A symbol of the transition is the rise of Charlie Chaplin as a film star. In 1910 he was an increasingly popular star of the British music halls. He made two tours of the US with the Fred Karno troupe and in 1914 he entered the US film industry. It was there that he became the greatest star of the new entertainment medium.

It was in this period that the US industry, mainly centred on New York, moved its production base to California and the small town of Hollywood. The first recorded film shot there appears to have been a version of *The Count of Monte Cristo* by Selig Polyscope in 1908. D. W. Griffith was one film-maker who wintered in California from 1910, where the climate and scenery were ideally suited to location filming (his *The Country Doctor*, 1909, shows this landscape). Kevin Brownlow notes how the Los Angeles Chamber of Commerce advertised to 'Motion Pictures the vital importance of having every member of an organisation awake in the morning and start work in a flood of happy sunshine' (Brownlow, 1968: 32–33).

Reputedly other film-makers liked the state because they could quickly cross the border to evade the Pinkerton detectives sent out by the Motion Picture Trust to pursue patent evaders. Apart from these favourable factors California also offered an open society for a new and changing industry. Unlike the eastern seaboard, there was no establishment, and little in the way of regulation of business. Wages were lower than in the east.

Entrepreneurs could develop and exploit the medium freely. (John Steinbeck's novel *The Grapes of Wrath* describes a California that is a paradise, not for the migrating Oakies, but for the hard-fisted capitalists who exploit them.)

Selig Polyscope constructed a studio near Hollywood in 1908. The first studio constructed in the town itself was in 1911, by the Centaur Film Company. Mack Sennett moved into a neighbouring studio in 1912-13. Another newcomer was Cecil B. De Mille. He was a partner with Jesse Lasky and Samuel Goldfish (later Goldwyn) in the new Jesse L. Lasky Feature Play Company. Their first production was to be a western based on a 1905 stage hit *The Squaw Man*. After a train journey of several days out west they set up production in a barn on the corner of Selma and Vine Street in Hollywood. They had to endure sabotage by agents of the Trust during filming. DeMille describes such activities on this production:

> Our film was processed in the dark little laboratory next to the barn. One morning when I went in there, before my eyes had become accustomed to the dim light which was all we could use in the laboratory, my feet scuffled over something that made a rustling sound. When my fingers touched it, I did not need a light to tell me what it was. It was our film – it was *The Squaw Man* – unwound, thrown in a heap on the floor, and, as fingers and eyes soon told me, scraped, pitted, disfigured, as if someone had put it on the floor, put his heel on it, and dragged it between heel and floor. It was completely ruined. So would our company have been if I had not had the extra negative at home. (DeMille, 1960: 77-78)

The first screening was a failure because, new to the industry, the print had incorrect sprocket holes.[1] But, released in February 1914, the film was a major box office success. It established the young company; soon they merged with Adolph Zukor's Famous Players Company. This firm had also had a big hit with the distribution of a French film, *Queen Elizabeth* (1912), starring Sarah Bernhardt. The combined company then took over the Paramount Distribution Company. By this stage Famous Players was vertically integrated.

Westerns like *The Squaw Man* (1914) were a popular genre in the early teens. They were filmed not only in California, but also by studios still operating around New York and other eastern cities. Most were one reelers, running for approximately 15 minutes. Rather differently from the westerns of classical Hollywood many of these were fairly sympathetic to the Indians. One illustration of this was *White Fawn's Devotion* (1910).[2]

This film was made by Pathé Frères and directed by James Young Deer. It offered 'a play acted by a tribe of 'Red Indians' in America'.[3] White Fawn is an Indian woman married to a white settler who sacrifices herself to save her husband, a scenario that was used in several early films about Indians including *The Squaw Man* and which was still in use in the 1950 *Broken Arrow*.

The other genre that continued to dominate one reel films was comedy. These often only loosely followed strict narratives. Indeed, they offered many of the pleasures associated with the earlier cinema of attractions: caricatures, jokes, chases, crashes and spectacular mishaps. *The Keystone Kops* typified these crazy, frantic and anarchic films. Keystone was founded in 1912, with Mack Sennett as the director. He was one of the most important developers of silent slapstick comedy. Keystone was absorbed by Triangle in 1915. In 1917 Sennett set up as an independent producer distributing through Paramount. Some of the greatest comics of the silent era worked for Sennett: Roscoe 'Fatty' Arbuckle, Mabel Normand, Charlie Chase and others.

In 1914 Charlie Chaplin joined the company and worked with them for a year. In 1915 he signed with the Essanay Company, enjoying a raise in salary and a bonus. It was Essanay's ownership of the Chaplin films that was a key element in the company being able to introduce and enforce a block booking system in the UK. Rachael Low quotes their announcement: '… it is impossible to place subjects of such importance and magnitude on the open market. … We shall therefore in future RELEASE THE WHOLE OF OUR OUTPUT DIRECT TO THE EXHIBITOR' (Low, 1947: 43).

In 1916 Chaplin moved to Mutual, contracted to make one film a month on a salary of half a million dollars, and in 1918 he signed with First National for over a million dollars. In that period, he made about 70 films, mostly one and two reel comedies. His impact on audiences was easily equal to the pay increases he earned. He became the most famous film star, possibly the most famous person, on the planet. Chaplin's success was built on abilities shared with other silent comics: superb timing, comic grace and evocative mime. However, he also added a distinctive onscreen character, the Tramp. `The little fellow` was anarchic, anti-authoritarian and irrepressible. He was susceptible to feminine woes and offered heroines a shabby gentility. The character became an everyman for the twentieth century.

Already, in 1912, producer Carl Laemmle formed the Universal Film Manufacturing Company for film distribution. In 1915 the firm built Universal City on a 230-acre site in Hollywood. This was a large, purpose built studio for making films. This vast site provided space for scriptwriters, set builders, costumiers, cinematographic stores and backlots for the different movie genres. Like Paramount, Universal developed both distribution and exhibition arms to consolidate its power in the market. The latter sides of the business were run from the New York office. Thus, while the Hollywood site was the visible part of the growing film empire, the head office and accountants were back in the east.

Another studio, built in 1915, was located in Culver City, constructed for the Triangle Film Company by producer / director Thomas H. Ince. Later it was used by Goldwyn Productions and then became part of Metro-Goldwyn-Mayer. The organisation of production involved the rationalisation of the production process. A key player in this process was Ince. He was particularly influential in the use of a continuity script to control production. This broke the actions of the film down into a series of scenes and shots, which allowed for careful organisation of production design, construction and filming. It also led to a high degree of specialisation among the workforce. An early film-maker like

Méliès did almost everything himself, or used member of his family. In the developing studio system there was markedly increased division of labour. Craftsman like Billy Bitzer specialised in cinematography and later lighting. And they also acquired assistants, to carry the equipment, change the focus, and the lenses. Similar division and developments took place in editing, set construction, art design, costumes, props and other tasks in pre- and post-production.

As discussed earlier, D. W. Griffith was the director who most greatly influenced the development of the conventions that the mature Hollywood would follow. He viewed with interest some of the developments found in films from Europe, including the far greater length used in Italian epic films. Biograph was quite satisfied with the short films that Griffith made as they still produced a profit. But he had ambitions for bigger and longer films. In 1914 he directed a four reeler for Biograph, *Judith of Bethulia*. This film was based on the biblical story of Judith, who cut off the head of the invading monarch, Holofernes. A film he made in 1913 was *The Battle at Elderbush Gulch*. This has an impressive climax, intercutting beleaguered settlers under attack by Indians, and the US cavalry riding to the rescue. Such a dramatic ending was to appear again in his 1915 epic, *The Birth of a Nation*, the latter film made after he broke with Biograph.

The Birth of a Nation ran to 12 reels and for three hours, almost unprecedented in that early period. The film's story follows the fortunes of a southern family who are caught up in the US Civil War. Friends enlist on opposing sides, Unionist and Confederate. The first part includes a recreation of Civil War battles. These were mammoth affairs, with assistants using semaphore to signal to the numerous extras spread over sizeable spaces. On the set were men who would become major directors in their own right, like Erich von Stroheim, an extra on this film. Another assistant from earlier films, Raoul Walsh, also acted, appearing as John Wilkes Booth, the assassin of President Lincoln. The cast included a number of stars from Griffith's earlier short films. One was Lillian Gish, who played the threatened white heroine, a role that cemented her as a key female star of the silent era.

However, the threat to her in the second part of the film was from freed black slaves. Her sister in the film, played by another Griffith star Mae Marsh, chose death rather than such a fate. These racist incidents were central to the film's portrait of the post Civil War reconstruction. The film's source was a revisionist Civil War novel and play, *The Clansman*. Both the play and the film are full of derogatory portraits of black people. In the film black characters with distinct action in the plot are played by blacked-up whites, whilst the crowd of extras include actual Negroes. Apparently they were segregated even on the sets. And, as in the play, the Ku Klux Klan saved the endangered white women. A specially arranged score performed by a live orchestra accompanied screenings of the film in important film theatres. The ride of the Klan through the night had the orchestra playing Wagner's *Ride of the Valkyries*.

When the film was released it created a sensation. Major city shows were charged at two dollars admission, way above the usual prices. The film made a fortune for many distributors and exhibitors. The combination of powerful melodrama and spectacle, combined around a romanticised and conservative historical tale, was great box office. With his partners Griffith made use of the roadshow feature. In this system the producer dealt directly with exhibitors, rather than through distributors. The production company took a percentage of the box office or even ran the theatre entirely. This 'roadshow' system made use of an extremely extensive publicity process. Since it tended to use large theatres rather than nickelodeons, it could benefit from the large-scale orchestral score available and from the more expensive ticket price. One estimate has the overall gross at $18,000,000, with Griffith taking about a million as his share. All this was from an investment of $100,000 which had been seen as extravagant before the film's success.

However, its clearly racist narrative and images also created a storm. Black associations organised protests and boycotts, and there were ugly riots when the film was exhibited in some US cities. Despite this the film was extremely influential. The racist portrayal of black people was, unfortunately, a staple of classic Hollywood. But Griffith's film also influenced the narrative structure and the stylistic language of film for years to come.

Griffith followed The Birth of a Nation with another long epic, Intolerance (1916). The new film addressed persecution and bigotry through the ages, as if in mea culpa for the earlier film. Intolerance weaves together four stories: from ancient Babylon; from the New Testament; from sixteenth century France and the massacre of the Huguenots; and from the contemporary period, as an innocent man faces hanging. The latter episodes contain a caricature of female 'busy bodies' laying down moral values. Griffith had also published a pamphlet on free speech, an expression that indicated that he was more resentful than penitent over the (justified) criticism of The Birth of a Nation.

While Intolerance offered the epic sprawl of Griffith's previous film, it also included even more sophisticated intercutting. In the long climax of the film Griffith cut between the four stories, as in each case the characters are involved are in rescue attempts, and in a race to save the victims. Even by modern standards this is an extremely complex piece of narrative. But the film failed to emulate the success of Birth of a Nation, possibly because audiences found the storytelling too challenging.

Although Griffith's masterworks dominate our sense of Hollywood in the teens, there were numerous other directors at work producing popular films, both for the domestic exhibition and export. Raoul Walsh produced and directed Regeneration (1915). This story of criminality and salvation in the urban slums was distinguished by the authentic city settings in which the action played out.

A rather different director from Griffith in this period, both in production scale and values, was Lois Weber. She started as an actress in 1911, usually opposite her husband, Philip Smalley, but turned to direction in 1913 with the Universal Studio. Its founder, Carl Laemmle, started out in nickelodeons. Later he expanded with the Independent Motion Picture Company. In 1913 he created the Universal Film Company and in 1915 built

Universal City in the hills above Hollywood. Weber worked in Hollywood until the late 1920s and was one of only a few women to climb to the key positions of producer or director. Weber tended towards social topics and directed and often scripted films that dealt with controversial topics like capital punishment, opium addition and child labour. . The situation of women was a recurring issue. One of her noted films was *Where are My Children?* (1916), dealing with the subject of birth control and abortion. This five-reel film, which ran for 65 minutes, dramatised issues about women's access to family planning. The title comes from the despairing cry of the male protagonist, a District Attorney. He has just discovered that his wife, along with other middle-class women, has been using abortion to control pregnancy. Earlier in the film the DA has successfully prosecuted an advocate of birth control and then a doctor who practises abortion. The latter follows a botched abortion on a young girl who has been impregnated by the DA's wife's younger and callow brother. The film ends with the ageing couple mourning their unborn children, as ghostly representatives of babies and then young people are superimposed on screen.

The DA, Richard Walton, was played by Tyrone Power (father of the more famous star son) and Mrs Walton by his actual wife, Helen Riaume. The narrative is not always completely clear, presumably due at least in part to problems of censorship. The prosecutions in the film mirror actual cases in the same period. However, the film fairly clearly advocates birth control rather than abortion. Walton initially is a supporter of eugenics and early in the film there are images of deprived and 'feckless' working class families who thoughtlessly bring 'unwanted' children are into the world. But the majority of the film focuses on the issue in relation to middle class women like the Attorney's wife.

On release the film ran into some problems with State Review committees, but did receive a fairly wide release. It was extremely successful, despite (or maybe because of) the distributors advertising that it was not suitable for children. The box office return was in excess of $3,000,000. Apparently there were at least two other women producer/directors at the Universal Studio at this time, but generally Weber can be considered an exception to the male dominance in the industry.[4]

One of the most successful film-makers was Cecil B. De Mille. As the Jesse L. Lasky Feature Play Company merged with Zukor's company to become Paramount, De Mille became the key person in the studio's production process. He was both producer and director, worked at scriptwriting and assisted in the work of other directors. He was a key force in the development of films from the two reelers to the six and seven reelers that became standard for features. He also was an important innovator in the area of film style, especially in the use of lighting to create light and shadow (chiaroscuro).

One film with a strong visual style was *The Cheat* (1915). Based on an original story the film centres on a rich society woman, who borrows money against her own sexual virtue. As well as being visually distinctive, the film offered a risqué topic, which appealed to audiences. De Mille throughout his career was able to combine flamboyance in the story line with flamboyance in production to great effect.

In 1918 De Mille directed an adaptation of a novel called *The Whispering Chorus*.[5] The tale follows a man who fakes his own death to avoid prison and then is accused of his own murder. The film used a strong alternation of light and dark to create the dangerous world into which the protagonist falls. It looks and plays rather like an example of *film noir*, a genre that helped to define Hollywood in the 1940s. The film failed at the box office, rather like Griffith's follow-up: perhaps for the same reason, that audiences found it too challenging.

These films featured far more complex characters and sequences of events than previously. They also occupied the audience's attention for far longer. *The Whispering Chorus'* six reels took over 80 minutes to unspool. The effective imparting of these dramas depended to a great degree on the use of conventions of narrative and film style which audiences recognised and readily understood. The emphasis on continuity in Hollywood studios ensured that great care and attention were paid to the presentation of story, character and action.

The staging in films was carefully organised. Thus, in the teens one finds the rise of the art director. De Mille's art director on *The Whispering Chorus* was Wilfred Buckland. Buckland's credit in the titles read 'Technical Director', but this included the visual look and especially the use of lighting. Buckland was an established theatrical designer who joined Famous Players Lasky in 1914 and later worked on Douglas Fairbanks' expensive and lavish *Robin Hood* (1922). He was one of a number of designers who were able to produce sets and scenery that both fitted the story but also enabled technicians to capture this on film. The work of costume designers, props departments and so on were equally important in this respect. And their work was both rigorous and ample. In the teens one can see the development of high production values in Hollywood films. The profitably of the films enabled studios to set standards that competitors found hard to match.

Equally important was the work of the lighting cameramen and editors. Billy Bitzer, who worked on Griffith's films, had over a decade of experience and expertise that he brought to filming. He introduced backlighting to Hollywood. 'Bitzer evolved a more efficient method of backlighting with mirrors. One mirror would reflect the sun into another, and this would be aimed at the back of the player's head. The men holding the mirrors could move around with the sun, enabling shooting to continue as long as the sun shone' (Brownlow, 1968: 247). Hollywood's fine weather meant that the studio backlots were usually open to the sky and the sun.

During this period the Hollywood production personnel developed and polished ways of filming that enabled audiences to clearly follow onscreen action. There was a consistency in the placement of cameras, thus enabling audiences to understand the spatial arrangement of the story and follow changes in set-up, angle and distance from the subject. Camera positions tended to adhere to one side of the action, so that both foreground and background were seen from the same point of view, even in a new shot; a convention known as the 180-degree rule. Scenes were established by long shots and used a conventional mix of mid-shots and close-ups. Increasingly when characters interacted the camera swapped back and forth between protagonists in shot / reverse shot.

The careful composition and recording of onscreen space were matched by the offscreen space. In both the placement of the camera and in the editing of shots film-makers carefully preserved an identifiable spatial world. If a character looked offscreen, when the person or object appeared it 'matched' the preceding look. And the film-makers carefully avoided over-emphatic changes. In most films the constantly changing camera did not attract the attention of audiences, who were able to focus primarily on the star characters, hardly consciously noting the changes in filming characters and sets.

Lighting was another area where conventions of use developed techniques that was 'invisible' to audiences. This was built round 'three point lighting', the use of key, fill and rear lighting. There were key lights for all the major characters or objects; fill lights removed shadows and even the spill. Rear lights made characters and object stand out from the set. High key lighting was very bright; low-key lighting was shadowy. This was less to do with the level of illumination than the combination of lights, the best analogy is like key in music, high is bright and cheerful, low is dark and sombre.

Another key contributor was the scriptwriter. At this stage her work was called a 'scenario', a sequence of scenes rather than a shooting script. One of the most successful in Hollywood in this period was Frances Marion. Overall she worked on over 150 movies. She was a journalist who transferred to screen writing in the teens. Among her scripts were a number of Mary Pickford films. In the late twenties she wrote one of the acknowledged classics of the silent era, *The Wind* (1928). Writing was one area where women could succeed and make a career. The skills involved included not just well constructed stories and convincing dialogue, but a structure that could be plotted and organised into the Hollywood system of production. The writer also needed to play to the strengths of genre and star, as Marion did so convincingly with Pickford. *Poor Little Rich Girl* (1917) allows Pickford to exploit her screen character's child-like spontaneity and resilience. Pickford overcomes the obstacles and grief as a young girl is separated from her father.

By 1918 the overall standard of Hollywood productions was extremely high This can be seen by comparing examples of Hollywood and, say, British films (a comparison that was frequently made by contemporary critics). A good example of the standard of Hollywood production values is to be seen in De Mille's *The Whispering Chorus*. This is not a star-led or big-budget film, but the quality is clearly seen in the sets, costumes, and in particular in the lighting, which uses bright illuminations at some points, and light and shadow at others. To this was added the economic advantage of the largest market. By the time the films came to be exported they had often already recouped their cost. Thus, the Hollywood producers could undercut competitors in other markets with films that were polished, professional and appeared extremely good value for the entrance admission.

In the USA the rise in costs from one reelers to four or more was noticeable. Between 1908 and 1910 a quality one reeler could be produced for between $1,000 and $1,500 dollars (Finler, p. 53). By the mid-teens a five reeler production could cost between $20,000 and $30,000. *The Birth of a Nation* was reckoned to cost $100,000, though it took millions in revenues. Louis B. Mayer alone apparently made over a $1,000,000 from the distribution rights. *Intolerance* was made for about $400,000, which it failed to recoup. These two films demonstrated the extremes of the business, and the attraction of large profits.

2. EUROPEAN INDUSTRIES

The competence in production and distribution were to be key in the way that Hollywood achieved dominance over the European films industries. And the disruptions of war provided the opportunity. However, on the eve of war there was still expansion, if uneven development.

i. Britain

In Britain 60 to 70 per cent of cinema admissions were reckoned to be for US films. A number of the larger British renters increasingly relied on US imports as the mainstay of their business. The Kinematograph Renter Society, formed in 1914, was a forum for frequent complaints about the US invasion. However, the Society was split between large and small renters with disparate interests and rarely achieved a consensus on what do to. It is clear that British film production companies found it increasingly difficult to maintain bookings. They were slower than the US to move to the longer three and four reel features.

The Kinematograph Renter Society also dealt with government intervention in the industry. The first piece of legislation in Britain was the 1909 Cinematograph Film Act. This was concerned with health and safety, especially the dangers of fire. Licensing powers were vested in Local Authorities, though they quickly interpreted the act in order to control content (see Part VI, Censorship below). The war initially raised questions about film entertainment, but it soon became clear that it was an important leisure activity in this situation. In 1915 the government introduced the McKenna Duty, a tax on luxury items which included cinema, then in 1916 they introduced a general entertainment tax levied on seat prices. The Kinematograph Renter Society organised vigorous opposition, but only obtained concessions after the war.

In the first months after war was declared — autumn 1914 — there was a spate of war films. This included the last film of Bamforth's Winky, *Sharps and Flats* (1914). It was remarkably unpatriotic, as in the film Winky and a friend leaves their wives on the pretext of enlisting, but then goes carousing away from home. The film was apparently popular, but after this Winky himself went AWOL from the screen. As the conflict settled down into the long haul the British producers tended to carry on with the staple genres. The Hepworth Manufacturing Company remained one of the most important. A key film was an adaptation of a novel by Helen Mathers, *Comin' Thro' the Rye* (1916), a tragic love story.

There was a continued reliance on literary and theatrical adaptations in the British industry and fewer original screenplays than in, say, Hollywood.[6] Generally, the film industry had a close relationship to the British theatre. Most of the studios were sited in London suburbs and relied to a great extent on stage actors. Critics remarked that these actors were given to more flamboyant gestures than were their US rivals. British films failed to keep pace with the development in techniques and increase in production values, nor did they develop or enjoy the virtues of the continuity system in terms of the look of the film and organisation of a film story.

The production values on Bamforth's Winky films are a case in point. Vanessa Toulmin, a fairground and film historian remarked (in *Holmfirth Hollywood*, 2006) that they still had the look and techniques of productions from 1900. It is revealing that when, later in the war, directors were sought for two important productions supported by the Ministry of Information, they hired Hollywood film-makers. D. W. Griffith made *Hearts of the World* in 1917, and Herbert Brenon directed *The Invasion of Britain* (1918). The latter was not finished until the end of the war and was never publicly exhibited.

Factual films also developed from the typical one reeler in these years. Films about the war were difficult at first because the military declined to assist cameramen in filming at the front. After continued protests by the trade the War Office Topical Committee was set up in 1915 and access was opened up. One of the key films that resulted from this was *The Battle of the Somme* (1916). A five reel production, filmed during the actual battle (though not all the footage is actually from the front line), it made a great impression on audiences. It was shown to packed cinemas and at special events. It generated more enthusiasm for the war, but it also brought home to audiences the grim nature of modern warfare.

Topical films went back to earliest cinema. Newsreels had emerged as a regular part of the exhibition programme circa 1910. They arrived with the introduction of *Pathé's Animated Gazette*. The British firm Topical Budget produced and distributed a weekly news digest from 1911 to 1931.[7]

ii. France

Just prior to the war the French film company Pathé Frères shifted its focus from production to distribution and exhibition. It also withdrew from the Motion Picture Patents Company in the USA. This move, designed to consolidate its power in the home market, weakened both French exports and domestic film production. The advent of war undermined production even more, as film theatres were closed. They did reopen after a few months, but French film production was considerably reduced in this period.

Pathé was still involved in the developments in French film-making, particularly in relation to two new popular genres: the detective story and the serial. There was a spate of films featuring detectives in the early teens; revealingly even European films often featured US detectives. The French company Éclair produced a series of films from 1908 onwards, based on the detective *Dick Winter*. This genre crossed over with the serial. This was a multi-part story of up to a dozen episodes. Later versions were extremely lengthy with each episode lasting two or even three reels. These serials usually involved mystery and detection, and after the outbreak of war spies were added to the mix. The stories had heroes and heroines, but often the villain was the most charismatic character. An expert in this field was the Louis Feuillade, who worked for Pathé's rival Gaumont. His great serial is *Fantomas* (1913), a master criminal capable of amazing feats and disguises. And there is *Les Vampires* (1915) where the central character is an equally resourceful and attractive woman, played by the actress Musidora dressed in an all black skin-tight outfit. Serials offered many of the pleasures of early cinema, with daring stunts, surprise twists, disguises and exotic themes. The narratives, over so many episodes, were often quite rambling. These serials were immensely popular in the early and mid-teens.[8]

Pathé produced and distributed in both Belgium and Holland. The French filmmaker Albert Machin directed films in both countries. A key and impressive work was his *Maudite soit la guerre*, 1913, filmed in Pathécolor. This was a melodrama with a pacifist slant set in a fictional war, but which clearly commented on the militarism across Europe. In an impressively varied career Machin also filmed wild life documentaries in Africa and made some rather bizarre dramas that featured animals.

iii. Italy

The Italian cinema made a serious impact in the international film market in the early teens. This was especially true of the new genre of historical epic. In 1913 the novel *Quo Vadis?* was filmed, for the first time of many. And in 1914 came *Cabiria*, a massively popular film, at home and abroad. It was set in Rome of the third century before Christ. There were enormous set pieces, which showed off the Italian film-maker's abilities in set construction. The film made particular use of forward and reverse tracking shots, a technique little used before this time. Audiences so took to the lead character, Maciste, that a whole series of films followed featuring him.

Another distinctive genre among Italian film-makers was the melodrama that featured a 'diva'. An early example was *But My Love Does not Die* (*Ma l'amor mio non muore*, 1913). This made a star of Lyda Borelli, who suffers and dies in the film with magnificent abandon. Typical plots involved passion and intrigue in an upper class or aristocratic setting, providing the opportunity for sumptuous staging. In part this seemed an attempt to attract more affluent patrons by rivalling the experience of Italian theatre and opera. Divas like Borelli, and her rival Francesca Bertini, were central to Italian films for a number of years. But its developing industry failed to maintain its impetus and declined after the war.

iv. Russia

The Russian film industry developed during the war years, partly due to a reduction in the volume of imported films. The first Russian film production company Drankov Studio appeared in 1907. By late 1914 there were three important production companies: Drankov, Khanzhonkov and Yermoliev. Russian feature films had a distinctive style and content. They were noted for offering audiences sad or tragic endings. It is recorded that imported films often had happy endings changed for sadder ones, and that exports had happy endings to replace the original downbeat ones for domestic audiences. Russian films also had a tendency towards tableaux staging, with both long takes and deep staging. Early film and lenses frequently offered deep focus, where the depth of field in the frame is extensive. However, Russian films exploited this to an unusual degree.

One of the key directors in this period was Yevgeni Bauer. He combined staging in depth with distinctive lighting, often from side on. (Staging in depth is when the film offers material of interest in the back of the frame, there is an example in the discussion of Bauer's film, *After Death*. Bauer also frequently uses a technique often associated with deep staging, deep focus; this being when the image provides enough depth of field to clearly discern material in the rear of the frame.) And he combined long takes with some unusual (for the period) tracking shots. In *Daydreams* (*Gryozy*, 1915) Bauer offers a morbid story of a husband who tries to recreate his dead wife in another woman (the film looks forward to Hitchcock's 1958 masterpiece, *Vertigo*). The husband's fetishism is summed up in a lock of hair that he keeps from the dead wife. Such psychological depictions were unusual for the period.

Another key director was Yakov Protazanov. He directed one of the several film adaptations of Pushkin's *The Queen of Spades* (1916). This tale of a man's obsession with a supposedly magical card combination contained an intense performance by Ivan Mozhukhin as the protagonist. He was one of the popular actors of the period as Russian cinema developed its own star system.[9]

An abrupt disruption to the industry occurred with the revolution of 1917. A new and very different cinema emerged after this. Many of the personnel of the industry fled abroad with Tsarist émigrés. Protazanov was one of the few pre-revolutionary directors to return and work in the new industry.

v. Scandinavia

The Scandinavian film industries were in a state of flux in these years. Denmark had sizeable and important parts of both the German and Russian film markets. The Danish directors were in the forefront of developments of film lighting. In particular Benjamin Christensen in *The Mysterious X* (1913) made dramatic use of light and shadow in a story that combined suspense with the macabre. As the war progressed this business was increasingly disrupted as the industry relied heavily on the Russian and German markets. The main production company, Nordisk, had an international success with *Atlantis* (1913), directed by August Blom. The film made great use of well-designed sets and spectacular action, including the sinking of an ocean-going liner, clearly referring to the Titanic disaster of the previous year. The star Asta Nielsen was Blom's protégé. But there was an exodus from the Danish film industry, either to Sweden or to Germany.

The Swedish industry was developing in this period. The Svenska Biografteatern Company was founded in 1907 (it still produces today as Svenska). Three key directors worked at Svenska: Georg AF Klercker, Mauritz Stiller and Victor Sjöström. Stiller and Sjöström were especially important in the late teens and 1920s. However, in 1913 Sjöström had already made one key silent masterwork, *Ingeborg Holm* (1913). This was a five reeler recounting the travails of a middle class family. The husband dies, and the wife and mother descends into poverty and then madness. The film crosses over with the contemporary work of British director Ken Loach in dealing directly with social problems. It uses both long takes and deep staging to build up a powerful picture of the tragedy.

vi. Germany

The war and the policy of retrenchment actually aided the German film industry. Prior to 1914 the market was dominated by imports. This was partly due to the low artistic status of film in Germany, and theatrical people actually boycotted making films. This boycott broke down in the teens, and then in 1916 foreign imports were banned.

Among the developments in the industry was the rise of a type of art film, parallel to the Film d'Art in France. A key example is *The Student of Prague* (*Der Student von Prag*, 1913). The film stars featured actor Paul Wegener as a student involved in a Faust-like bargain. Wegener both played the student and his 'doppelgänger' (mirror image). This was achieved by sophisticated in-camera special effects.

In the later stages of the war the pressure from the military high command, worried about the superiority of the Allied war propaganda, led to the setting up of a Photographic and Film Office, BUFA. This was to be the basis for the great film company Ufa, which with both commercial and Government funds acquired a number of production, distribution and exhibition companies to become the dominant studio in Germany and across Europe in the 1920s.

STUDY FILM: THE BIRTH OF A NATION

David W. Griffith Corp. USA 1915. 12 reels, 11,700 feet, running time of 190 minutes at 16 fps.

Directed by D. W. Griffith. Writers D. W. Griffith assisted by Frank Woods.

The Birth of a Nation was based on two novels, *The Leopard's Spots* and *The Clansman*, which was also a stage play, by Thomas Dixon. Filming took place between July and November 1914 and the film was premiered in February 1915. Originally it was released as *The Clansman* and then re-titled as *The Birth of a Nation*. The film cost around $110,000 dollars, though there was also an expensive marketing campaign with intensive publicity, attractions like the specially prepared musical accompaniment and extended road-show screenings.

The film starred Griffith regulars Henry B. Walthall and Lillian Gish, with Robert Harron, Miriam Cooper and relative newcomer Mae Marsh as the little sister. Black characters were white actors in 'black-face', though there were also genuine black people among the extras.

The Birth of a Nation is both famous and infamous. Its success, innovation and grandiose epic proportions have made it one of the most influential films in US history. But its racist treatment of the US Civil War and post war construction have made it a notorious and problematic classic. There have been quite a number of attempts to play down the racism in the film and/or to excuse Griffith for the content. I incline with the comment in an excellent book by Scott Simmon (*The Films of D. W. Griffith*) who discusses some of these 'defenders': 'what is evident to all but the most determined apologists: *The Birth of a Nation* has evolved into one of the ugliest artefacts of American popular art.' Paul Gilroy, in his introduction to Channel 4's screening of the Thames Silents version (1993), commented that it was a 'white supremacist text', but also a film masterpiece. He pointed out how the film sexualises the conflict through the use of melodrama. Yet the film is an enduring presence in US popular art, and it needs to be confronted. Simmon's book is helpful because he studies the film in some detail, examining its influences and recognising those aspects that contributed to its power and success.

The surviving film is not complete; the version most widely available is from the 1921 reissue. Griffith cut some scenes because of the complaints about the film, but it is not completely clear what has been excised. The remaining film still offers a clear narrative. In a manner reminiscent of much of his work at Biograph, Griffith presents his picture of the US Civil War and the reconstruction of the defeated South in terms of family melodrama.[10]

The film opens in 1860 before the start of the war between the States and introduces us to the Cameron family (southerners) and the Stoneman family (northerners). The opening two reels allow the development of audience identification, especially with the Cameron family. We witness a visit by the Stoneman sons to the Cameron household in Piedmont, South Carolina. In the manner of the earlier Biograph films some of the characters have appellations rather than names in the intertitles. For the contemporary audience a programme provided the cast list. The doctor and his wife head the Cameron family. The eldest Cameron son is Ben, who, during the war years, becomes 'the little colonel'. The youngest Cameron's son, Duke, and the youngest Stoneman strike up a friendship and earn the title 'chums'. We only learn the name of the eldest Cameron son, Phil, later during a Civil War battle. And the Cameron second son Wade is scarcely identified and remains a minor character. The youngest Cameron daughter Flora is only shown as the 'Little Sister' in the title cards. A romance develops between Phil and the eldest Cameron daughter, Margaret. And Ben is smitten when he sees Phil's portrait of the absent Elsie, who is with her father senator Stoneman in Washington.

The Cameron family is given a positive, warm representation, which includes loyal, uncritical black slaves. There is also an early example of a long Hollywood line of identifications, sympathetic characters presented with their pets. (The main villain, a mulatto Silas Lynch, is later shown mistreating a dog!) However, the representation of the Stoneman family is more problematic. There is no mother, though her absence is not explained. In keeping with his roots in nineteenth century melodrama, mother figures are central to Griffith's notions of the wholesome family. Stoneman walks with a stick, often associated with either weakness or villainy. In reel 2 a title card warns the audience of Stoneman's 'fatal weakness' – a mulatto servant, Lydia Brown, who becomes his mistress. This is the viper in the nest. And the representation picks up on a warning placed clearly in the opening title of the surviving film: 'The bringing of the African sowed the first seed of disunion.' Black people are the central problem in the film, and they create disunity within the 'American family'. It is important to remember that the Civil War was fought initially over the Union and the South's attempt at secession, not directly over slavery.

Scott Simmon relates Griffith's film to the developing genres of the Civil War film and to the costume dramas set in the South. He details some of the contemporary films that dealt with similar material. Miscegenation is clearly a common issue in these films. *At the Cross Roads* (1914) has white-skinned Annabel discover 'tainted blood' and she tells her white-skinned fiancé 'as long as there is a stain of Negro blood we can be nothing more than friends'. Clearly, popular film tended to reproduce the dominant racism of wider society. There is also the myth of the pre-war south, a paradise of courtly gentlemen, dainty belles and happy, unthreatening slaves. A key sequence in the film is the ball before the Southern gentlemen ride off to war; a spectacle repeated in innumerable later films. The ball is intercut with a bonfire and celebrations in the streets, tinted red in the original. Despite the plotline including both families, the film clearly privileges the experience of the South, an odd predilection that continues to this day, as in the more recent Civil War films: *Gods and Generals* (2003) and *Gettysburg* (1993).

In the third, fourth and fifth reels, Griffith presents some aspects of this war. In classic melodramatic convention the 'chums' meet and die on the front line in opposing armies. The final shot of the battle shows the fallen bodies in a deathly embrace. The second Cameron son dies in a scene depicting Sherman's 'march to the sea'. This is a powerful sequence, using superimposition and crosscutting, that depicts Sherman's army and the burning of Atlanta. Gilroy's point about 'sexualising' the conflict is borne out here in a title card: 'The torch of war against the breast of Atlanta.' Griffith also uses the powerful image of a harassed mother and children, both intercutting with the soldiers, and superimposing the image within the same frame as the battle.

There is a guerrilla raid on the town of Piedmont, where the Cameron family resides. The raid is led by a 'scallywag white captain', in charge of black militia, who reappears late in the film. The Cameron women hide in the cellar as the black soldiers' loot and pillage. Confederate irregulars run to the rescue and repulse the raid. This is clearly a precursor for the scenes that follow in the post Civil War south.

There is only one major battle sequence, which is Petersburg. As Simmon points out though, it acts more like a generic battle of the whole Civil War. Again the emphasis is on the heroic south, even as they lose. Colonel Ben Cameron is the key figure in a courageous but hopeless charge against the Union lines. The battlefield meeting convention recurs as the Colonel falls wounded at the feet of Captain Phil Stoneman. Ben convalesces in a Washington hospital and he is able to develop a relationship with Elsie, who is a nurse there.

Reel 6 dramatises the assassination of Lincoln, and the ascendance to power of 'carpetbaggers' in Washington. Once again history is personalised as Elsie and Phil are in the theatre audience. Lincoln's death makes Stoneman a key political figure determined that the South should be 'treated as conquered provinces' and to 'put the white South under the heel of the black south'. His mulatto mistress is shown as a noxious influence, encouraging a black opportunist, Silas Lynch. This sets the scene for the way in which Griffith's film develops a more shocking dimension in the second part, titled *Reconstruction*.

Ben Cameron returns to the defeated south, family loss and a home ruined by war. For Griffith and the Cameron family the southern blacks are incapable of either equality or democracy. There is a manichean split in the representation of black characters in the film. They are either unquestioningly devoted and loyal servants, or they are given to feckless singing, dancing, drinking, and in some cases even to rape and violence. Their excessive acting style emphasises these characteristics. One scene has a Cameron servant whipped for loyalty to his white master. The black population is seen as at the mercy of leaders and carpetbaggers, who 'cozen, beguile and use the Negro'. This threat to family and southern order creates the response, the Ku Klux Klan – heroic defenders of the endangered white community.

In line with generic conventions this threat is personalised in attacks on white women. Gus, 'the renegade', pursues the little sister who jumps to her death rather than face dishonour. And Stoneman's black protégé, Silas Lynch, menaces Elsie Stoneman. Interestingly, neither black character appears to be bent on rape, but rather on marriage to a white woman. But the staging and editing used by Griffith generate a sense of violation. In addition, Mae Marsh demonstrates a more melodramatic acting style than other leading white characters, and her death becomes an orgy of hysteria. This is cemented in melodramatic fashion as 'the little colonel' cradles the dying body of his 'little sister'.

There follows a night-time scene of the trial of Gus. Then the Klan leader holds aloft the 'flag that bears the red stain of a southern woman' and the call goes out for a ride to save the South. These final three reels of the film prepare and then launch a bravura intercutting of the Klan riding thunderously to rescue Elsie from 'a fate worse than death'; white townspeople harassed and victimised by black riffraff; and, a besieged cabin where both southerners and northerners are fending off crazed black soldiers. The cabin suggests an image of a reconstructed 'American family' as Union veterans, with a young daughter, offer shelter to the Camerons, who are accompanied by Phil Stoneman, now in opposition to his father. They 'defend their Aryan birthright'. Predictably all are saved and the black soldiery is put to flight. This victory and the renewed union between north and south are cemented by the marriages of Ben and Elsie, Margaret and Phil. The film ends with a rhetorical flourish to antiwar sentiment and Christian piety rather at odds with the bloodthirsty actions of the Clan.

Stylistically the film uses the form familiar from Griffith's Biograph work. The intertitles tend to explain the action, often prompting the audience prior to the scenes in question. There are only occasional camera movements, such as pans across the battle action and one reverse track during the final conflict. Exciting motion, such as the ride of the Clan, adheres to the style of early film, with the camera almost frontal to the movement. The most sophisticated aspects are in the editing, the masking of images and superimposition.

Griffith's editing of the final reels – which depict, in quick succession, the Klan, the distraught Elsie, the panicking townsfolk and the besieged cabin – generates excitement and dynamism. This was amplified at the premiere as an orchestra filled the theatre with Wagner's *Ride of the Valkyries*. Elsewhere Griffith uses similar techniques to dramatise the death of little sister and the heroic actions of Colonel Ben Cameron. In the sequence in which Elsie flees from Gus, intercut with the Colonel's search for her, Griffith alternates mid-shots of the characters, iris style close-ups showing their emotional state, and long shots that place the characters in the landscape of trees and rocks. Editing is also used to reinforce the stereotypes of the black characters: early in the film cutting to their simple frolicking dances and later to their more menacing drunkenness and violence.

Griffith, as in his Biograph films, has a real fondness for the use of masks within the frame. What the viewer sees appears to reduce the image within the frame by closing down the iris, though masks came in a number of shapes and sizes. The Sherman sequence is visually very sophisticated with the Union army, the burning Atlanta, refugees and the distraught mother and children. He uses a soft edged iris to focus on particular action or objects. In many scenes such techniques function as a form of close-up, showing us a character or an important object. There is a particular fine iris out in the theatre sequence, which gives the impression of a reverse tracking shot. The film also uses extensive tinting of the image. The bonfires in Piedmont are tinted red, as are a number of shots in the battle sequences, notably for the burning of Atlanta. Red tinting is also used for the 'ride of the Klan', including a famous shot of horse riders silhouetted against the skyline and a striking full moon.

Griffith brings a particularly powerful set of techniques to the staging of melodramatic moments. As in his earlier films he makes good use of natural scenery and of well designed interiors. The representation of the Cameron family is enhanced by the way characters are sited in domestic settings and against natural landscape. As the narrative develops, Griffith emphasises emotion through the use of *mise-en-scène*. The scene of Ben returning to his home in the aftermath of war is very powerful. He walks along the deserted street, to the dilapidated house, with the strains of 'There's no place like home' played in the original music score. Little sister runs out to greet him and leads him inside. As they cross the door frame a second arm appears and pulls him inside, presumably the arm of his mother. The flight of little sister and the search of the Colonel for her take place among trees and rocks, and there is a powerful sense of wilderness. Gus (the black assailant) is given a masked shot in close-up in which his face is framed menacing by hanging branches.

Griffith also uses the facsimile; a reconstruction based on well-known historical or cultural representations. Thus, we get the carefully designed and constructed Ford Theatre, where Lincoln was assassinated. This was a common device in silent film and played on audience fore knowledge. However, as Simmon points out, there is a serious discrepancy in Griffith's use of this device. In the first part of the film the facsimiles are based on well know photographs or paintings; however, in the second part of the film, especially those depicting the black people in political situations, the reconstructions are taken from political lampoons. It should be noted that facsimiles in the first part of the film credit their source. In the second part a reconstruction of the South Carolina House of Representatives is credited to a photographic source, but there is no reference to the political lampoons identified by Simmon. This further feeds into the myth-making function of the film, passed off to contemporary audiences as historical reconstruction.

The film was an undoubted success. A Hearst reviewer in *The Evening Journal* wrote: '*The Birth of a Nation* will thrill you, startle you, make you hold onto your seats. It will make you cry. It will make you angry. It will make you glad. It will make you hate. It will make you love. It is not only worth riding miles to see, but it is worth walking miles to see' (in Bowser, Gaines and Musser, 2001: 69). Karl Brown describes at least some of these emotions in his recollection of the opening night and the film's climax: 'When the clansmen began to ride, the cheers began from all over that packed house. This was not a ride to save Little Sister but to avenge her death, and every soul in that audience was in the saddle with the clansmen and pounding hell-for-leather on an errand of stern justice, lighted on their way by the holy flames of a burning cross' (*Adventures with D. W. Griffith*, p. 94).

But much of this emotion was generated by a racist, white supremacist assault on black people. And there was fierce contemporary criticism and controversy over the film. The National Association for the Advancement of Coloured People organised protests against the film. There were riots in some cities over screenings. The American Film Institute Catalog, *Within Our Gates*, has a fairly detailed account of such activities. In some cities opponents were successful in having cuts enforced in the film or its screenings cancelled. But many Censor Boards were happy to pass the film as it stood. There is also an account of a visit by Thomas Dixon to accompany a screening of the film in Boston. In an interview he opposed intermarriage (between white and black) and proceeded to argue his desire to secure the removal of all of the Negroes from the United States (Simmon, 1993: 126). In the 1920s the film was certainly used by the Ku Klux Klan in its recruiting drives.

It is likely that the controversy also attracted attention and more customers. Griffith was probably well aware of this: Karl Brown recalled '... when the director was told that the film might cause riots in Atlanta, his reaction was "I hope to God it does"' (*Sight & Sound*, June 1994). Certainly, despite the offence caused, the film was extremely profitable. And that profitability was carefully handled in a way that was to become Hollywood's trademark.

> During all this Griffith was still in and out of town, managing the various business details of showing *The Clansman*. Too big and much too important to be handled through normal booking channels, *The Clansman* was peddled out to various moneyed men on a franchise basis, in which the purchaser got the right to exhibit the picture within

certain defined territories, plus a percentage of the earnings over an agreed-upon ceiling. The New England rights went to a former junk-dealer name Mayer, who made a fortune out of his investment. (*Adventures...* , p.128)

Louis B. Mayer's fortune became the basis for the Hollywood major studio, M-G-M, and much of the film's profit funded his first forays in production around 1916-17. The seminal influence of *The Birth of a Nation* on Hollywood can be traced in many ways. As with the example of Mayer, the economic success fed into the development of the Hollywood industry and majors, which remain to this day. In both the form of its narrative and in its style Griffith's film had a powerful impact on contemporary and subsequent film-makers. Steven Spielberg's depiction of the family in films such as *E.T.* (1982) follows in Griffith's footsteps, and that film actually contains a homage to the earlier film as the boys and E.T. fly in front of the face of the moon on their bicycles, a parallel to a shot in *Birth of a Nation* where the Klansmen ride across the face of the moon. But unfortunately the value system embedded in the film also remains potent in Hollywood. The stereotypes of both black people and the South carried on in Hollywood for decades, and we are not entirely free of them even today.

STUDY FILM: MAD LOVE

The currently available DVD contains *Twilight of a Woman's Soul / Sumerki zhenskoi Dushi* (1913), *The Dying Swan / Umirayushchii Lebed* (1917) and *After Death / Posle smerty* (1915).

Russia. Directed by Yevgeni Bauer.

Twilight of a Woman's Soul appears to be missing the third reel and should probably have a running time of about an hour (there is no information on the DVD about this). *The Dying Swan* is probably the most morbid film of the three, and gives a sense of the preoccupation with fetishism and death found in these films. The film on which I wish to focus is *After Death*.

All three films are in tinted versions and there is purposely composed music performed by a piano and string trio. The extras on the disc include a half-hour illustrated discussion of the films by Yuri Tsivian, one of the leading film historians on early Russian and Soviet cinemas. Tsivian's commentary is very helpful, as it deals in detail with the techniques and style in the films, provides some sort of context and fills out the cultural references.

After Death is a three reel film running for 46 minutes. It was probably screened about 16 frames per second, typical for that period. Vera Karalli heads the cast as a young actress and Vitold Polonskii is the male protagonist Andrei: both were regular leading actors in Bauer's films. Karalli was a major star of the growing industry. For the later *Dying Swan* she gave ballet performances to accompany screenings of the film, which were hugely popular. The story is taken from a tale by Turgenev, *Klara Milich*, and the DVD commentary by Tsivian points up some important differences in the film version.

Andrei is a young recluse, cared for by an aunt, and obsessed with his dead mother, whose portrait dominates his room. Dragged to a social event by a friend, he meets a young actress. Each is struck by the other. Shortly after the actress meets Andrei and declares her love. Andrei rejects her love and she commits suicide. He is stricken by remorse and finds himself haunted by strange dreams of her. Inexorably, he is driven to his death.

In fact, all three of the Bauer films are obsessed with death and suggestions of necrophilia. Bauer's obsession reflected a dark fascination in Russian elite culture and in the important art movement of Symbolism. Symbolists were especially interested in moods and psychological states, a staple of Bauer's films. The drive of artworks was to express the mystical or the abstract rather than the realistic. Whilst Bauer's stories are naturalistic, in the sense that we view recognisable characters, places and events, their powerful sequences are often bizarre, even dreamlike.

This downbeat, even tragic stance, is one that Bauer shared with a range of other Russian films of the period, and to a lesser degree with other European films. This is film that might be considered a form of art cinema. By 1910 film was moving into purpose-built venues, and increasingly these promised more opulent surroundings, partly with the aim of attracting more bourgeois customers. At the same time films began to offer a more extravagant staging and design, and stories closer to classic literature and theatre, rather than just straight popular melodrama.

In *After Death* one can see the affluent world of the bourgeoisie on display with the type of characters found not only in novels by Turgenev, but also Tolstoy and in literature and opera across nineteenth century Europe. But Bauer also provides in his films interesting and polished cinematic techniques. Tsivian discuss in detail a scene early in the film when Andrei accompanies his friend to a social function. This includes a three minute reverse tracking shot with pans to both left and right. This is an unusually sophisticated camera shot and movement for the period. Italian films had developed the use of tracking shots, for both their Roman epics and bourgeois dramas, but rarely with this complexity and assuredness. The shot is the more effective because Bauer works consistently with deep focus and deep staging. Whilst this is also a not uncommon technique for the period, Bauer's use of it is exemplary. Commentator Tsivian also discusses deep staging at another bourgeois social function in *Twilight of a Woman's Soul*. He points out how, just as the track in *After Death* expressed Andrei's psychological state, the staging in the former film comments psychologically on the character.

Bauer had worked in design for the theatre and then in film before becoming a director. Tsivian notes admiringly his command of spatial relations in his films. He also shows a mastery of lighting, using distinctive and evocative settings. There are contrasts between light and dark not only between scenes but also within the staging of particular scenes. In the original Turgenev novel, Andrei was a scientist, but in the Bauer film he has become a photographer. In one scene he uses a lantern to examine a photograph of the dead actress, paralleling the projection with which the story itself is on display. It also heightens the emphasis in the film on fetishism. This is another common element in Bauer's films. At one point in the story Andrei has a dream of visitation from the dead actress. Crossing the boundary between reality and fantasy, he is left with a lock of her hair in his hand. This echoes the fetishism of the husband in *Daydreams* who, obsessed with his dead wife, strangles his current mistress with a lock of her hair that he has kept in a box on his desk.

FOOTNOTES

1. In 1912 Bell and Howell developed a perforator that standardised sprocket holes.

2. *White Fawn's Devotion* is included on *Treasures of the American Archives*, and is provided with background information on the film and its production.

3. The contemporary description of the indigenous North Americans is Native Americans. In the teens and twenties 'Indians' or 'Red Indians' was used, a continuation of the mistake made by European explorers who thought they had arrived in Asia, not a 'New World'.

4. *Where are my Children?* features on *New Women* disc II, in the Library of Congress *Treasures III: Social Issues* collection.

5. *The Whispering Chorus* is available on a Region I DVD from Image Entertainment. It demonstrates the very high production values to be found in Hollywood films by this date.

6. An example would be films adapted from stories by Charles Dickens. There are examples on the BFI *Dickens Before Sound* DVD. Included are extracts from a 1913 version of *David Copperfield* by the Hepworth Company. This was unusually long at eight reels and with higher than average production values.

7. There is a book on *Topical Budget* (BFI, 1992) with an accompanying VHS video.

8. *Fantomas* and *Les Vampires* are available on DVD. An episode of a US serial, *The Wild Engine*, Episode #26 from the serial *The Hazards of Helen* (14 min., 1915) is available on *More Treasures from the American Film Archives*.

9. The BFI has produced a series of videos that provide an anthology of early Russian films. The set, *Early Russian Cinema*, comes in 10 VHS cassettes. It includes the earlier Russian short films, key films of the teens, like those of Evgenij Bauer, and films that preceded the Soviet Revolution in 1917. The sleeve notes are fairly detailed with names, dates and some production details. Both Protazanov's *The Queen of Spades* and Bauer's *Daydreams* are included.

10. The Eureka DVD has a version of *The Birth of a Nation* based on the 1921 reissue, with an adaptation of the original score arranged by Joseph Carl Breil. This is a plain black and white print and the framing is not consistent, sometimes slightly cropping edges of the frame. The better version is the Photoplay restoration (by Kevin Brownlow and David Gill), which is also from the 1921 reissue. This offers the original tinting, exact framing and (for my money) a better musical score adapted by Joseph Lanchbery from the surviving records of Briel's arrangements.

4. THE MATURE SILENT CINEMA

The Gold Rush

INTRODUCTION

From the end of the World War I until the end of the silent era in 1927 – and beyond – Hollywood dominated the international film industry. The Hollywood studios reached their peak, both in their organisation and efficiency, and in the sheer quality of their product. But this quality was fed from both within and without. Part of the response to Hollywood dominance was for other film industries to develop and exploit their own distinctive features, ranging from English idiosyncrasy, through art films in Germany and France, to complete contradiction in the Soviet Union. This section discusses those cinemas which were part of an international industry dominated by commerce.

One of the important features of Hollywood is the consolidation of the studio system. This includes its economic organisation, its organisation of both workforce and resources, and the form of its product. Each can be a substantial area of study.

As with earlier periods it is possible to study this industry by using examples. Paramount is a good case study in terms of the importance of vertical integration, and the control of the distribution and exhibition markets. M-G-M is a good example of the ruthless but effective efficiency pursued in a major studio. Case studies on the likes of Thalberg or Mayer would be illuminating.

While many of the films of the period are only accessible in specialist venues there are a substantial number of quality films on DVD and Blu-Ray. Both director studies, like Griffith or de Mille, and star studies, like Chaplin or Pickford, are really useful. All are relatively well represented in both formats. It is worth noting that even in the 1920s there was a degree of specialisation with both stars and studios tending to favour particular genres.

Beyond Hollywood, Britain is clearly an interesting subject. There are not that many British films easily available, but there is a great deal of material on the industry. This is a worthwhile study because of the parallels with contemporary British cinema and because the historical roots of the industry's weaknesses are apparent in this period. The one film-maker with ample work available is Alfred Hitchcock. In an earlier period his British work was dismissed in comparison to his Hollywood films, or studied merely as an apprenticeship for that work. Several recent studies have discussed the films on their own merits. Hitchcock is a good subject because of the obvious quality of his work on narrative and style. He is also interesting because one can see him learning from other cinemas, especially German expressionism and Soviet montage (see Chapter Five) but at the same time he is able to provide a distinctive and realistic sense of contemporary Britain.

Of the other European industries, the country with most material available on DVD is Germany, in particular the expressionist cinema. This has the advantage that the influence of its conventions can still be seen clearly in modern horror, one reason being the long shelf life of *Nosferatu* (1922), directed by F. W. Murnau. Other films by Murnau are also available on DVD and he is one of the exponents of the 'unchained camera'. Films like *The Last Laugh* (1924) or *Faust* (1926) stand up well and have a rich style for study.

I. POST WORLD WAR I HOLLYWOOD: THE STUDIO AND STAR SYSTEMS

In 1918, by the end World War I, the US film industry, with its production base in Hollywood, dominated its own vast domestic market and the international film market. Film-makers in other countries and industries still turned out successful movies, but they almost all did so in the shadow of Hollywood.

During the 1920s Hollywood consolidated into a small group of vertically integrated companies which produced films to meet the weekly requirement of distributors and exhibitors. Around these 'majors' (as they became known) were smaller production companies who specialised in particular genres or modes of film, for example comedies and animation. The key figures in developing the major companies were the studio heads, i.e. the 'moguls'.

Adolph Zukor was an East European migrant who eventually became one such film mogul. He opened a nickelodeon in New York in the early years of the twentieth century. Then he founded the Famous Players Company and built success partly on the basis of having contracted the rising star Mary Pickford. The company merged with that of Jesse Lasky and then the Paramount Studios. Famous Players-Lasky was the pacesetter in Hollywood in the late teens, partly because of the strength of its theatre chain and its leading stars.

The majors concentrated particularly on 'first run' theatres, sited in city centres, charging high prices and setting the baseline for marketing. The new purpose-built theatres of the 1920s were extremely large, a number seating over 5000 customers. They were decked out in opulence and luxury. One patron remembered this was the first time working people walked on carpets (*The People's Century*, 'The Great Escape', BBC 25 October 1995). The major city theatres took over half of the admission income in this period. So whilst the majors did not own a majority of the theatres they exerted a powerful influence. Famous Players-Lasky also pioneered a system of block booking, where exhibitors had to commit to a whole year's product in order to obtain the company's most expensive and high profile pictures.

At the end of the teens the keenest rivalry was between Famous Players-Lasky and the First National Exhibitors Circuit. The latter was set up by leading exhibitors aiming to produce their own pictures. In this way they hoped to avoid the market power of the major studios. Initially, First National benefited from a number of contracted stars with a strong box office appeal. These included Charlie Chaplin and Mary Pickford. However, First National never achieved Famous Players-Lasky's strength in vertical integration. It was eventually taken over by Warner Bros. in 1928.

One of the most important studios in the long term was to be Metro-Goldwyn-Mayer. This was the product of the merger of Metro Pictures, Goldwyn Pictures and Louis B. Mayer Productions in 1924. Metro was already associated with Loew Enterprises, which controlled a chain of cinemas. Thus, M-G-M was also vertically integrated. Mayer was the key person in the merger and was another powerful mogul (Sam Goldwyn had already left M-G-M by this point). With the arrival of M-G-M the studio system model was fully established.

These three studios were part of larger companies with both distribution outlets and exhibition chains. Other important studios did not have the same exhibition power. One company, Universal, was led by mogul Carl Laemmle, who opened his first nickelodeon in Chicago. In 1909 he founded the Independent Motion Picture Company. A series of mergers in 1912 with other small companies provided the basis for the Universal Picture Company. The first feature film from the new company was *Traffic in Souls* (1913). This story of the 'white slave traffic' was a tremendous box office hit. The profits helped pay for one of the earliest purpose built Hollywood studios.

Another studio was the Fox Film Corporation, established in 1916. The founder, William Fox, opened his first nickelodeon in New York in 1904. He then set up the Greater New York Film Rental Company. In 1914 he started film production and in 1916 the company moved its production base to Hollywood.

In 1919 Chaplin and Pickford founded a rather different company, United Artists. This company emerged in response to the growing power of Paramount and First National. The dominance of these new studios threatened the many independent companies involved in film production in Hollywood. Four of the most powerful stars of the industry set up United Artists to act as a distributor for their films. Besides Chaplin and Pickford, there was Douglas Fairbanks and the director, D. W. Griffith. Metro President Richard Rowland famously quipped 'So, the lunatics have taken charge of the asylum' (Finler, 1992: 322).

The moguls who ran the studios had worked up through the industry, first in exhibition, then in distribution and production. They had a keen sense of the public tastes and knew what sort of product would sell well. They also organised and controlled the production process with close attention to detail. This was achieved by a chain of command built on a highly developed division of labour in the studio.

In 1919 Carl Laemmle at Universal brought in Irving Thalberg, who became general manager of the Universal City Studio. Thalberg maintained a strict balance between the lavish expenditure of the studio's glossy pictures and the income generated through their distribution and exhibition. In the mid-twenties he moved to M-G-M, where he set similar standards. Executive producers like Thalberg were an integral part of the studio system. At Famous Players-Lasky, Adolph Zukor brought B. P. Schulberg from the eastern office and he became head of the studio production, fulfilling a similar role to that of Thalberg.

The studios built and retained a high level of craft skills in their films through the contract system. Foremost among the contract staff were the stars. Assets like Chaplin and Pickford were key in selling popular movies to large audiences. Chaplin and Pickford moved between companies earning high salaries and increasingly controlling their own productions. As the industry developed the contracts were tightened so that the large sums invested in the player could be protected over long periods. Increasingly, studios sought to tie a star under contract, typically running for seven years.

Equally the studios attempted to build up teams of successful craftsmen. Director Raoul Walsh worked for the Fox Company from 1915 to 1920. Cecil B. De Mille was with Lasky or Paramount from 1913 to 1926. Famous Players also had Karl Brown, a cameraman who worked with Griffith, employed from 1920 to 1925. And at the beginning of the twenties they had two of the newly important and skilled art directors, Ben Carré and Robert Haas.

As the studios developed their craft teams they were able to efficiently organise and deliver on a sort of assembly line. Individual products followed a general blueprint, which included generic features, narrative conventions, stylistic conventions and the centrality of the studio stars. Each picture fitted the general plan but was individually designed and built (a process known as serial production). This ensured that the films would roll out of the studio with the regularity required by the cinema chains. By 1920 Famous Players-Lasky could deliver a new film every week of the year.

The movie theatres changed programmes twice weekly on average so most movie theatres used more than one company for product. However, the close co-operation between studios meant that they controlled the bulk of the US film business. Average weekly attendances rose in the 1920s from 40 million admissions to 80 million. As firms expanded and developed to exploit this market the capital investment in the industry increased ten-fold (Thompson and Bordwell, 1993: 158).

2. NARRATIVE AND STYLE IN THE 1920S MAINSTREAM FILMS

With the rise and consolidation of the studio system the classical Hollywood style was fully developed. It offered audiences clear, well laid out stories constructed with careful continuity. Continuity was at the centre of this model. The continuity of the studio process allowed films to be produced quickly and efficiently as the craft team followed the established conventions. The shared conventions meant that set builders knew the basic rules to follow. That the lighting cameraman could move into those sets and illuminate and record in a set fashion. And that the actors, costumiers and props staff could work easily, following set ways of performing. Just as film-makers learnt these conventions so did audiences, though presumably with less conscious application.

The films' narratives were constructed with a clear chain of events. The action centred on a few well-defined characters whose motivation drove the story. In bigger budget pictures, stars played the key characters. Scenarios or photoplays became an important aspect of film-making, as writers ensured that the action was comprehensible and that the individual actions fitted into the overall chain. In most cases convention dictated that the film ended with a happy outcome. In all cases the films offered 'closure', the resolution of the action with the important aspects all tied up. Manuals on scriptwriting appeared: 'Elinor Glyn published a series of books entitled The Elinor Glyn System of Writing. The third volume was devoted to the photoplay…' (Brownlow, 1968: 316).

The system of conventions and editing was perfected. Camera positions and movements followed set ways that preserved a sense of integral screen space for the audience. And the offscreen space was included by a system of matching shots, cuts and movements.

Many films were now being shot at the studio sites, either on backlots or in enclosed studios, which replaced the earlier glass-sided buildings. The latter now relied entirely on artificial light. This allowed control over technical matters. In particular, lighting was an important aspect. The studios developed a pattern of what was known as three-point lighting. This allowed key lights for important characters, and side and fill lights to fill out and give a sense of depth. Under this system the studios were able to produce images that were well lit, with an emphasis on the star, but at the same time achieve a 'natural' look. This was time consuming because lights were changed between each shot to maintain the clear, even spread. However, the continuity system allowed this to be done in the most efficient fashion.

An important development was in the change of film stock which occurred in the mid-twenties. Early film stock was orthochromatic, which was insensitive to the red colour range. This tended to give a high contrast and required the use of heavy make-up on Caucasian skins to neutralise the red tones. This also favoured studio filming, where the lighting could be more strictly controlled. Panchromatic film stock was now widely adopted. It was sensitive to the whole colour range and able to render flesh tones fairly naturalistically. But it was less senstitive to light levels. So, this required either greater lighting or the use of wider camera apertures. The latter reduced the depth of field and therefore made 'deep focus' filming less common.[1]

The change in make-up techniques developed alongside a growing restraint in gesture and performance. With the increasing use of close-ups, fuller lighting and editing that constantly moved the focus, actors developed a style closer to that of today. Acting in the 1920s is still expressive but it seems less flamboyant than in the dramas of the teens.

Also coming into use in the 1920s was colour film, two-tone Technicolor. This used two negatives, controlled by a beam splitter in the camera and in projection. It was used for particularly important scenes in big budget films, and in the later 1920s for whole films, notably Douglas Fairbanks' *The Black Pirate* (1926). Three-colour Technicolor film only became available in the 1930s.[2]

The major studios produced films across a range of genres. Programmes included the main feature, comic shorts, newsreels, music played by the accompanist or ensemble, and frequently some live entertainment acts. There were big budget features with the most popular stars, which were expected to run for weeks. And there were lower budget features, with less well-known stars, which provided the staple fare for theatres.

The Four Horsemen of the Apocalypse (1921) was one of the major films released early in the new decade. It was produced by Metro Pictures, directed by Rex Ingram and made stars of Rudolph Valentino and Alice Terry. The film lasted 11 reels running for well over two hours. The story was taken from a best-selling novel and follows the action and loves of a young Argentinean (with French ancestry) involved in the battles of World War I. It included strong scenes of melodrama, a famous and sensuous tango by Valentino and epic battle scenes. The film also featured a strong anti-war climax, inaugurating a theme that recurred consistently through the 1920s.

D. W. Griffith directed a series of classic melodramas. The most famous was *Broken Blossoms*. The cameraman Billy Bitzer provided striking images of the foggy and shadowy Limehouse district of London, filmed on studio sets. The story follows the doomed relationship between a Chinese Buddhist and a brutalised young girl. They die tragically (and conventionally given their different ethnic origins) without any sexual activity. Lillian Gish delivered an incredible performance as the young girl victimised by her father. This role set the seal on Gish's career playing melodramatic victims and confirmed her as one of the most important female stars of the silent era. Following the conventions of Hollywood in that period, a white, western actor, Richard Barthelmess, played the Chinese man.

Cecil B. De Mille directed a series of sex comedies in the late teens and early twenties. Gloria Swanson's reputation was built in these films. They were sophisticated and seduced audiences with reels of opulent imagery. The 'moral' stance of the films can be gauged from two titles, *Don't Change Your Husband* (1919) and *Why Change Your Wife?* (1920). These slightly racy films were one factor in the rise of a campaign for increased film censorship (see Chapter 6).

With great aplomb de Mille responded by developing the religious epic, combining immorality – which the film condemned – and morality – endorsed by the film's closure. *The Ten Commandments* (1923) was the epitome of this type of film. There were epic scenes of the Israelites leaving Egypt under Moses; exotic orgies as the Israelites sinned beneath Mount Sinai; and the voice of morality and God with the handing down of the Commandments themselves. The film used two-tone Technicolor for certain sequences. The biblical story was framed within a contemporary story of sin, punishment and penance. De Mille followed this success with *The King of Kings* (1927), a film about the life of Christ himself. (He remade *The Ten Commandments* with great success in the 1956.)

One new director to make his mark was Erich von Stroheim, once an assistant to D. W. Griffith. He had success with *Blind Husbands* (1919) for Universal. This story of a wife tempted by an affair whilst on holiday did well at the box office. Von Stroheim not only directed but also starred as the evil seducer, a role he replayed many times. He was then allowed to film *Foolish Wives* (1922) with a much larger budget. Von Stroheim now revealed a passionate desire for ultra-realism, building massive sets and ordering sumptuous costumes and props. Universal reckoned the film had cost over a million dollars before Irving Thalberg, the studio head of production, halted filming. Thalberg took the film away from von Stroheim and had the 30 reels cut down to 10.[3]

This inflexible approach as director and the attitudes of the studio managers became a serious problem in Stroheim's directorial career. His films are incredibly powerful narratives, filmed with magnificent style and attention to detail. But they strain at, or break, the Hollywood conventions, usually resulting in enforced cuts. Von Stroheim's masterwork is *Greed* (1924). Based on the novel *McTeague* by Frank Norris, it recounts the tragic consequences of the love of money. Early in the film McTeague marries Trina. As the wedding couple stand making their vows a funeral procession passes in the background. This is one of a number of symbols used in the film to signal to the audience. The central symbol is the hoard of gold dollars accumulated by Trina. They lead inexorably to tragedy. The films end with a climactic fight in Death Valley. The final version was incredibly long; claims vary from seven to 11 hours or even more. Stroheim had started filming under the Goldwyn Company, but, by the time he completed the film, it was under M-G-M. Irving Thalberg, now at M-G-M, insisted on cuts, and then more cuts. The final release version was just over two hours. There have been repeated attempts to reconstruct the original masterpiece. At present the longest version is a 200 minute video print, including stills and captions for missing segments.

Ingram, Griffith and, most of all, De Mille, demonstrated that highly talented film-makers could work in the Hollywood system, abide by its conventions and yet make distinctive films with their own stamp upon them. Von Stroheim's career demonstrates what happens when a film genius comes into continual conflict with the system. This was an example repeated over the years with a number of talents. Stroheim pointedly appeared in Paramount's *Sunset Boulevard* (1950), where Gloria Swanson plays the ageing silent screen star and Stroheim the director reduced to working as her butler.

Alongside the epics, equivalent in some ways to today's blockbuster, were a series of genre movies. These covered both main features with established stars and lower-budget variants, often produced by smaller independent studios.

There were a series of costume dramas that combined adventure, romance and swashbuckling action. Douglas Fairbanks was the key star for this genre. He was noted for performing his own stunts, which were spectacular and, as in *Robin Hood* (1922), quite dangerous. He appeared in a chain of film adaptations that have been recycled since: *The Mark of Zorro* (1920), *The Three Musketeers* (1921) and *The Thief of Baghdad* (1924).

The western developed and rose in status during the 1920s. Fairbanks made a number early in his career. The key successes were films that exploited the romance of the frontier and the spectacle of the expanding west. In 1923 Famous Players-Lasky produced *The Covered Wagon*, directed by James Cruze. This followed the westward trek of a wagon train, a story that reappeared in countless later westerns. At Fox an established director, John Ford, had his first major box office success with *The Iron Horse* (1924). This recounted the construction of the great transcontinental railroad. It was embellished with the feel for landscape that also graced the great westerns Ford made in the sound era.

There were stars like William S. Hart who worked primarily in this genre. He started acting in films with Thomas Ince in 1914. As a young man he had travelled in the real 'wild west'. His later films, which he frequently directed as well as starred in, were notable for the efforts he made to achieve a realistic representation. Typically Hart plays a 'road agent' (bandit) who reforms through the influence of a good woman. In his early films the protagonist often pays for his crimes in death; in the later films his conversion allows him a settled life with his woman and his pony. *Hell's Hinges* (1916) contrasts the contradictory careers of a gunman and a religious minister. One finds and one loses salvation. The film included some powerful set pieces of confrontation and mob violence, with an apocalyptic last reel where church and town are burnt down.[4] Hart's career tailed off in the 1920s but he made one final masterwork, *Tumbleweeds* (1925), with its story set during the Oklahoma land rush, which was popular with the public and critics alike.

The foundation of popular film-going in the 1920s was clearly comedy. Most programmes were supported by one and two reel shorts. Their popularity, even after the end of the silent era, means that they offer the iconic image of early film. Small specialist studios produced many of these. The most successful of these producers was Mack Sennett. After the parent company of Keystone ran into difficulties in 1917 Sennett set up Mack Sennett Comedies, releasing his films first through Paramount and then Pathé. His major star in this period was Harry Langdon. Langdon played the wide-eyed simpleton, a recurring character in silent slapstick comedy.

One of Sennett's early discoveries, Charlie Chaplin, had dominated the short comic film during the teens. In the 1920s he moved into feature film-making. Probably the most famous example is *The Gold Rush* (1925). This five reel comedy was shot in various Hollywood studios, but also included some adventurous and impressive location sequences. One scene has become the iconic image of Chaplin and silent comedy. Trapped with a prospector in a frozen cabin caught in a blizzard, Chaplin cooks then eats a boot for want of any food.

The film was a tremendous success. Chaplin scripted and directed as well as starred in the film, and when it was re-released in the sound era he also composed the music. In retrospect it is clear that his success, which appeared to embody spontaneous pantomime, was built on hard, painstaking production work. He endlessly repeated scenes until he was satisfied with the effect. This generated an enormous amount of film footage (the material provides a unique portrait in Kevin Brownlow's *The Unknown Chaplin*).

The other comic superstar of the 1920s was Buster Keaton. Fans argue the respective merits of Keaton and Chaplin; however, they have very different styles. Keaton was nicknamed 'the Great Stone Face', because of his ability to appear impassive as the world collapsed about him. Keaton started his career with Fatty Arbuckle. In the 1920s he both directed and starred in a series of two reel comedies. Then, like Chaplin, he moved into feature production. His great silent comedy is *The General* (1927), the story of a railway engine and its southern driver captured by the Union forces. The film has great comic moments, but it is also a very stylish (if somewhat romantic) representation of the Confederacy and the Civil War. The train chase scene where Keaton pursues his stolen engine rivals Chaplin's frozen cabin sequences for iconic images. Keaton moved to the M-G-M studio in 1928 but, like von Stroheim before him, he found the studio did not allow for the idiosyncrasies of such an artist.

There were also films that combined comic moments with drama. In the late 1920s there were a series of such films centred on the new modern miss, the flapper. These bore some relation to the sexual comedies of De Mille in the late teens, but they were about young romances with marriage providing the film's closure. One of the most successful stars in this genre was Clara Bow at Paramount Studios. She was attractive, bubbly and modern. Her most famous picture was *It* (1927), based on a book by columnist Elinor Glyn. 'It' was what made women (and men) attractive to the opposite sex. It was, in a sense, sex appeal, though there was not any actual sexual activity. Despite many mishaps, including being mistaken for a single mother, shop girl Clara finally marries the boss.

Some of these films focused less on comedy and more on the melodramatic situations.

In *Our Dancing Daughters* (1928) Joan Crawford is an attractive, single, 'free soul' but her very freedom haunts her position and relationships as her conduct strays across conventions. Both of these films celebrated the modern, but cherished the conventional mores of Hollywood.

Chaplin also made one rather less typical non-comic film, *A Woman of Paris* (1923), during this period. This melodrama traces the career of a woman who becomes a mistress to a wealthy Paris playboy. This luxurious existence is disrupted when her old love reappears. Chaplin had only an unaccredited walk-on part. The film was constructed around Edna Purviance as the heroine. Purviance had a professional and emotional relationship with Chaplin. She had appeared in most of his comedies since 1915. Adolphe Menjou was cast as the playboy. Menjou was so adept in the part that he continued to play this character through a string of films in both the silent and sound era.

A melodramatic tendency crept into many films. This created a wider approach, which crossed over many genres, similar to how melodrama operated in popular nineteenth century theatre. Chaplin's film constantly alternated comic moments with those of sentimental melodrama. Melodrama remained central to the films of Griffith, who in 1921 made a film version of the classic, *Orphans of the Storm*.

An actress who was extremely melodramatic onscreen was Pola Negri. She was Polish, and established herself first in that industry, then in Germany. There she worked with Ernst Lubitsch. She then signed a contract with Paramount. Her typical screen character focused on intense love affairs. In both *Hotel Imperial* and *Barbed Wire* (1927) her passionate loves are bound up with the war and a military hero. She was as passionate offscreen, enjoying well-publicised affairs with both Charlie Chaplin and Rudolph Valentino.

One especially striking drama was *The Crowd*, which combined a type of social realism with a melodramatic plot. *The Crowd* is a good example of the standard of film techniques in late twenties Hollywood. The acting is noticeably restrained, a change in style as the twenties progressed. The director, King Vidor is one of the film-makers whose films demonstrate these changes. Part of the pleasure of watching *The Crowd* is the powerful naturalism of the film (see case study, page 102).

Vidor had been allowed to make this slightly offbeat movie because of the success of his previous film, *The Big Parade* (1925), an epic portrayal of the US soldiers during the latter part of World War 1. It had a romantic sub-plot, but what impressed in the film was the depiction of the soldiers' life and the battles. There is a memorable tracking shot late in the film that follows the US soldiers as they advance through a wood towards the front and battle.

The film took over $3,000,000 at the box office and was an important factor in reviving war pictures. Another genre that developed in the 1920s was the aerial combat film. The most notable example of this was *Wings* from Paramount (1927). The action and costs of aerial combat were interspersed with romance and melodrama. Clara Bow played the heroine, who waits as two boyhood friends go off to fight and possibly die in the skies above Europe. Made in the late silent era the film actually had a recorded music track that played in theatres equipped for this technology.

One other genre that emerged in the late silent era was the gangster film. Josef von Sternberg made *Underworld* for Paramount, also in 1927. The film introduced what were to become the characteristic types of the genre: the bank robber, his moll and the crooked lawyer. It also exploited the violence of gangsters in Chicago for exciting action sequences. However, the genre really took off in the sound era when the new technology provided for both snappy dialogue and the impact of gunshots and squealing tyres.

There was a part of Hollywood beyond the majors: low-budget subsidiaries which produced the 'no-star label' films that would later become known as B-movies. Realart was set up in 1919 by Paramount to produce just this type of low-budget release. Like the later B-movies of the sound era this could result in very interesting and slightly unconventional fare. In 1920 Realart released *The Soul of Youth*, a six-reeler running for 80 minutes, written by Julia Crawford Ivers and directed by William Desmond Taylor. The film is a social problem drama, tracing the young life of Ed Simpson (Lewis Sargeant). An unwanted child, Ed is left at an orphanage. In his teens he runs away and lives by itinerant street work. A failed minor theft brings him to court, where a liberal judge offers him the opportunity of family life and social redemption. One of the film's most interesting aspects is that it features a real-life judge, Ben B. Lindsay, a keen advocate of the juvenile court system and of reclamation for young offenders (apparently other films also featured the liberal judge). The film also includes a more melodramatic plot line, as the family that adopts Ed is that of a liberal politician who is working against a crooked opponent. The film shades over into areas of educational and state and voluntary organisation sponsored films. Julia Crawford Ivers is another example of a relatively successful woman in the industry; she was a writer-cum-producer and also directed some films.

As the silent era drew to a close in the late 1920s Hollywood dreamt up one of its longest running creations, the Academy Awards ceremony. The first of these was held in 1929 for films released during 1927-28 and *Wings* was awarded Best Production. The Best Actress went to Janet Gaynor for two melodramatic roles, as the wife in Murnau's *Sunrise* (winner of Unique and Artistic Production, effectively co-winner of Best Picture with *Wings*) and as the woman waiting at home for her man who is at the front line of the war in *Seventh Heaven*. The Best Director went to Frank Borzage for *Seventh Heaven*. The Best Actor went to Emil Jannings for roles in *The Last Command* and *The Way of all Flesh*. Like Ernst Lubitsch and Pola Negri, Jannings had moved from Germany to Hollywood. The cinematographer on *Sunrise*, Charles Rosher, also won the Oscar. Notably, considering our subject matter, only one film released during the qualifying period was deemed ineligible for nominations – *The Jazz Singer* (1927).

3. EUROPEAN CINEMA IN THE 1920S

Hollywood films dominated all European markets to some degree. For example, in 1928 Hollywood produced 641 films, while Germany produced 221, France produced 94 and Britain produced 72. This was partly due to Hollywood's overwhelming economic advantages, displayed in the amount of money spent on individual productions. In the late 1920s Hollywood features averaged costs of around $350,000 or the equivalent of $4,000,000 today; French productions were estimated to average $30,000 to $40,000: in comparison, German films cost up to $50,000 while an apparently expensive British production cost $85,000.[5] This advantage was itself affected by other factors that varied from country to country. Likewise, the responses of film-makers varied, as did the type of films these responses produced.

i. Britain in the 1920s

Essentially, in the 1920s US films increased their dominance at the British box office. A US survey (as featured in Dickinson, 1985: 42) noted, in 1926:

Total features shown in UK	742
US Features shown	620
US per cent market	83.5
UK per cent market	4.8

It seems very similar to the figures for more recent decades.

The UK industry had not developed to the same degree as that in the US, where vertical integration was more advanced. One important consequence of this was that the surety offered by a vertically integrated company and the theatrical properties that it owned opened up financial markets. In 1926 it was reckoned that there was $1.5 billion (£308 million) invested in the US industry. The UK by comparison was only £35 million. The USA did enjoy the advantages of a large market, which was estimated at 20,000 cinemas catering for not far below 80,000,000 customers. In Britain there were 4,000 theatres catering for 20 million customers. But what we notice about these figures are the disparities and the variations. The USA has more screens per head of its customer base. British screens may have had a higher occupancy rate but whilst these serve a film-going public a quarter of the size of the USA, the film production sector can only manage a tenth of the investment that its more successful rival achieves.

This related to the larger factor of Britain's loss of industrial and financial supremacy. Up until World War I London had been the most important clearinghouse for film, both from the UK and abroad. US companies regularly sent negatives to London, where the positive prints required for projection were produced and then were distributed, home and abroad. By the 1920s the sizeable US firms produced their own exhibition prints at home and distributed them direct to the various markets.

British producers were not only undercapitalised. They had problems in the nature of the market. As features grew longer and the US studios introduced measures such as block bookings, British firms had difficulties in finding spaces in the exhibition sector for their films. A number of firms collapsed because the delay in financial return prevented investment in their next round of productions. Increasingly in the 1920s the renters of the US major companies dominated the UK market. Vitagraph opened their rental company in Britain in 1912, Fox in 1916 and Paramount in 1919, but they only distributed US films. Even a British firm, Stoll and Butcher, who distributed 49 films in 1926, only had seven UK films on the books that year.

The US companies also acquired the British equivalent of first-run theatres in major cities. The UK market was moving over to larger theatres. There was a spate of building in the 1920s. Cinemas with seating for thousands, as in the US, were to be found in major cities. Many smaller cinemas were run by independents but increasingly chains dominated the exhibition sector. The number of cinemas tied to large chains doubled in number during this period.

This expansion also led to the first serious vertical integration in the UK. There were two major companies: Gaumont and the Associated British Picture Corporation. Gaumont had grown out of the distribution subsidiary of the French company. By the 1920s it controlled 287 cinemas. It then added to these a renter firm and an interest in Gainsborough, the British production company founded by Michael Balcon. Associated British Picture Corporation (ABPC) was formed in 1912. By the end of the 1920s the latter firm controlled 147 cinemas as well as the Wardour Renter Company and the British National Pictures Studio.

In the late 1920s there was an increase in the prospects for capital investment in these companies. This grew out of the increasing disquiet about the US dominance in the British market and action to curb this. There were two important groups representing industry interests: the Cinematograph Exhibitors Association was formed in 1912, whilst the Kinematograph Renters Society was founded in 1915. However, the two associations had very different interests. The renters included the US subsidiaries so there were rather different standpoints on any attempts to control the market.

At the same time concerns about US film exports to the UK were shared by industry and by government. It was part of a larger anxiety as the US replaced Britain as the dominant economic power. Various policies aimed at protecting British manufacture and export were floated. In the case of cinema, there were additional concerns about the cultural influence of film. This was heightened because US films not only dominated in the UK but also across the Commonwealth.

After much discussion and debate over a range of options, the government introduced legislation in 1927. The key policies were the imposition of quotas on both renters and exhibitors for British films. In fact, it proved difficult to make adequate definitions of 'British'. Moreover, as some had feared, the act did not really lay down standards of quality. In the sound era the legislation produced a sizeable number of films made purely to satisfy quota demands. They were cheap and generally inferior and were nicknamed 'Quota Quickies'. Tales were told of exhibitors screening such films before the public performances commenced, to empty houses, just to satisfy the law. However, in 1927 the legislation appeared to offer new prospects for British film. There was an influx of capital and the formation of a number of new film production companies, many of which did not last long.

This decade saw the changeover in Britain from an average film length of three reels to five and more. The development did not just mean longer films. The programming in theatres changed, with the main focus on the full-length feature. In earlier times cinema still offered a number of attractions but increasingly the programme was primarily about the main feature, with its well-publicised story, genre and star.

This was another area where British films lagged behind the USA. There were few known domestic actors who could rival the magnetism of the Hollywood icons. Those with star potential usually migrated to the USA. Ronald Colman appeared in some British shorts and features after the war, but he became a major star and romantic idol in Hollywood. One of the few British stars to achieve real popularity with the public was Ivor Novello. He was an actor and writer and became a matinee idol on the West End stage. He started out appearing in films, first in France then in Britain from 1920. Key movies in his film career were *The Rat* (1925) and *The Return of the Rat* (1929). In these films Novello plays a slum criminal who becomes involved with a bourgeois woman. Novello projected a magnetic personality onscreen. His sensuousness was most apparent in a performance of an Apache dance in the films. The Apache dance was associated with criminality; it openly flaunted both female sexuality and male violence.

According to critics, British films generally lacked the production values found in Hollywood films. Rachael Low records Joseph Schenk writing in *The Bioscope* in 1925: 'British producers do not consider what the public requires. They do not produce good pictures. They simply produce pictures and shove them out into the world. You have no personalities to put on the screen. The stage actors and actresses are no good on screen. Your effects are no good, and you do not spend nearly so much money' (Low, in a chapter entitled *The Quality of British Film*, 1971). Low suggests that a number of factors worked against British films. Hollywood's ability to undercut the cost of films to exhibitors: the block booking system; the lack of managerial talent: the influence of the British theatre scene; the shortage of capital: and the loss of talent to Hollywood itself.

Such problems were partly a question of finance, but it was also suggested that British producers had not mastered the professional methods of working that made Hollywood studios so effective. A number of the stalwarts of British film, like Hepworth, carried on making films in the 1920s, but they were far less successful in this decade, and Hepworth had withdrawn from the industry by the mid-twenties. The more effective and successful

British films tended to come from the new companies associated with the growing combines. Gaumont British, which eventually became part of a fully integrated company, was one. And British International Pictures, which was part of ABPC, was another.

The importance of capable producers was a key factor in the British fortunes. One of the most successful was Michael Balcon. He started out with a regional film company in Birmingham. In 1924 he was part-founder of Gainsborough Pictures at the Islington Studio. After this company was taken over by Gaumont British he was appointed director of production. In both the silent and sound eras Balcon supervised and supported a cycle of British films with above average production values, and which also offered a distinctive British ethos. In the sound era he ran Ealing Studios, one of the most successful British production companies ever. At Gainsborough one of his protégés was the young Alfred Hitchcock.

Herbert Wilcox was both a producer and director. Wilcox started out in film renting and then moved into production. In 1926 he established Elstree Studios, which was to lead to a more substantial output in the 1930s. It was then that he teamed up with Anna Neagle for a string of very successful movies, frequently biopics, such as the popular portraits of Florence Nightingale or Queen Victoria.

Some of the successful directors in the British industry had developed fairly substantial careers. Maurice Elvey started in films in 1913. He was to carry on directing until the 1950s. In the late twenties he made a number of distinctive and successful film dramas. One of the best is a screen adaptation of a classic northern play, *Hindle Wakes* (1927). The play follows an illicit affair between mill girl Fanny and boss's son, Allan. Like the stage play, the film captures the early twentieth century Lancashire mill town. The working environment is unusually well set and photographed. And there is a finely filmed and edited sequence at the Blackpool holiday resort. The film is also remarkable, for its time, for the determined independence of the heroine.

The most critically acknowledged of British films in this decade were those of Alfred Hitchcock. He started in films as a writer of titles at the London base of Famous Players Lasky. The studio was taken over by Michael Balcon and Hitchcock soon graduated to direction. In 1926 he married Alma Reville, a fellow scriptwriter and editor. She worked on a number of Hitchcock's films. Hitchcock is most famous for the films made after he migrated to Hollywood in the 1940s, however, his British silent films had a masterly control of narrative and style. And they were extremely popular with the public. His first major success was with *The Lodger* (1927), starring Ivor Novello. It was a film about a serial killer, though the story is really about suspicion and wrongful arrest, a theme Hitchcock would return to over and over again. The quality of the staging, camerawork and editing is very high. The film opens with a sequence of changing shots and locales, which deftly set out the drama the film is to follow.[6]

The writer Eliot Stannard scripted all Hitchcock's early films. He was apparently a key craftsman in the 1920s industry. Different sources credit him with from between 100 and 300 film scripts in the late teens and twenties. A fellow writer of the period, Sidney Gilliat (later a director) recalled: '… a great character. He seemed to be writing or rewriting everything. If something went wrong on a picture, Stannard was called up – like Shakespeare would have been – and asked to come in and pep up a scene a bit' (Barr, 1999). As with much of British film output of the period, little of Stannard's work survives (with the exception of the Hitchcock films). He did produce a short guide, 'Writing Screen Plays', for the Standard Art Book Company in 1920 on film acting and associated skills. He appears to advocate a strong sense of continuity: 'A successful film-play depends as much on the soundness of its central theme as a stage-play or novel, and that theme must never be lost sight of by the Scenario writer, for every scene which does not bear upon it is a blemish to the scenario' (ibid.)..Certainly one of the virtues that stand out in the Hitchcock films is the coherence and drive of the narrative. Stannard is overdue for a reappraisal.

Another new arrival was Anthony Asquith. Asquith actually went to study film in Hollywood, where he clearly learnt well from the US example. His first film in the UK was *Shooting Stars* (1927). This follows a sexual triangle in a fictional British film studio and includes a bravura tracking shot through the studio as the audience follows the twists in an attempted murder. Asquith was to continue to be an important British director until the 1950s. One of the stars of the film was Brian Aherne, who left to become a Hollywood star. And the film itself features the theme of British stars migrating to Hollywood.

These directors and writers were able to appeal successfully to British audiences. That they stand out from the ordinary run of British film work is partly due to their undoubted talent. However, another factor was the generally weaker standards of British film production. It might have been that an industry in which the values of Stannard were the norm would have achieved a level of production standards closer to Hollywood.

The majority of cinema-goers preferred and enjoyed the US imports. The attraction of the major stars was important. Women often copied the fashions in hair and clothing set by the stars. Men modelled both their 'chatting up' methods and their smoking habits on stars. Cinema remained relatively cheap entertainment. Prices ranged from 2p in the cheapest seats and cinemas to over 2s plus in West End theatres in 1916. In 1924 the cheapest seats had risen to around 6p but apparently the expensive seats had fallen to just over a shilling. For this outlay, audiences enjoyed a programme of over two hours, with the feature film, comedies and newsreels, plus some sort of musical entertainment. And in many cinemas the comfort of the surroundings was well above their everyday experience.

ii. French Impressionism

France's film production had been cut back considerably during the war. In the post war world the two largest French companies, Pathé and Gaumont, concentrated on the most reliable and profitable areas of the industry, distribution and exhibition. Thus, whilst Hollywood was cementing its vertical integration the French industry failed to develop in this way. French film-making was split between the few large companies and many smaller companies. The latter often only survived long enough to make a single feature. As in Britain the technical facilities were vastly inferior to those of Hollywood. Many firms still used the out-dated glass-sided studios.

There were nonetheless popular and successful French films. The serial continued to be popular into the early 1920s and there was a cycle of expensive historical epics, often adopted from literary classics. Both the *Three Musketeers* and *Les Misérables* enjoyed film adaptations. In 1924 there was a lavish medieval adaptation, *The Miracle of the Wolves* (*Le Miracle de loups*), costing 8 million francs, but whilst successful at home the film failed to break into the US market. There were a series of realist films, frequently set in rural landscapes and using actual locations. One impressive feature was an adaptation of Emile Zola's *La Terre* (*Earth*) in 1921.

The one area where French film-makers were more successful was in making films with different conventions from Hollywood. This was a movement called French Impressionism (after the earlier movement in painting). These film-makers self-consciously regarded film as an art form: a form for expressing and conveying a personal vision. They were keen to be cinematic; that is, that they transformed the subject not by theatrical or literary methods but through 'visual rhythms'. They especially like close point of view shots, to suggest subjective or dreamlike states. And they used superimposition, special lenses, and even gauzes to achieve this.

An important factor in the relative success of these films was the rise of a film club movement in France. In the early 1920s there were a number of intellectuals who took an interest in cinema as an artistic activity. Key among these was Louis Delluc. Delluc wrote pioneering columns in a Paris newspaper *Paris-Midi*. This spread to articles in literary magazines. Then in 1919 the film journal *Ciné-pour-tous* appeared. Rivals followed and there began an extremely lively discourse of French film criticism. Delluc was joined by a number of fellow writers and film-makers, including Jean Epstein, Marcel L'Herbier and René Clair. All of them were later to make impressionist films, though they are also worked on more mainstreams productions. And in the mid-twenties, Jean Renoir, son of the famous impressionist painter, started a career that ran on to the 1960s, including an excursion in Hollywood.

Out of all this activity grew the *ciné-club* movement. The clubs provided screenings, lectures and discussions. They also inspired *Le Journal du Ciné-Club*. There were a number of these, both in Paris and in provincial centres. Club screenings included French films, like those of Epstein or Delluc, and foreign art films, like the German *The Cabinet of Doctor Caligari* (1919, see Germany below). Following on from this activity in 1924 the first specialised cinema opened in Paris, the *Vieux-Colombier*. The access to alternative film and discussion provided a base for the work of the French impressionists.

Delluc directed several films, and scripted a number more, in the early 20s but his films had little impact or success. He died young, at age 33. Jean Epstein was more successful. His 1921 *Coeur fidèle* (1923) was highly praised. One critic described it as 'the high point of the impressionism of movement' (Katz, 1994). The film added to the impressionist style very fast editing. This included a series of shots lasting under a second, and alternating disparate images and framing.

Fast editing was also found in the films of Abel Gance. He was the most popular of the impressionist directors, placed high in a public poll of favourite films. However, his films were long and expensive. *La Roue* (*The Wheel*, 1923) in its original release version was 32 reels and ran for about five hours. The film opens with a spectacular train crash, hence the title, which also refers to a recurring symbol in the film. The story follows the lives of a railway driver and the girl he adopts, orphaned in the crash. The early part of the film is set in the world of the railway. It used very fast, and sometimes disruptive, edits to create impact. These included not just action sequences like the crash, but the depiction of mental states, as when the driver becomes hysterical at the controls of his engine. In the second part of the film the driver, now an old man, and his adopted daughter move to the Alps where more tragic events occurred. The film's style, and Gance's use of symbolism, were both influential in the 1920s.

Another important director in French cinema was the Belgium-born Jacques Feyder. He worked in the pre-war French industry and after war service returned in 1919. He made a number of key films in the 1920s, including *Visage d'Enfant* (*Faces of Children*, 1925). His work is seen as a precursor to the 1930s French Poetic Realism. However, his satirical *Les Nouveaux Messieurs* (*The New Gentlemen*, 1928) was banned and for a time he worked in Hollywood, returning to France during the sound era.

iii. Germany

Germany's film industry had benefited and expanded during the war from an allied blockade and a ban on imports. In 1917 the government provided finance to assist in the merger of a number of studios into the giant Universum Film Aktien Gesellschaft (UFA). UFA went on to acquire Decla-Bioscop, a studio founded by Erich Pommer. He was an important and successful producer in the 1920s. The new company then branched out into distribution and exhibition. UFA was the centre of a German film revival in the early 1920s. It also benefited from import restrictions that ran from 1921 to 1928. Even so, by the mid-1920s UFA was in financial difficulties and required investment from its Hollywood rivals, Paramount and M-G-M. In 1927 it was saved from further financial problems by a Trust led by one Dr Alfred Hugenberg. Hugenberg was a Nazi sympathiser and used UFA to develop a strain of nationalist propaganda in the 1930s. Anti-Semitic representations became virulent in the 1930s, but they are present to some degree in the films of 1920s Weimar Germany.

As UFA expanded it acquired a studio facility at Neubabelsberg, near Berlin. This was developed into the largest and most sophisticated studio in Europe. Directors from other countries bought their productions here because of the facilities. The young Hitchcock worked here before directing his British films. UFA also acquired the German facilities of the Danish Company Nordisk, long heavily involved in the German market. This increased their dominance in Germany, but also helped build their distribution and exhibition network across continental Europe. UFA was the dominant European studio in the 1920s, and enjoyed the most advanced production facilities. This contributed to a high standard of production values in UFA films.

UFA produced a range of films in the silent period, including sophisticated comedies. The greatest exponent of these was Ernst Lubitsch. Lubitsch started as an actor and progressed to direction. He worked in several genres, but it was *Die Austerprinzessin (The Oyster Princess,* 1919) that displayed his gift for visual wit and irony. Lubitsch subsequently left for Hollywood, working first for Warner Brothers, then Paramount.

However, the most noteworthy German productions were a series of films labelled Expressionist, after the central European art movement of the late nineteenth century. It was especially influential in the field of painting and theatre. In 1919 Decla-Bioscop produced *Das Kabinett des Dr. Caligari (The Cabinet of Doctor Caligari).* The scriptwriter was Carl Mayer who was an important writer and influence throughout this period. Characters in a lunatic asylum recount a story of somnambulism and murder. In their story Caligari is a fairground entertainer whose creature Cesare carries out a series of murders in a small German town. The story was gloomy and dark, but what struck audiences was the staging - angular and abstract non-realistic sets, in an expressionist style. This was equally true of the acting, notably Conrad Veidt as Cesare, a role that established him as a new star. And the camerawork used a chiaroscuro effect of light and shadow that was very unusual at this period and remains distinctive today.

Caligari did fairly well in the international film market. It could be seen as a harbinger of an art film cycle offering an alternative narrative and film style to the dominant Hollywood commercial model. A chain of expressionist movies, with downbeat stories and a stark style followed it. The most successful, and a film that still attracts audiences, was *Nosferatu,* an unofficial remake of Bram Stoker's cult novel, *Dracula.* F. W. Murnau directed this early vampire movie in an expressionist style. The centre of the film is the ghostly undead count. Both the staging and the performances created a memorable and seminal film. Murnau was also a key exponent in the development of more mobile camerawork.

The Cabinet of Dr Caligari

The influx of US investment also bought UFA access to Hollywood technology. The German film-makers then developed a series of innovations termed *entfesselte camera* ('unchained camera'). These included the use of dolly shots and what were effectively crane shots. Murnau's *Der Letze Mann* (*The Last Laugh* – the change in title in translation is due to there already being a Hollywood production with the title) has several famous sequences, including one where the mobile camera creates the subjective viewpoint of a drunken character. The director, the star (Emil Jannings) and the designer all worked on the subsequent *Faust*. This was an epic recreation of the story made famous by Goethe. It too demonstrated German prowess in set design, lighting and camerawork.

An equally talented director in this period was Fritz Lang. He made his name with a number of films that played to the popular genre of detective cum spy stories. Over a decade he made two films centred on a criminal mastermind, Dr Mabuse. This world of criminality and bizarre behaviour was shot in an expressionist style. Lang also showed effective use of editing, using fast cutting in a powerful sequence depicting a stock market frenzy in *Doktor Mabuse, Der Spieler* (*Doctor Mabuse, The Gambler*, 1922). In 1926 Lang made one of the earliest science fiction films, *Metropolis*. At the heart of this film was a mad and evil inventor, but most impressive was the creation of a future world with a huge underground city where the workers were enslaved by a master race. The film demonstrated UFA's ability to create vast and impressive sets in their large studio. However, the film was too costly to return a profit and was a major factor in UFA's subsequent financial problems.

The expressionist trend died out in German films in the mid-1920s. An important new cycle was a series of 'street films' exploring the underworld of criminality, vice and prostitution. They did use the chiaroscuro style developed under expressionism, but they were far more realistic in both their staging and acting. Another director of immense talent, G. W. Pabst, was central to this genre. His most famous film is probably *Die Büchse der Pandore* (*Pandora's Box*, 1929), adapted from an already notorious play that chronicled the short, dark life of a femme fatale. For the title role, Pabst used a Hollywood actress, Louise Brooks. She had already appeared in US films, but it would seem that the studios did not know how to exploit her unusual combination of naivety and sexual allure. She made two films with Pabst and became an icon of late silent cinema.

iv. Scandinavia

The Danish industry suffered during the war as the markets of Russia and Germany were closed off to its products. In the 1920s it was not especially influential. However, it produced one director of real stature, Carl Theodor Dreyer. He started working as a journalist and then took up script writing. He directed his first feature, *Proesidenten* (*The President*), in 1919. A major silent film is *Du Sjak Aere Din Hastru* (*Master of the House*, 1925), a beautifully composed melodrama where an unfeeling husband learns to care for his wife and family. In 1928 Dreyer directed *The Passion of Joan of Arc* (*La Passion de Jeanne d'Arc*) for French producers. The film is one of the masterworks of silent cinema. It is full of intense close-ups with a powerful performance by Renée Falconetti as Joan. The film epitomises Dreyer's minimalist style with his concentration on setting and character.

The Swedish industry enjoyed a successful period in the early 1920s, but this was dissipated later in the decade as it attempted unsuccessfully to gain a larger foothold in the international market. It was gifted with two outstanding directors: Mauritz Stiller and Victor Sjöström. Both directors had a particular feel for landscape. Stiller's films made great use of meadows, forests and water. In the twenties he scripted and directed a number of films by the popular Swedish novelist Selma Lagerlöf. In 1919 there was *Herr Arnes Pengar* (*Sir Arne's Treasure*), a violent and tragic drama that followed the actions of a band of Scottish freebooters. And in 1923 he directed *Gösta Berling's Saga*. It was released in two parts, and ran for over 10 reels. The film had a notable and climactic sequence built round the burning of the manor, as a symbol of the forces unleashed in the film. It also had a charismatic cast, including the Swedish star Lars Hansen and a new discovery, Greta Garbo.

Sjöström usually both starred in and directed his films. He also made a number of adaptations from the novels of Lagerlöf. His style was restrained but he had a great ability to draw compelling performances and site them in memorable locations. *Ingmarssönerna* (*The Sons of Ingmar*, 1919) was in two parts. In the second part there was a wonderfully moving scene between a reunited husband and wife, which is set amongst trees. It looks and feels like the inspiration for Hitchcock's great and similar scene in *North by Northwest* (1959). In 1921 Sjöström wrote and directed *Körkalen* (*The Phantom Carriage*). The situation was reminiscent of Dickens' *A Christmas Carol* - a wastrel confronted by death and visions of his life on New Year's Eve. Sjöström played the protagonist with great feeling. The complex editing and organisation of the narrative unfolded the story and character in a way that demanded concentration.

In fact both the directors and the two stars took up Hollywood offers as the Swedish industry declined. Years later Sjöström would memorably play the protagonist in Bergman's great masterpiece *Smultronstället* (*Wild Strawberries,* 1957), and only Garbo would not again work in the Scandinavian industry.

4. Émigrés

Hollywood's dominance in Europe extended beyond the renters and exhibitors. Increasingly in the late silent era the studios poached the best talent from the European industries. This included stars, directors, cameramen, scriptwriters, set designers and musicians. Two early recruits from the German industry were Lubitsch and Murnau. Murnau worked for Fox Studios and there directed one of the classics of silent cinema, *Sunrise.* The film combined Hollywood storytelling and production values with the innovative style of German film. The story followed the impact of a city vamp on a farmer and his wife. The film included a striking visit to the city with impressive sets, the moving camera and sophisticated editing.

The cream of the German film industry, including Fritz Lang, was to follow these pioneers in the 1930s. They were escaping from the dark, murderous world of the Third Reich, but they also took their mastery of the dark German cinema of the 1920s, which fed into the great *film noir* cycle of the 1940s. And there was a German diva, Marlene Dietrich, who bought a special sexual magic to Hollywood drama in the 1930s.

The Swedish émigrés included the directors Stiller and Sjöström. Sjöström settled fairly well in Hollywood at Goldwyn Studios, later taken over by M-G-M. He also used the Americanised name, Seastrom. He made some fine films with major Hollywood stars. This included one of the best vehicles for Lon Chaney, the master of make-up and disguise, *He Who Gets Slapped* (1924). Sjöström's greatest Hollywood film featured Lillian Gish as the heroine in *The Wind.* Gish played a migrant married to a farmer out in the wilds. Lars Hansen played the farmer. At the climax Gish was faced by breakdown and the emotional force of the drama is emphasised by the wind. There was a drama with Garbo, *The Divine Woman* (1928). This is one of the lost masterworks, with only a single reel surviving.

Stiller's most important input into Hollywood was probably the stars he brought from Sweden. Hansen returned to Sweden, but Garbo became the face of Hollywood stardom, both in the silent era and on into the sound era. One of her key films of the 1920s is *Flesh and the Devil* (1927). Her co-star was John Gilbert, with whom she also enjoyed an offscreen romance. Onscreen, the romance was torrid and passionate. Garbo remains one of the iconic faces of the twentieth century.

There was one other important group of émigrés. These were the Russians who migrated when the Communists won the post-revolution civil war. The majority settled in Paris and turned out a series of well-made and popular films. The actor Ivan Mozhukhin was a prominent member of this production circle.

STUDY FILM: THE KID

Chaplin–First National. USA 1921. 5,250 feet, running time of 63 minutes at 22fps.

Directed and scripted by Charles Chaplin. Cinematography Roland Totheroh. Production Design Charles B. Hall. Filmed in the Chaplin Studio.

Cast: Charles Chaplin (The Tramp), Jackie Coogan (The Kid), Edna Purviance (Mother).

The Kid was Chaplin's first proper feature length film. He had, though, appeared in a six reel film by Mack Sennett, *Tillie's Punctured Romance* (1914), early in his career. Also, his own productions had been increasing in length, the extremely successful *Shoulder Arms* (1918) being a three reeler. Since 1918 he had been based in his own studio making a series of films distributed by First National. He also enjoyed the support of a regular crew of production personnel and a fairly regular cast of supporting actors.

A meeting with a new talent, the four-year-old son of a vaudeville family, Jackie Coogan, inspired *The Kid*. There seems to have been an immediate rapport between the two. Chaplin himself was mourning the recent death of his first child, by Mildred Harris. Shortly after the meeting he started work on a new project, then titled *The Waif*, and the young Jackie was lined up to become Chaplin's most famous co-star.

As Chaplin's career progressed he became more and more exacting in his search for comic perfection. He would not only rehearse scenes endlessly, but film them repeatedly as well. His then current project, entitled *Charlie's Picnic*, was already up to over 6,000 feet of film. Finally released as *A Day's Pleasure*, the released cut was only 1,714 feet in length. The entire final negatives for what would be *The Kid* were 400,000 feet of film. It was Chaplin's phenomenal earlier success that enabled him to pursue a production process that might well have bankrupted smaller outfits.

Chaplin started work on *The Kid* at the end of July 1919; production work carried on for about nine months, and post production until about November 1920. The post production was fraught. Chaplin was in fear, both from divorce proceedings from his wife and actions by the distributor First National. The editors, the entire set of rushes and Chaplin secretly set up in a hotel, where they edited the film. (Richard Attenborough's *Chaplin*, 1992, has a reconstruction of these events.) The finished film was released in January 1921. During this time Chaplin also finished and released *A Day's Pleasure*.

The film's story is very simple. 'The woman – whose sin was motherhood' leaves a charity hospital with her fatherless child. Desperate, she leaves the baby in a rich family's car. Repenting of her folly she returns to find the car and baby stolen. The baby, dumped in the street, is then found by the Tramp. The Tramp now learns how to care for the abandoned baby. Five years on the Tramp and the Kid survive in a threadbare and slightly disreputable existence.

The mother, now a 'prominent star', meets the Kid whilst carrying out charity work, but fails to recognise him. The Kid is taken ill and the visiting doctor notifies the authorities about the child. They arrive to take the Kid away to an orphanage. Desperate the Tramp chases and steals back the youngster. Shortly after the Kid is reunited with his mother.

The film was reissued in 1971 (to coincide with Chaplin's honorary Academy Award of 1972), for which Chaplin composed an orchestral score. He also cut three scenes that expand the 'woman's' story. In two short scenes we see the mother passing first a wedding, then a nurse and child, aggravating her emotional state. In the third, years later, she again meets the man who fathered her child. There is a suggestion of their coming together again.

The influence of D. W. Griffith is apparent in the story's sentimental emphasis. And in 1919, Griffith, along with Pickford and Fairbanks, was the partner with Chaplin in the star's own studio, United Artists. The film uses a number of stock melodramatic conventions: the abandoned and desperate mother; the child left to the care of a wealthy family; the coincidences that bring the child to the tramp; and the oppressive moral hand of authority. These are also parallels with the hardships of Chaplin's own upbringing in East London. There are familiar melodramatic motifs. In the deleted scene of a wedding we see a young bride married to an older man; the groom steps on a flower, symbolic of the deflowering that is taking place.

Within this frame Chaplin places his iconoclastic comic creation, the Tramp. Coogan clearly learnt and represented a number of the Tramp's characteristics. When Chaplin finds the abandoned child his instinct is to pass it on to someone else. These efforts are thwarted by the regular reappearance of a policeman. Saddled with the child there is then a sequence that displays Chaplin's comic mastery, as he ingeniously uses the few sparse objects of his attic room to produce infant necessities. A suspended coffee pot that acts as a substitute baby's bottle is masterful.

After a five year ellipsis (the child now being Coogan's actual age), we are shown the Tramp and the Kid surviving in the slums. In a typical Chaplin quirk, they earn an 'honest living' as the Tramp repairs widows, but these are windows that have been broken only a short time before by the Kid. And there are comic variations on familiar Chaplin situations, one being a fight with a larger and more brutal opponent. This is paralleled as the Kid takes on a larger, bullying boy.

The entry of authority figures, backed up by the policeman, ushers in the melodramatic high point of the film. Both the Tramp and the Kid are overcome by the trauma, which demonstrates great pathos. But in his resilient manner the Tramp returns to rescue the boy, and they set off together. In this case they go to a penny-lodging house. A reward posted by the mother prompts the owner to turn the Kid into the police.

Alone once more, the Tramp has a dream, a sort of heavenly version of the slum where they live. Here, in counterpoint to 'real life', all is heavenly white and charity abounds. Even so, 'sin creeps in' as the devil introduces discord. It would seem Chaplin wanted to provide a counterpoint to the grim realities of life, but he lacked confidence in such a positive world. More melodramatic coincidence allows the reuniting of mother and son. And in a variation from the usual closure of Chaplin films, the Tramp also is brought into this new, affluent household.

The style of the film follows that of Chaplin's one reelers, and is similar to the early style of Griffith. Long shots and mid-shots are predominant, and the camera almost acts as a proscenium for the staging. There are a number of iris effects, usually marking the opening or closing of a sequence. Other transitions are marked by a fade. There are occasional close-ups to present the emotional responses of the characters or to show important detail. In one or two scenes this is achieved by an iris mask rather than a proper close-up. In an early scene there is a dissolve as the man, whom we assume has fathered the child, burns a photograph of the mother, but essentially the camera's function is to record the physical movement, which is Chaplin's forte.

Before release, Chaplin had to negotiate with First National for an increase in his salary. The cost of the film vastly exceeded the budget of the proposed two reeler. First National only agreed to increases after favourable previews. Chaplin, in the end, was paid over a million dollars. The film justified the expense. It was one of Chaplin's most successful films and grossed over two and half million dollars on its initial release.

Chaplin went on to make a series of successful silent comic features, including two (*City Lights*, 1931 and *Modern Times*, 1936) after the arrival of sound. Jackie Coogan worked for First National and then Metro in the 1920s, but his career came to a temporary halt in 1927.[7] A Hollywood wag remarked that 'senility hit him at thirteen'. The music on most versions is that composed for the film by Chaplin and the print most frequently seen today is the 1971 version. This means that the film runs at 24fps, which is a little too fast. There are a number of comic moments that are not held quite long enough for effect.

STUDY FILM: OUR HOSPITALITY

Metro. USA 1923. 7 reels, 6,220 feet, running time of 75 minutes at 22fps.

Directed by Buster Keaton and John Blystone. Scripted by Clyde Bruckman, Joseph Mitchell and Jean Havez.

Cast: Buster Keaton (Willie McKay), Natalie Talmadge (Virginia Canfield), Joe Roberts (Joseph Canfield), Leonard Clapham (James Canfield), Craig Ward (Lee Canfield).

Keaton started his film career with Roscoe 'Fatty' Arbuckle, which led to him working for producer Joseph M. Schenck. Schenck was a business associate of Marcus Loew. He was an independent producer, distributing through Metro, later part of M-G-M. Schenck went on to become head of the Board, first at United Artists then at Fox / Twentieth Century Fox. Unlike Chaplin, Keaton worked within the established production companies and studio system. In 1921 he formed Buster Keaton Productions, which operated until 1928, when it was incorporated into M-G-M.

In his early days Keaton enjoyed a great deal of freedom, and he seems to have been in control even when, officially, the films had a different director. There was a fairly regular production team, with Bruckman, Havez and Mitchell as scriptwriters. Havez came up with the idea for *Our Hospitality,* based on the 'famous feuding families of the old South' (Robinson, 1973: 82). Fred Gabourie was in charge of technical direction and Elgin Lesley with an associate handled cinematography. At least one regular in the cast was Buster's father, Joe Keaton, whose renowned vaudeville high kick features in the scene where the train arrives in the town of Rockville.

Buster had worked in the late teens in a successful series of one and two reel comedies. *Our Hospitality* was the third in a series of feature length comedies, a format which Harold Lloyd had been the first Hollywood star to trial. By now Keaton's screen persona was firmly established, the 'old stoneface' who could walk with little apparent emotion and a deadpan face through the most outrageous and calamitous events. Like many of the successful silent clowns he had learnt his trade in vaudeville. He was a master of mime, acrobatic stunts, and had perfect timing. All these are on display in *Our Hospitality*.

The film opens with a prologue set in 1810. Somewhere in the south a family feud, carried on from generation to generation, produces its latest tragedy. John McKay, father of Willie, and his clan enemy, Jim Canfield, shoot each other. Willie's mother flees to New York, where his aunt raises Willie. In Rockville Jim's surviving brother Joseph decides: 'My two sons must be taught to avenge the dead.' This is despite the wall motto, 'Love Thy Neighbour as Thyself', which he earlier pointed out to Jim.

Twenty years on the story resumes when Willie (Keaton) receives a letter regarding his father's estate. Before he sets out for the south his aunt tells him the story of the family feud. His fellow passenger on the train journey is Virginia Canfield, though neither realises that their companion is from the other feuding family. When they arrive in Rockville the story has two strands, the developing romance, and the attempts by the male Canfields to kill young McKay. Willie survives all their attempts for a happy ending with Virginia.

From the opening prologue Keaton demonstrates his mastery of a lengthy narrative. One and two reel comedies often had disjointed plot lines, with narrative interruptions and digressions for chases and slapstick sequences. *Our Hospitality* establishes a strong plot line with clear characterisations. All through the film the comic sequences flow naturally from the developing plot. Most of the second reel is taken with the train journey south. The film-makers used a copy of Robert Stephenson's Rocket as the engine. The comedy plays with and exploits the period quaintness. There are gags about the rail tracks, a tunnel and the passing landscape, including a stubborn mule that holds up the train. There is also a running gag, literally, as Willie's pet dog follows the train all the way south. In another Hollywood tradition the dog disappears from the plot around reel five.

On arrival Willie is identified by one of the Canfield brothers, and there are a series of gags as he, and then also his father and brother, fail in their attempts to shoot Willie. At one point, the breaking of a dam creates a flood that hides Willie from the searchers. This is executed to excellent effect and is an example of Keaton's flair for the action scenes.

Virginia, still ignorant of Willie's family background, invites him to supper. Once in the house the Canfield males are faced by a problem: 'Our code of honor prevents us shooting him whilst he's a guest – in our house.' This inspires a whole series of gags as Willie tries to avoid leaving and the Canfields attempt to force him from the house.

The last two reels are a pursuit as Willie, now aided by Virginia, flees the vengeful father and sons. There is an exciting chase on a cliff, the reappearance of the train and a finale where Willie and Virginia end up in a river. This climaxes with a brilliant gag and stunt, executed with superb timing, at a waterfall. Finally married, the father and brothers have to give up on the feud. The moment is reinforced with a return shot of the motto, 'Love they neighbour…'. Then the film has one final joke with the guns.

Keaton's film makes excellent use of both the natural settings of California and studio sets. This combination of the natural and the constructed is done with real mastery and the viewer's attention is rarely distracted from the action. The waterfall sequence is typical of Keaton's films, both spectacular and funny. Keaton nearly always performed his own stunts, even when, as here, they are fairly exposed. At one point he actually fell into the real rapids shown in the sequence, and narrowly avoided drowning.

Our Hospitality uses a number of contrasts, including a familiar Hollywood couplet, north and south. Keaton's film, and the later *The General*, seem to subscribe to Hollywood's mythic representation of the Confederate states. Keaton remarked of the latter film: 'You can always make villains out of the Northerners, but you cannot make a villain out of the South' (Robinson, 1973, p. 143). He was presumably referring to well-established myths around reconstruction, reinforced by Griffith's *Birth of a Nation*.

Keaton's films have a well thought out and effective staging. The opening death sequence takes place in a storm. It is also shot with low-key lighting, making for dramatic effect. Much of the comic action takes place in daylight, and with high key three-point lighting. But at the point of final confrontation there is another low-key shot that echoes the sombre opening.

Keaton also uses deep staging to develop plot and comedy. Several times in the chases by the Canfields one character is positioned in the foreground whilst another performs in the background. Both are equally important. Such an effect is achieved when the erupting water cascade from the dam hides Willie from the searching brothers. Later in the film a shot shows us, from the point of view of the Canfield men, Willie and Virginia in a room. They are placed upstage, at the back of the frame. The next shot places them centre stage and also reveals the parson who announces their marriage. This sort of narrative surprise for comic effect is something that Keaton and his crew produce frequently. There is also visual humour exploiting well-established traditions in film. Thus, the New York sequence opens with an antique-style print to jokingly introduce the primitive city.

Keaton's choice of shots and edits is carefully structured around the development of the comic possibilities. The predominant technique is moving between long shot and mid-shot, with less frequent close-ups for important emotions. Whilst the editing retains visual continuity, there is only limited use of shot, reverse shot. Frequently for an exchange Keaton will use a two-shot followed by a mid-shot of one of the characters. And for particular moments, like the final confrontation, Keaton will use a long take rather than a succession of short takes.[8]

Our Hospitality retains its freshness both because of its very effective humour and its simplicity of style, which enables the spectator to focus on the comedy. It is certainly one of the films that shows Keaton's mastery of both visual humour and cinematic technique. The film, distributed by Metro, was a box office success. Keaton's features tended to cost around $200,000 (slightly expensive for the period), but generally took over a million at the box office.

STUDY FILM: DER LETZTE MANN / THE LAST LAUGH

Germany 1924. Directed F. W. Murnau. Scripted by Carl Mayer. Cinematography Karl Freund. Production Design Robert Herlth and Walter Röhrig.

Cast: Emil Jannings (Doorman), Maly Delschaft (his niece), Max Hiller (her fiancé), Emilie Kurz (his aunt).

This classic German silent represents a number of strands from the 1920s. The film uses a number of expressionist techniques, but it is not really about the dark, dreamlike worlds found in the earlier films (one of the production designers, Walter Röhrig, had worked on *The Cabinet of Doctor Caligari*). The film really falls into a short cycle of films known as *Kammerspeil* (or chamber play) in the mid-1920s. These films showed an interest in disturbed minds and emotions as in expressionism but were predominantly realistic in presentation. And the film, in its depiction of working class tenements, looks forward to the 'street films' of the late twenties. Most notably it was the film which demonstrated the use of the 'unchained camera'.

The *Last Laugh*'s English title does not literally translate the German (referring to status) but reflects another aspect of the film. It was a fairly expensive production, costing over one million marks. It also demonstrated that the star system was just as important in German cinema, with Emil Jannings receiving 600,000 marks for his starring role, which was over half the film's budget. The film was expensive in part because of the use of large sets, special effects and the time spent developing technical innovations. Shooting lasted 180 days and the film was shot at UFA's Neubabelsberg studio.

The production benefited from a number of areas of technical excellence in German film. Many of the large-scale sets involve models and the careful creation of a false perspective. Lighting, including low-key effects, were techniques in which German films excelled and which influenced film-makers in other industries, including Hollywood. There were special effects created in the use of camera lenses and film processing, and there were new developments in moving the camera. Karl Freund and the production team created overhead riggings and mobile platforms in order to perform what were very complicated manoeuvres. For one scene of subjective camera, Freund designed a special harness which enabled him to strap the camera to his chest (in 1925 Eduard Tissé used something similar for the Odessa Steps sequence in *The Battleship Potemkin*).

The film's story is very simple. Emil Jannings plays the Doorman at the Atlantic Hotel. He is immensely proud of his uniform, which also contributes to his status in the block of flats where he lives. One day the manager sees him struggling to lift a heavy trunk from a taxi, so the Doorman is demoted, now having to work as a lavatory attendant below stairs. This entails surrendering his splendid uniform for a plain white jacket. He hides his fall from status by stealing back his uniform and lodging it in a station left luggage office during the day. He then assumes this 'disguise' to return home in the evenings, but his secret is exposed and he becomes the object of ridicule. Rather than ending on this note of despair the film-makers introduce a happy ending where he is left a large inheritance and is able to enjoy the luxury once reserved for the hotel customers on whom he waited.

None of the characters have names and the relationships are sketchy. An important event is a wedding involving the Doorman's niece. But some reviews credit her as the Doorman's 'daughter'. And the Doorman is exposed by a visit to the hotel of the fiancé's aunt. Her relationship to the Doorman is unclear, though she appears to harbour romantic intent towards him until she discovers his degradation. This generalised sense of the story is emphasised by the absence of intertitles. In fact there are only two proper title cards. There is the opening title, which makes a moral point, rather than providing plot information. And then there is the epilogue title, which explains the addition of a 'happy ending'. These are supplemented by the iced writing on the wedding cake, the typed notice to the Doorman of his change of position, and a newspaper report in the epilogue explaining the inheritance. Few silent films manage to cover this sort of narrative territory with so little written information. It is a tribute to the structure of the screenplay, the acting and the visual plotting of the film that the story unfolds with such clarity.

The story is a variation on Nikolai Gogol's *The Overcoat* (there are at least two other film versions). The emphasis on uniform is reckoned to be a particularly Germanic inflection. Certainly, in the 1920s, after World War I and with the increasing militarisation of political organisation in Germany, the Doorman's fetishistic regard for his great coat and hat is very pointed. The comments on the characters are equally scathing. The working class people of the tenement seem friendly and co-operative, especially at the wedding of the niece, but the exposure of the Doorman brings petty and malicious jealousies to the fore. The hotel manager treats staff with a complete lack of sensitivity or understanding. He sends the oldest employee of the company to a shelter in order to create the Doorman's post in the lavatory. And the hotel guests wallow in decadent luxury.

The film employs an impressive range of notable techniques and embodies a number of stylistic strands from German film. The UFA studio was large and was noteworthy for the skill with which it recreated other worlds in sets. The production personnel were particularly good at creating impressions through set design and miniatures. So what appears to be a large traffic junction outside the hotel, or a busy railway station, involves the use of miniatures, including for people, to great effect.

Lighting in German films was also striking. The expressionist films, like *Nosferatu*, also directed by F. W. Murnau, offered a canvas of chiaroscuro, the interplay of light and shadow. They had developed notable effects using low-key lighting, rather distinct from the three-point high-key lighting favoured by Hollywood. In *The Last Laugh* the lighting is important in helping create the special effects and scenes involving deep staging. Especially notable are the sequences involving low-key lighting. The production involved a number of night-time shoots, and the exteriors outside the hotel are impressive. Here the recreation of the night-time city is very effective and the noir look comments on the situation of the Doorman, at one point seen creeping in the shadows. The apparent depth of field is aided both by the lighting and its reflection in water.[9]

The different locales in the film are important to plot and character. The Doorman is the only person to bridge the divide between the affluent world of the hotel and the more deprived world of the slum. The aunt does in fact cross this divide, but her treatment, first by the new Doorman and then inside the hotel, makes her an invader in this space. And at the end of the film, when the Doorman and his protégé, the night-watchman, enjoy the good life in the hotel, it is as if they have clearly left behind the world of the tenements. In effect, the ridicule experienced by the Doorman serves as an expulsion from that community.

Within both areas the staging reinforces such divides. When the Doorman loses his position, he is moved from his public position at the hotel entrance to the washroom, hidden away down a forbidding flight of stairs. We see several characters crossing and descending to this nether world. Interestingly, when the Doorman returns to the tenement late in the film, to find that his deception is exposed, he has to climb up stairs to reach the flat of his niece and her husband. These two contrary movements are expressive of the situation of the main character. Of course, we never see the Doorman ascending into the upper regions of the hotel. In fact, the camera reinforces this point, as the film opens with a vertical track, followed by a horizontal track that takes us into the public space of the hotel from the interior of the building. The only parts of this interior that we see are the manager's office, the downstairs lavatory and corridors in between and the hotel's restaurant in the epilogue.

The way the camera is used to plot character and action was the aspect of the film that created most impact on its release. The film uses camera position, deep focus and special lens effects. But the movement of the camera is the most striking technique. When the Doorman is summoned to the manager's office, he is sited behind a glass door, cutting him off from his prior position of status and the public. The camera tracks forward and a dissolve carries us past the door to a close-up as he reads the notification.

The extended sequence in the tenement demonstrates an especially expressive camera. After the wedding reception the musicians serenade departing guests. Freund uses the overhead camera positions to achieve a shot that carries the onlooker along with the music. It is a reverse aerial track, a sort of crane shot. Then we have the subjective depiction of what appears to be the Doorman's dream. The camera staggers with the Doorman, and a special lens and superimposition create the world of his fantasy. Less flamboyant use of tracks, pans and cranes occur throughout the film.

One of the reasons that UFA was happy to accommodate the experimentation and cost was that they were hoping to break into the US market. So one function of the film's style was to impress US moguls. This it clearly did. Murnau, Freund and Jannings were all recruited by Hollywood studios, though Freund was the only one to enjoy a long career in the film capital. The film was very successful, both in Germany and abroad, including in the USA. However, only a few German films were able to exploit the US market. A couple of years later the failure of *Metropolis* led to the company becoming dependent on Hollywood majors, including M-G-M.

STUDY FILM: *VISAGES D'ENFANTS / FACES OF CHILDREN*

Les Grands Films, France, 1925. 2500 metres, 121 minutes at 18fps. Black and white, with tinting.

Director: Jacques Feyder. Scenario: Jacques Feyder, Françoise Rosay. Cinematography: Léonce-Henri Burel, Paul Parguel. Editing: Jacques Feyder.

Cast: Pierre Amsler (Victor Vina), Jean (Jean Forest), Jeanne Dutois (Rachel Devirys), Arlette Dutois (Arlette Peyran), Pierrette (Pierrette Houyez), Canon Tailleur (Henri Duval).

Visages d'enfants is a fine realist drama set in a village in the Swiss Mountains of Haut-Valois. The feature fitted into a cycle of films set in mountain areas in the Pyrenees and Switzerland which were part of a larger cycle of French realist productions of stories set in rural settings, using extensive actual locations and capturing a sense of country life, its rhythms and its landscapes.

The film was written and directed by Jacques Feyder. Born in Belgium, he entered the French theatre and film industries in 1911 as a supporting actor. World War I gave him the opportunity to graduate to director. In 1917 he married the actress Françoise Rosay. He then served in a Belgium army military troupe. In the 1920s he established a reputation with *L'Atlantide* (1921), notable for its use of actual Sahara locations: and *Crainquebille* (1922) the story of the friendship between an old street vendor and a young orphan. The latter film worked against the usual conventions of such stories and was praised for its sense of authenticity. The film also introduced the young Jean Forest to a screen career and enjoyed fine location filming by L. H. Burel, who had started his career in cinematography with Abel Gance. Both Forest and Burel are central to the achievements of *Visages d'enfants*.

Visages d'enfants is an original scenario, written by Feyder with his wife Françoise Rosay. It is set in the village of Saint-Luc, found in a steep-sided valley far from the bustle of modern urban life. The story follows the rhythms of this village community: changes are marked by the changes in the seasons. Events are marked by Saints Days, in a community bound partly by a shared Catholic faith and devotion. There is a clear separation between the worlds of the men and that of the women. Though a community, economic differences are apparent with a hierarchy amongst its members.

The basic plot is simple. The Mayor, Pierre Amsler, has just lost his wife (Suzy Vernon). His son, Jean, misses her deeply, but Jean's young sister, Pierrette, who is told her mother is merely 'away', seems to adjust more easily. After a while the Mayor remarries, partly in order to provide for the care of his children and his house. His new wife is Jeanne Dutois, a widow with her own daughter, Arlette, about the same age as Jean. Jean's resistance to the 'interlopers' takes the form of an antagonism to Arlette; he is responsible when she is lost at night and nearly killed in an avalanche. Although Arlette returns safety, Jean is consumed with guilt. He decides to leave home and attempts to commit suicide in a nearby torrent. It is his stepmother who saves him and the family are finally reconciled.

The developing relations and conflicts are re-inforced in the film through the use of landscape, and the rhythms of life and the seasons. The plot runs for about a year, from late winter when the funeral takes place, through summer and the marriage, to the winter of the lost child and finally the reconciliation, which occurs in the spring. The characters' travails across the landscape mirror their emotional lives. Thus Amsler cannot bring himself to tell his son about his forthcoming marriage. He asks the kindly Canon to help, and he takes Jean on a visit to a nearby valley for several weeks. As they leave the village the struggle uphill comments on the struggle that is faced by the canon and then by Jean. On their return Jean descends into the valley alone, and his position in the landscape suggests the emotional isolation that he feels.

The father, Amsler, is a distant and fairly stern figure. The one emotional outburst we see is when he weeps at his first wife's funeral. Otherwise he seems more concerned with practicalities than emotions. His sensitive son's emotional turmoil is clearly beyond his ken. He is Mayor of this community, but also seems to be the local bourgeois. He apparently owns the local logging yard, and he also collects rents from the tenant farmers.

His new wife, Jeanne, is the widow of a workman who died in an accident. Her situation is expressed clearly at our first sight of her, at the rent payment on St Martin's day. The male tenants sit in a line on a bench, but she is seated separately and across from the men. This strict gender separation recurs constantly throughout the film.

In contrast to Amsler, Jeanne is frequently shown in cheerful moods and laughing. She is firm but caring with her new stepchildren. At one point, when Jean's antagonism provokes his father, she steps between them to stop Amsler striking his son. At the dramatic climax she becomes hysterical at her fears for her missing daughter, and is supported and comforted by the village women.

Jean is deeply attached to his lost mother. One important object in the film is her portrait. When, after the marriage, Jean is moved to a rear room he takes down and moves the portrait with him. The film uses subjective viewpoints frequently, and at several points we see the portrait as Jean imagines it, with his mother's responses, smiling at him at one point, but looking distant after his actions towards Arlette. This last shot is followed by Jean's tussle with his conscience, and the portrait, moved from its usual position for this shot, looks on. Finally he rises and goes to confess to this father about tricking Arlette.

Early on in Jeanne's life with the family, Jean sees her wearing a broach that belonged to his mother, which aggravates his grief and resentment. There is a potent scene where Jean caresses an old dress of his dead mother in the attic. Later the practical Jeanne decides it can be turned into dresses for the girls. In a fit of rage Jean cuts and tears up the dress, producing more antagonism from his father.

The youngest girl, Pierrette, seems to adjust happily to the situation without great thought. She misses her dead mother but quickly accepts her new mother. She plays with Arlette, but on another occasion joins with Jean when he persecutes his stepsister. The greetings between Jean and Pierrette after absences show that there is a strong bond between them.

Arlette antagonises Jean unintentionally. Their first meeting goes badly. She is home alone when he returns from his trip with the Canon. Not knowing him she refuses to open the door. Things get worse. In one scene Jean has to take her lunch while she is watching the cows and goats in the hills. Her treasured possession is a doll, which Jean surreptitiously takes and ties to the horns of a Billy goat. The sequence ends with Arlette vainly chasing after the goat and her doll. It is the doll that occasions the climatic sequence of the film. Amsler is returning on a winter evening in his sleigh with Jean and Arlette. As she sleeps Jean deliberately drops her doll in the snow and later at home he encourages her to sneak out to look for it. Becoming lost, Arlette is almost caught in an avalanche. She shelters in a mountain shrine to the Virgin Mary, where the village men find her and from where Amsler carries her home to her mother.

The majority of the film was shot on location, and the studio sets are carefully integrated with these. The landscapes are both attractive and evocative. The film opens with a long shot of the village as it lies in the steep-sided valley. There are recurring locations, the most important being the local graveyard. It is here at the funeral of his mother that Jean faints and is taken ill. Subsequently he and his father visit every Sunday to lay flowers at the grave. Significantly Amsler's proposal to Jeanne is made on a Sunday. He leaves Jean to visit the graveyard on his own, and as they part each follow a separate path – Jean's uphill, Amsler's down.

Such divisions in the narrative are emphasised by the editing. The film frequently uses parallel cutting to accentuate the situations and conflicts within the film. The notable example is the wedding of Amsler and Jeanne, an event is paralleled by the kindly Canon breaking the news to Jean far away in the neighbouring valley. The scene cuts back and forth between the two events. The wedding is a gay, joyful occasion to which the whole commune appears to be invited. Interestingly this is the only occasion that we see the village policeman, there among the guests. In contrast, in a quiet, almost empty space the Canon gravely sits Jean on his knee and tells him of his father's remarriage. It is at this point that Jean asks, 'Do I have to call her mama, too?' There is a similar, if more dramatic, sequence of parallel cutting between the village men searching in the night-time snows for Arlette and her mother, at home surrounded by the women of the village.

Much of the film is shot in a conventional style. Long shots and mid-shots predominate, with less frequent close-ups. The editing follows the conventions of the 180 degree rule and on and off-screen matches. However, there are a number of sequences of more distinctive camera work and editing, especially to emphasise the subjective viewpoint or feeling of characters. Thus, at the film's opening we watch as father, son and neighbours wait in the house for the coffin to be bought downstairs. As the men carrying the coffin manoeuvre on the narrow stairs there are telling close-ups of their shuffling feet. This scene also introduces the use of subjective camera angles, with low-angle shots of the father from Jean's perspective, and high-angle shots of Jean from the adult.

The subjective style is most noticeable in the sequence of Jean's illness. Here the camerawork and editing resemble some of the avant-garde style found in such film-makers as Jean Epstein. There is very rapid cutting, distinctive camera angles and an almost feverish sense of the boy's situation.

The subjective recurs frequently in the film. At the final climax we follow Jean as he walks down to and then along the rapid river. Here is a waterfall, which we have already visited in the shots that open the film. A number of subjective shots give Jean's impression of the foaming torrent and suggest the despair in his state of mind. Once more parallel editing shows us both the daughters telling their mother Jean has left and her rush after Jean, and the boy as he contemplates plunging into the water. Finally Jeanne leaps into the river, right below the waterfall, to rescue Jean and carry him home. It is here, in his little room, below the portrait of his dead mother, that Jean finally calls Jeanne 'mama'. The portrait 'smiles' as they embrace. The finale packs great emotional resonance. Intriguingly, though, Jean's father is completely absent: another parallel cut has shown him driving his cart along a peaceful road lined with poplars, the last we see of him. This is not, then, strictly an oedipal drama, but the working out of a recurring drama of sons and mothers.

Visages d'enfants enjoyed limited success on its release, partly due to lukewarm support from the financiers of the Film Company. Feyder had gone over budget and the film was completed in 1923 but not released until 1925. But over the years it has gathered increasing praise and the status of a classic. Subsequently, Feyder's political satire *Nouveaux Messieurs* (1929) was refused an exhibition licence for a short while, prompting Feyder to work in Hollywood at M-G-M for a period. He continued directing in the sound era; his most famous film being *La Kermesse héroïque* (*Carnival in Flanders*, 1935), a satire on war set in the seventeenth century.

STUDY FILM: THE CROWD

USA 1928. M-G-M. Nine reels, 8540 feet (approximately), running time of 93 minutes

Directed by King Vidor. Scripted by King Vidor and John V. A. Weaver (uncredited Harry Behn). Titles Joseph Farnham. Cinematography Henry Sharp. Editor Hugh Wynn. Settings Cedric Gibbons and Arnold Gillespie.

Cast: Eleanor Boardman (Mary), James Murray (John), Bert Roach (Bart), Freddie Burke Frederick (Junior).

The Crowd was a minor success compared to Vidor's and M-G-M's predecessor, *The Big Parade*, which was a box office smash, but the later film took over a million dollars, twice its cost. Moreover, the film brings together a number of characteristics of late 1920s Hollywood. It also features representations that occurred both in the US and in European films of this period. While clearly melodramatic at times, the film is predominantly naturalistic in its plotting and acting. It retains the dominant conventions of the Hollywood style, but utilises the technical innovations of European film, in particular German cinema. And whilst it deals with the quintessential US dream, 'a little man the world's going to hear from', at its centre it offers both a critique and a fear of twentieth century mass, urban life.

The film is about ordinary working people, but there is little of the class-conscious attitudes found in Soviet films like *Strike*. In fact the Hollywood studio deliberately avoided any such class dimensions. King Vidor recalled: '"I've been thinking about the title",
[Thalberg] said. "Mob sounds too much like a capital-labor conflict." "Then how about 'One of the Crowd'?" I suggested' (Vidor, 1981: 146). The film parallels *The Last Laugh* in its choice of subject. John Sims, the protagonist, is an office worker who dreams of becoming 'somebody big'. He does not regard himself as part of the working masses,

though, unlike the Doorman, at the film's conclusion that is where he firmly remains.

The story opens with the birth of John to the Sims family on 4 July 1900. The date is significant, emphasised by the title 'celebrating America's 124th birthday'. His father's occupation is unknown, but the family home appears to be in an affluent suburb. We cut from Johnny's birth to 1912, when his father dies after an accident. Presumably this blights his adolescence, but an ellipsis takes us forward to his twenty-first year. Now John arrives as a migrant in New York, a city where 'you've got to be good in that town if you want to beat the crowd'. John works in a large office at the Atlas Insurance Company. He meets Mary on a foursome with his friend Bert. John and Mary marry and have two children, a boy and a girl. Five years on and the daughter is killed in a road accident. Traumatised, John quits his job and becomes unemployed. His marriage threatens to break up and John contemplates suicide. The love of his young son, Junior, revitalises him. He gets a job, but only as a sandwich board man. This is the very work that he laughingly pointed out to Mary on their first date, 'poor sap'. The film ends with the reconciled husband and wife, plus Junior, sitting among a laughing audience in a vaudeville theatre.

The film's representation of the 'crowd' is fairly negative. It shares a view widely held in 1920s of the mass of urban dwellers being atomised and alienated individuals. John's first view of New York is from the ferry, equating him with masses of migrants who flocked to that city in the early twentieth century. One title tells the audience, 'The crowd laughs with you always, but it will cry with you for only a day'. There are a number of scenes where the lead characters are lost and submerged in a larger group. The office where John works gives an impression of desks and workers stretching away into infinity. In a similar manner when Mary has their first child, John searches desperately for her at the hospital. She is clearly swallowed up in this large institution. And when he finds her she is lost in a large ward of new mothers. The film also makes play with common habitual behaviour. His co-workers rag John, all in the same manner. He and Bert arrive to collect their dates in the manner already displayed by a queue of young men.

There is also a threatening edge to this mass anonymity. When John hears the news of his father's accident he climbs a staircase into the house, with a sea of curious onlookers below. A similar shot positions John and his injured daughter after the accident against another sea of onlookers. In the following scene John pleads helplessly for quiet in the street, only to be unsympathetically silenced by a policeman. These earlier scenes undermine the final upbeat shot of John, Mary and Junior lost in the sea of laughing spectators at the theatre.

The sense of alienation is reinforced by the style of the film. Overall The Crowd follows the dominant conventions of Hollywood. The leads are nearly always carefully positioned in high-key three-point lighting. This is the case even when shadows obtrude into the periphery of the scene, as when John returns home late after carousing with Bert. The street scene after his daughter's accident is low-key lighting, but even here key lights are positioned to illuminate the faces of John and the policeman. And the onscreen action is organised in terms of the 180-degree rule, and on- and offscreen matches. Exchanges between characters are either in a two-shot or the increasingly familiar shot to reverse shot.

An expressionist feel creeps into some scenes. Thus, as the young John climbs up to his injured father, the stairwell becomes distorted, created by the use of a high-angle long shot and a painted backdrop similar to those used in early expressionist films. The repetition of such a high-angle long shot recreates this feel when John's daughter is injured. Vidor recalled how the vast alienated spaces in a modern city were partly created through the use of models and intricate camera movements in the manner of the mid-twenties UFA films:

'This camera manoeuvre [the camera crane up the Atlas Building] was designed to illustrate our theme – one of the mob, one of the crowd – and it was accomplished in the following manner: a scene was made in New York City at the entrance of the Equitable Life Insurance Building at lunch hour. The camera started its upwards swing and when the screen was filled with nothing but windows, we managed an imperceptible dissolve to a scale model in the studio. This miniature was placed flat on the floor with the camera rolling horizontally over it. In the selected window was placed an enlargement of the single frame of the previously photographed interior view. As the camera moved close to the window another smooth dissolve was made to the interior scene of the immense office. The desks occupied a complete, bare stage and the illusion was accomplished by using the stage walls and floor, without constructing a special set. To move the camera down to Murray (John), an overhead wire trolley was rigged with a moving camera platform beneath it '(Vidor, 1981: 151).

And, in a similar fashion, they use the technique of false perspective in the hospital scene: 'We wanted a tremendously long corridor stretching, as it seems, to infinity. Cedric Gibbons, head of the art department at M-G-M, designed and constructed a corridor in forced perspective, with each receding door becoming smaller and smaller' (ibid: 152). But the film also uses location shooting in New York. There is a documentary feel to many of the street scenes. Vidor again recalls: 'For the scenes of the sidewalks of New York, we designed a pushcart perambulator carrying what appeared to be inoffensive packing boxes. Inside the hollowed-out boxes there was room for one small-sized cameraman and one silent camera. We pushed this contraption from the Bowery to Times Square and no one ever detected our subterfuge' (ibid.).

The production crew used a real funfair, though not Coney Island, for the scenes of John and Mary's first date. The location shots are edited into a sort of montage through the use of superimpositions. There are fairly frequent tracks into or away from the action. The crane shot into the Atlas building is mirrored by a reverse crane shot at the end in the vaudeville auditorium.

More typical Hollywood techniques figure when the camera moves close for personal drama. In the honeymoon trip to Niagara, what we see is clearly a back projection of the great waterfalls. While the film sets up the vast alienated space of the city it also offers a very personal story within this. Thus, the domestic situation of John and Mary is developed in some detail. There are a number of scenes of home life, which emphasise both the ordinariness of their lives, but also the way that relative deprivation exacerbates tensions. Their honeymoon is followed by an unsuccessful Christmas when Mary's family visits. Then an ellipsis take us forward to April, John and Mary cooped up in a small, dingy bedsit. The various problems of the flat, such as a broken cistern, beds that won't fold, cupboard doors that won't close, the overhead railway directly opposite, lead to a tiff and outright quarrel. Here the romantic inclinations of Hollywood intrude and Mary's revelation of her pregnancy lead to reconciliation. Similar scenes of the wear and tear of domestic married life recur during the movie. As John quips, 'Marriage is not a word – it's a sentence.'

The gender representations in the film are important in this plotting. John is easygoing, almost feckless at times. When Bert suggests the double date that leads to his meeting with Mary, John demurs because of 'studying nights'. However, he is soon seduced by the spiel of Bert. Then at the end of the evening, on the homeward journey an advert ('You furnish the girl – we furnish the home') prompts his proposal of marriage to Mary. Mary, however, matures with marriage and motherhood. During the traumas of child loss and John's unemployment she is clearly the strong centre of the family.

The film manages to marry light comic moments with scenes of great melodrama, but this leaves the film poised between romantic happiness and more cynical tragedy. Apparently, seven different endings were considered for the film. These included quite upbeat endings where John became affluent from the success of ad-slogan writing. This is a hobby and opportunity path he pursues through the whole film. The one moment of affluence follows when he actually wins $500 for 'Sleight o' Hand – The Magic Cleaner'. Apparently exhibitors were able to choose between two of the alternatives. However, the one that survives in the print is very apt, as it reemphasises the 'little man' lost in *The Crowd*.[10]

FOOTNOTES

1. The changes in film stock gradually encouraged the superseding of the carbon-arc lighting with its 'yellowish' tinge by tungsten lamps. This, together with the new filmstocks, affected actors' make-up. In earlier films certain colours like red were problematic, pancake was needed to prevent skin tones appearing anaemic, and the eyes used extensive shadowing. Less make-up was now needed, which aided the changes in acting style.

2. *More Treasures from the American Film Archives* has examples of early colour film formats.

3. *Foolish Wives* is an example of a particular technique of the period, using different camera takes for the prints for the domestic and export markets. Thus there are surviving and different versions of the film from the 'American' market and the European market.

4.   *Hell's Hinges* features on *Treasures from the American Film Archives*. Note, Clint Eastwood's *High Plains Drifter*, 1972, appears to recycle this film's plot.

5.   The German and British figures are approximations, using the Exchange Rates listed in the 1928 *League of Nations Statistical Year Book*.

6.   The majority of Hitchcock's films are available on DVD and, increasingly, Blu-Ray. In 2012 the British Film Institute screened restored versions of his surviving silent films and, at the time of writing, there are plans for release on DVD and Blu-Ray.

7.   Coogan stars in the 1922 *Oliver Twist*, featured on the BFI *Dickens Before Sound* disc.

8.   All the editions of *Film Art* by Bordwell and Thompson have an interesting discussion of this film's *mise-en-scène*.

9.   The Eureka DVD uses the restored print from the Friedrich-Wilhelm-Murnau-Stiftung (Foundation and Archive). The musical accompaniment is from the 1924 score by Giuseppe Becce. There is also a *Making of …* documentary. This illustrates some of the technical achievements of the film. It also explains how the restoration was accomplished. UFA made three master negatives of the film: one for the German market, one for export and one for the USA. In the manner of the 1920s these were constructed from different camera takes. Freund used two cameras on most shoots. The differences are clearly illustrated in the documentary.

10.   *The Crowd* was issued on NTSC VHS video in 1998 by Warner Home Video.

5. ALTERNATIVE CINEMAS

The Battleship Potemkin

INTRODUCTION

Despite differences mainstream British, French, German and Hollywood cinemas all shared a common purpose – making films for entertainment and profit. But in the 1920s there were a series of film movements that were motivated by very different interests, primarily political. The most important at the time and the one that has had an enduring influence in world cinema became known as Soviet Montage.

Commercial cinema continued in the Soviet Union after the 1917 Revolution, but there also developed a non-commercial politically fired cinema. This cinema was radically different from the mainstream in its motivation, form, style and content. The premise in this book is that Soviet film, and the other alternatives discussed, should be studied as distinct film forms, and that the content is central to an understanding (if not necessarily sympathy) of these films.

Because of their influence there is an extensive selection of Soviet montage films available. However, courses frequently concentrate on extracts, especially the Odessa Steps sequence from *The Battleship Potemkin*. Any study of these films should include full-length screenings. The complexities of what the Odessa Steps sequence achieves only becomes apparent when placed in the larger context of the overall film. In a similar fashion the film's impact needs to be placed in the context of other Soviet films and of opposition film outside the Soviet Union.

There is a lot of reading available as well. There is material by the actual film-makers, Eisenstein, Pudovkin and Vertov. And there are also a large number of books about the filmmakers and their films. David Bordwell's study of Eisenstein's films is very good. And

Nelmes (1996) has a good section on Soviet Montage. There are also some studies of individual films. The DVD/video of *Man With a Movie Camera* has a commentary by Yuri Tsivian. And *In the Picture* magazine has produced a study pack on Eisenstein and his work.

Eisenstein and Vertov would make a particularly good case study. They operate in different fields and have different ideas about montage but both are central to the montage movement. There is plenty of reading available and their films appear to still interest students. The BFI set of pre-revolutionary silent films provides a good contrast. The collection includes a film made by one director, Protazanov, on the eve of the revolution.

The avant-garde and the late silents are also fairly accessible in terms of materials. Surrealism is a frequent area of study even today. The alternative cinemas outside these two movements are rather specialist. Very little film material is available, and there are only a few detailed sources for study, with the exception of the large US avant-garde DVD collection, *Unseen Cinema*.

Documentary film and especially animation cross over with the mainstream cinema. Documentary is relatively well-researched; animation is more specialised, but both make good topics in their own right. The developments in the 1920s and John Grierson's founding of the British Documentary Film Movement initiates an important trend in documentary film that still influences film and television today. It also feeds into an idea of 'British realism' still apparent in British films.

1. THE SOVIET CINEMA

Most European film-makers followed conventions that were not dissimilar to those of Hollywood. However, there was one cinema that developed a set of radical alternatives to this mainstream model. In 1917, in Russia, a revolution led by the Bolshevik Party (later to become the Communist Party) successfully succeeded the Kerensky government, which had itself overthrown the old regime headed by the Tsar. The Bolsheviks also won the civil war that followed between 'reds' and 'whites', and successfully resisted attempts to invade the new state by Britain, the USA and France. Out of this emerged the Union of Soviet Socialist Republics (USSR). Essentially the new society aimed to abolish capitalism and construct a socialist state: production for use rather than profit.

In the 1920s, amid the chaos and destruction left by the civil war and invasions, the Bolsheviks opted for limited restrictions on the market and attempts to develop state alternatives.[1] The economy and most industries were near collapse. The film industry was almost non-existent. The major film companies had closed down or emigrated, and there was a shortage of film equipment and film stock. In the early 1920s foreign imported films dominated Soviet screens. However, steps were taken to develop a socialist cinema under the Commissar (head) Anatoli Lunarsky. Both newsreels and short propaganda films (known as 'agitki') were made, often by film-makers new to the medium. The agitki included factual films and reconstructions. Thus, *Workers of All Lands, Unite!* (*Proletarii Vseh Stran, Soedinyaites!*, 1919) was made to celebrate May Day, the 1st. It included scenes from the class struggle across the ages and quotations from *The Communist Manifesto*. The agitki also included dramas: a recurring story is of a father and son on opposing sides in the civil war. In *For the Red Flag* (*Za Krasnoe Znamya*, 1919) an old Bolshevik joins the Red army in his son's place and they meet in the climax on a snowy battlefield. These sort of films were shown not only in cinemas but toured the great spaces of the USSR on agit-trains and steamers, reaching parts commercial cinema did not.

In 1919 the Bolsheviks nationalised the film industry and also established the State Film School. Goskino, a central distribution monopoly, was set up, then replaced by Sovkino in 1925. Both organisations struggled with the lack of resources and the breakdown of networks. But, at the same time, a cultural revolution in the arts was fuelling a new, younger generation of artists. An important artistic movement in the 1920s was constructivism, which emphasised the social function of art. Constructivists compared themselves to artisans rather than artists. They compared art works to machines, and talked and wrote about assemblage (montage). An important theorist and practitioner was Vsevolod Meyerhold, a theatre director. He used machine-like sets in plays, and a performance style modelled on machines. A number of the important new directors in Soviet film worked with Meyerhold. To this was added the impact of the State Film School and a discourse of debate and argument in journals such as *Lef*.

In 1921, one of the School's film-makers, Lev Kuleshov, conducted a series of experiments in editing film. In one film he cut together shots of characters in different locations, in Moscow and Washington. He was attempting to 'create a non-existing city with film editing' (Giornate, 1996).[2] In another film he alternated shots of the actor Ivan Mozhukhin with shots of objects, a bowl of soup, a baby, a corpse, etc. The alternation aimed to produce a sense of Mozhukhin's emotions by cutting rather than by his expression. Both films exemplified the idea that the audience's responses to shots depended on the editing; that is, the relationships between shots. This was to become the fundamental idea behind the theory and practice for a cycle of revolutionary silent films.

The most famous film from this cycle was *The Battleship Potemkin* (*Bronenosets Potyomkin*, 1925). The film recounted events from 1905 when a mutiny on a battleship in the Black Sea sparked off an insurrection and repression in the town of Odessa. The young film-maker Sergei Eisenstein directed the film. Eisenstein made a series of silent and sound films over the next two decades, which are monuments of international cinema. What is especially striking in *Potemkin* is the way that Eisenstein uses editing to delineate the conflict, to make symbolic and ironic comments on the action, and to produce a shocking but rousing climax to the events. The most striking passage in the film is *Part 4, The Odessa Steps* (the five parts frequently had breaks between them when screened).

The Odessa Steps scene from The Battleship Potemkin

This sequence shows the solidarity of the Odessa people with the mutinying sailors and the shocking interruption as Tsarist troops massacre civilians on the steps of the port. Unfortunately, the sequence is now so famous that numbers of people have seen only this and not the whole film. In fact the sequence brings to a head the conflict on the ship and on shore presented in Parts 1 to 3, and prepares for Part 5, which concludes the film with 'Brotherhood', as the sailors of the Black Fleet salute those of Potemkin.

Eisenstein used non-professional actors for many parts. He practised what he termed *typage*, character types that represented people and even social classes. The film involved a number of ordinary citizens from Odessa itself, including an agitator from the actual events of 1905. Key characters are there as a focus for their social group. One such is the sailor Vakulinchuk, who is the martyr of the mutiny. Another is First Officer Giliarovsky, who shoots Vakulinchuk. The idea of using non-professionals is one that we now generally associate with documentary film, and Eisenstein's team used a number of techniques associated with this mode of film-making. Thus, whilst the style was often unconventional, the film generated a feeling of realism that was noted by contemporaries. It also took care to foreground not just key characters but the mass of the people. The central focus of the film was the conflict between sailors and townspeople on one hand, and the forces of Tsarist reaction on the other.

Both the film's style and content made a real impact in the mid-twenties. In fact, the film was a major success abroad, especially in Germany. This brought in much needed currency for Soviet film. For audiences it offered a radical alternative to the happy ending romances of Hollywood. The young Luis Buñuel, of surrealist fame, remembered that he and his companions were fired to build a barricade in the streets after watching the film (Buñuel, 1982: 87).[3]

Potemkin was part of Eisenstein's search to develop a montage theory of film. The idea was that especially through editing the film-makers could construct ways of politically motivating audiences. Montage became more than just editing, and Eisenstein wrote extensively about staging, editing, camerawork and the construction of narratives, as ways of achieving this impact. Eisenstein developed his theory through a number of silent films. Following *Potemkin* he made *October* (*Ten Days that Shook the World*, 1928) which recounts the events of the 1917 revolution. *October* includes intellectual montage, where the alternation of shots aims to effect abstract concepts rather than dramatic or character effects. Eisenstein also used the realistic characters and the actual settings in St Petersburg (Leningrad) for this film. Interestingly, the sequence of the attack on The Winter Palace has frequently turned up in non-fiction films as a factual record of the event. He then made *The General Line* (*The Old and the New*, 1929) about the collectivisation of agriculture. At this point he also theorised about the place of the new sound technology in the theory of montage. Together with his assistant director, Grigori Alexandrov, and Vsevolod Pudovkin he wrote a pamphlet about sound in film. Essentially they argued for an approach based on aural counterpoint rather than simple synchronisation.

Pudovkin was himself an important Soviet director. However, his use of montage or editing was closer to the conventions of Hollywood. In his film version of Maxim Gorky's *Mother* (*Mat*, 1926) the film centres on the individual characters, the mother and her son. And the editing, whilst dramatic, does have a certain continuity. As in *Potemkin* there was a climactic attack on workers by the Tsarist military, but whereas Eisenstein's film had major disruptions of continuity, *Mother* was relatively easy to follow from the point of view of an audience who are used to the mainstream conventions.

Eisenstein's ideas on montage utilised some techniques that were parallel to the 'cinema of attractions', and the Soviet directors used all sort of attractions to excite audiences. They were fond of circus effects and stylised acting. And there was a clear strand of eccentricity in their work. This was visible in Eisenstein's first feature length film, *Strike* (*Stacha*, 1925). It was also visible in the work of FEX (Factory of Eccentric Actors). Two friends from this group, Leonid Trauberg and Grigori Kozintsev made a series of silent films culminating in *New Babylon* (*Novyy Vavilon*, 1929), which dramatised the celebrated Paris Commune of 1870, a landmark in the development of revolutionary politics. The film used stylised acting, symbolism and montage to create the world of the great Paris insurrection.

These films suggest a fairly serious treatment of politics. However, there was lighter side of Soviet film, which still addressed the emerging new society. A key director is Boris Barnet, who started out as an actor with Lev Kuleshov and then graduated to direction. His films use montage, but he is clearly less avant-garde than, say, Eisenstein. A lyrical style and concern with ordinary, everyday life dominate his films. One of his outstanding films is *The House on Trubnaya Square* (*Dom na Trubnoj*, 1928). This takes a familiar Russian story, the travails of an innocent peasant girl in the large city, and develops a glorious comedy around the residents and activities of the block of flats in Trubnaya Square. The characters include both ordinary workers and the 'nepmen' who rose out of the return of market activity. The film's opening bears some comparison with the documentary work of Dziga Vertov, and then, in one of the best jokes in the film, montage is used to set off a tale of confusions and mistakes in the personal and social lives of the characters (see this writer's early & silent cinema blog).

Bed and Sofa (*Tretya Meshchanskaya*, 1927, director Abram Room) is a slightly satirical take on sexual relationships and the problems of the housing market in large cities. The film deals with a *ménage à trios* (as the film was indeed titled in France) and suffered attacks in the Soviet Union and from censorship abroad for broaching a subject that was problematic even for the radical Bolsheviks.

At the same time in the late 1920s, there were important documentary montage films. A key film-maker was Dziga Vertov, who had started out in the civil war working on Soviet newsreels. With several comrades he developed a Factory of Facts, dedicated to films of the reality of Soviet society. Their most famous film was *The Man with a Movie Camera* (*Chelovek s kino-apparatom*, 1929). This film presents a portrait of a Soviet city, but was also an exploration of the rhythms and conflicts of the new Soviet society, of cinema itself, and of audiences and their responses to film.[4]

The end of the cycle of montage films more or less coincided with the advent of sound. However, this was due less to the impact of the new technology than to a change in the cultural politics of the USSR. In the 1930s the proscribed line in cinema was social realism. This produced films with individual heroes and heroines who represented the working people and who engaged in conflicts with capitalists, reactionaries and fascists. Apart from their politics, these characters shared many qualities with the protagonists of mainstream films as represented by Hollywood. In addition, the films were constructed following conventions very similar to those of the continuity that governed Hollywood narrative and style. Directors like Eisenstein suffered in having their films cut or even banned. The great French film-maker Jean-Luc Godard rightly characterised this period as the 'Hollywood/Mosfilm Axis'.

2. LEFT-WING FILMS OUTSIDE THE SOVIET UNION

The Soviet films and film-makers not only excited audiences, they inspired other film-makers. Eisenstein toured Europe and North America. He even had a short sojourn in Hollywood. In Europe he found workers' movements that organised the exhibition of Soviet films. And later, there was a cycle of radical films that espoused the interest of the working classes and criticised the power of capital and the state.

One of the important supporters for Soviet film in Europe was the Workers'

The Man with a Movie Camera

International Relief (WIR). It was founded in 1921 to help during the Soviet famine. It went on to mobilise publicity and propaganda in support of the Soviet Union. In Germany in 1928 was founded Volkfilmverband (the Popular Association for Film Art). Its first film shows screened Pudovkin's *Konyets Sankt-Peterburgs* (*The End of St. Petersburg, 1927*)in Berlin, followed by screenings in Hamburg, Stuttgart, Frankfurt and Main. Also in 1928, in France, Communist sympathisers founded the Les Amis de Spartacus (after the leader of the great anti-Roman slave rebellion). At first they were very successful. The Paris section recruited about 8,000 members. However, the chief of police forced lockouts at the cinema Les Amis used, and it disbanded in 1929. The Netherlands set up Vereeniging voor Volks Cultur (the Association for Popular Culture). Their first screening was the Soviet film *Bed and Sofa* (*Tretya Meshchanskaya*, 1927, director Abram Room). This film had also fallen foul of the censors as it explicitly depicted free love and abortion.

In the UK, a film critic, Henry Dobb, with Kenneth Macpherson, campaigned to set up a workers' society, which became the Federation of Workers' Film Societies (FWFS). This was inaugurated in 1929. Initially they booked the Gaiety Cinema in Tottenham. However, the London County Council (LCC) refused to provide a licence. So the Society used the Co-op Hall. Problems with the LCC continued. One of the arguments of the LCC was that the screenings cost only a 1s, so cheap as to be equivalent to public admission. (They were happy to license the middle class Film Society that charged 25s subscription for six to eight screenings.) However, the LCC ban brought support for the workers' societies from prominent figures, including Sybil Thorndike, Bertrand Russell and George Bernard Shaw. Eventually the Labour controlled borough of West Ham agreed to provide licences for cinema exhibition. The Society went on to show a number of Soviet classics and films produced by left-wing film-makers in western Europe.

In 1923 the WIR distributed the *International May Day Film*, which showed demonstrations by workers in all the major capitals of Europe. There was also a *Children's Film of Russia* and the *Vorowski Film* (which detailed the assassination of a Soviet diplomat). The British Federation of Workers' Film Societies (FWFS) was stimulated to effect long discussed plans to use film for propaganda in Britain. Three issues of a *Workers' Topical News* were made in 1930 and 1931, all silent. These included sequences on the Hunger Marches that were an important political activity in the 1930s. Later in the 1930s the Workers' Film and Photo League made drama-documentaries for exhibition, *Bread* (1934) and *Fight* (*Strife*, 1935). These were silent films shot on 16 mm. They relied on the left-wing organisation Kino for distribution completely outside the mainstream networks (see chapter six, *The Wider Context – i. Censorship*).

Film on behalf of the working classes had a long tradition in the USA. In 1911 the American Federation of Labour produced a film that defended a victim of anti-union actions, *A Martyr to his Cause*. This was one of a number of one or two reel films that labour and progressive groups produced in this period. A cycle of dramas followed a genre of labour versus capital.

Upton Sinclair had written a novel, *The Jungle*, tracing the journey of a migrant family to the USA and the exploitation inflicted on them. The All-Star Feature Corporation made a five reel version in 1914. A 1916 film by William C. de Mille, *The Blacklist*, dramatised actual events from a lockout at a mine and the subsequent murder of strikers by company thugs.

Frank E. Wolfe, a journalist turned socialist candidate turned film-maker, made *From Dusk to Dawn* in 1913. The film had a romance as central to its plot. It also contained actual footage of the workers' slums, a successful strike and a socialist candidate who is elected as State Governor. *From Dusk to Dawn* was actually booked into the New York theatre chain of Marcus Loew and its box office success sparked more films from the workers' point of view. These included 'actualities' or documentaries on all sorts of labour activities. In 1920 the Labor Film Services (LFS) was set up, capitalised by $10 shares from workers. This produced *The Animated Labour Review*, a weekly newsreel. Their first feature film was *The Contrast* (1926), a drama about coal miners. The film was as much a social document as a drama, depicting the poverty and danger endured by miners. There were also documentaries made with International Workers' Aid in support of the Soviet Union.

The films directly produced by labour organisations were more difficult to programme into film theatres. The LFS and IWA (International Workers' Aid) also rented film theatres for workers' screenings. The audiences were smaller than those enjoyed by mainstream films, but they could be substantial on occasions. The re-release of *The Jungle* drew 5,000 advance bookings in New York in 1922. However, the development of the feature programme and Hollywood's increasing power in the exhibition sector contributed to the decline of the labour films. There were far fewer in the 1930s sound era.[65]

3. CHINA

China's fledgling film industry went though a particular interesting period in the 1920s. The exhibition sector was dominated by US imports. In 1929 about 90 per cent of the 500 or so films released were from the USA. However, there were sizeable film production companies and the centre for film-making was Shanghai. Chinese film included traditional stories with Confucian values, but the Shanghai studios also produced a cycle of melodramas. As in Japan, sound technology arrived quite late and films without soundtracks were produced up until 1935.

In China during this period there was a struggle between the reactionary Guomindong Government and progressives centred on the Chinese Communist Party. In 1931 the Japanese invaded Manchuria, sparking off patriotic resistance. Whilst the Guomindong imposed censorship and repressive measures, a Communist cultural group, the League of Left-wing Writers, worked to influence popular films. They succeeded in making a series of leftist melodramas, which combined social criticism with calls for national resistance against the Japanese invasion.

Chuncan (*Spring Silkworms*, 1933) was a documentary-style representation of a peasant family involved in rearing and harvesting silk. The film emphasised the dignity of labour and the inequities of the market. *Xiao Wanyi* (*Little Toys*, 1933) followed a group of toy makers whose lives are disrupted by the war. In their flight from the battles a mother and son are separated. Late in the film, there is a melodramatic moment when the mother sees her son, who does not recognise his mother. At this point the film brings together its protest against the exploitation of workers and the oppression produced by Japanese aggression.

Such films were part of a constant battle with Guomindong censorship. They centred on heroes and heroines, and even developed their own stars. However, these protagonists were frequently positioned in a larger group, typically a small circle of workers or friends, for example, the village of silk makers or the toy makers collective. This enabled the films to emphasise the social and the collective. This social strand continued into the sound era and is a recognisable feature of films made under the Communist leadership in the 1950s and 1960s.

4. AFRO-AMERICAN CINEMA

As segregated as the US labour films were those specifically for the North American black population. Mainstream Hollywood provided little in the way of significant roles for black people, restricting them to stock characters such as servants, criminals, or for background or comic effect. This reflected the segregation of white and black peoples in most amenities, including film theatres. In the southern states, despite the outcome of the Civil War, segregation was enshrined in legal enactment. In the north, whilst not required legally, segregation was the norm, and several independent film companies made films specifically for this audience.

What became known as 'race movies' started in Chicago in 1910. Between then and 1950 about 500 films specifically for black audiences were made. In the 1920s there were around 300 movie theatres that catered for these separate audiences and their films. The early 'race films' grew out of vaudeville, but soon small independent companies developed. From about 1915 such companies made serious dramas. Eventually 'race movies' covered a range of movies, including westerns. The films were usually made cheaply and consequently had low production values.

The first 'race' film-maker to produce feature length dramas was Oscar Micheaux. He had previously been a homesteader, and then used his experiences in fictional writing. He distributed his books by door-to-door selling. In 1918 he formed the Micheaux Book and Film Company, acting as producer, writer, director and distributor. He made over 40 films between then and the 1940s. Whilst cheaply made, with noticeable stylistic flaws, these films had sophisticated narratives and comment. Despite low productions values they were intelligent in their stance and dramatic in their content.

Micheaux's most important film was *Within Our Gates* (1920). This answered the call by leaders in the black communities for a riposte to Griffith's *The Birth of a Nation*. Micheaux used powerful crosscutting between scenes of the lynching of black people and the attempted rape of a black woman by a white landowner. Both were shown in unusually graphic detail. These sequences were not only great melodrama but it also inverted and subverted the stereotypes used in *The Birth of a Nation*. The graphic detail of the lynching and the rape caused protests. The racist riots of the 1919 'red summer' were fresh in memories. Micheaux often had to screen the film shortened from six to eight reels, with part of these sequences cut.

In his next film, *The Symbol of the Unconquered* (1920) Micheaux addressed 'passing for white'. A Negro[6] becomes embittered when the sight of his black mother alienates his white girlfriend. This plot device reappears frequently, recently in Philip Roth's novel, *The Human Stain*. Micheaux's protagonist, passing as white, becomes involved in the persecution of a black prospector. The climax, most of which is now missing, has the Ku Klux Klan attempting to steal the land of the black hero. Once again Micheaux challenged and subverted the racist images of the earlier Griffith film. Another major Micheaux film was *Body and Soul* (1925), starring Paul Robeson. Robeson played a black minister who swindled, seduced and exploited his congregation. It was a powerful indictment of the exploitative side of religion and provoked criticism from many in the black religious communities. However, it was one of the few films that provided Robeson with a role that befitted his talents.[7]

In the late 1920s new companies emerged and production values rose. However, the advent of sound and the 1929 financial crash wrecked the industry. Micheaux was bankrupted. He did start film-making again (but only with financial input from white cinema owners) and continued into the 1930s. Increasingly Hollywood turned its eyes on the 'race movie' audiences. Many of these films were now financed by white producers and some also employed the stereotypes common in mainstream Hollywood films. The whole industry faded away by the 1950s as mainstream cinemas were finally integrated.

5. THE AVANT-GARDE

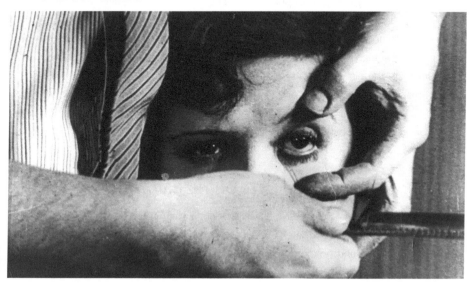

Un Chien andalou

Political film-making outside the mainstream crossed over into the experimental. There were a series of film movements that pushed the frontiers of film, though they had little immediate influence or impact on audiences. One centre for such activity was Paris. Some of the French impressionists, like Germaine Dulac, made films that were far outside the mainstream conventions. And in the early 1920s Paris was the centre for a new art movement, Dada. These artists challenged traditional values and elevated the absurd and the random. In 1923 the US artist Man Ray made *Retour à la raison* (*Return to Reason*) for a major Dada event. In what became almost a de rigueur encore for such events, there was a mini-riot in the auditorium. René Clair produced a film, *Entr'acte* (1924) designed to be shown in the intermission of a Dada ballet. It followed a group of animated and unexplained chases round Paris, ending up in a funeral. The film lacked plot, motivation or explanation, which fitted well with the Dada values. A painter Fernand Léger filmed *Ballet mécanique* (1924), which appeared to be a collage of objects and paintings

One of the audience members for the Man Ray film was the poet André Breton. He was a key member in the successor to Dada, Surrealism. The Surrealist emphasised chance and the random, but the idea of the unconscious and the importance of desire also fascinated them. There was also a strong political current in Surrealism. Several artists were members of the French Communist Party. Germaine Dulac and Man Ray both made surrealist films, but the most famous – or infamous – was *Un Chien andalou* (1928), by Luis Buñuel and Salvador Dali. Apparently they excluded anything from the film's script that had a possible rational explanation. The result was a dream-like film, shocking in parts, extremely comic in others and it launched Buñuel's career as a major European art film-maker. Even after 80 years it remains one of the most powerful films of the avant-garde.

There was an avant-garde journal published in English, *Close-up*. Its editor, Kenneth Macpherson, directed the film *Borderline* (1930). The film dealt with sexual relations between white and black people, a taboo subject in commercial films, but the events were presented in an elliptical style, and visually clearly displayed the influence of Soviet films. Unusually, the film presents sympathetic gay and lesbian characters. Paul Robeson played one of the hetrosexual characters. Unable to obtain serious roles in Hollywood, he made a number of films in the UK in the 1930s. Both Robeson and Macpherson were also involved in leftist politics.[8]

6. THE INFLUENCE OF RADICAL FILM ON THE MAINSTREAM

There were a number of progressive artists working in film in the late 1920s. Film-makers like Dulac, Epstein and, later, Buñuel, worked both on films that circulated in the commercial industry and on experimental works that were consumed only by a very specialised audience. Film-makers could move relatively freely between sectors of the industry and different national cinemas. Thus, the young British director Alfred Hitchcock worked at the UFA studio in Germany. The Danish director Carl Dreyer also made films in Germany and his famous *Joan of Arc* in France. The German director E. A. Dupont made two fine silent melodramas in London, *Moulin Rouge* (1928) and *Piccadilly* (1929).

In a similar way developments in film construction and style circulated among European directors. The chiaroscuro lighting of expressionism, the unchained camera of German cinema, the montage of Soviet films all had a marked influence across filmmaking. Hitchcock's *The Lodger* shows a debt both to expressionist lighting and a masterly use of fast editing. Of course, as in Hollywood, the transport of stylistic innovation often changed the way these functioned. In *The Lodger*, despite the use of light and dark, the film depicts a recognisable and realistic London. And the fast editing early in the film serves to develop rather than disrupt continuity. The appropriation of the most advanced innovations of the decade produced some of the most memorable films of the silent era. Hitchcock's films stand out in British production. Equally impressive were the late masterworks of Fritz Lang and G. W. Pabst in Germany.

In France, Abel Gance pushed the boundaries of film technology with a five hour epic film on the life of *Napoleon* (1929 – Kevin Brownlow's restoration in fact lasts over *six* hours). The early part of the film included a bravura sequence of a snow fight, beautifully edited and constructed to reveal the young man's early tactical genius. And the film ended with the invasion of Italy by Napoleon's armies, using a three-camera, three-screen set-up that anticipated Cinerama.

These developments and films benefited from an early art film culture. The Ciné Club movement in France had been an important factor in the growth of impressionist films. The surrealists' art depended on the support of rich patrons who sponsored films in a similar way to paintings. There were special cinematic events in Berlin in the early 1920s, which prominently featured the expressionist films. In 1925 the Film Arts Guild introduced Sunday afternoon screenings at a small New York theatre of the classic expressionist, montage and avant-garde films. Also in 1925 a group of British cineastes started The Film Society, based in London. It too showed the new European classics, including *Caligari* and *Potemkin*.

7. DOCUMENTARY

Both radical approaches to film and a mastery of construction and style can also be found in the development of documentary silent film. Prior to the 1920s non-fiction film was largely either newsreel or short films, like travelogues and actualities. In the 1920s new film-makers developed feature-length factual films, and the idea of a distinct factual genre emerged.

In 1922 Robert Flaherty released a film presenting the life of the Eskimos (Inuit) around Hudson Bay, *Nanook of the North*. The filming took nearly two years and included actual footage on the snow and ice, in igloos and following the Eskimo hunt. The film was not quite as objective as it appeared. All the sequences were pre-planned. And, for example, Flaherty filmed Nanook hunting with a harpoon when Inuits had already progressed to using a rifle in hunting. Even so, the film portrayed a seemingly realistic picture of an almost unknown world. It was distributed by the Independent Pathé Exchange and was very successful. Flaherty followed this up with *Moana* in 1926, shot in Samoa in the South Seas. And in the early thirties he collaborated with F. W. Murnau on a dramatic film, *Tabu* (1931). However, the fictional and factual film-makers fell out and Murnau finished the film alone, accompanying it with a musical soundtrack.

Flaherty's example was followed by the team of Ernest B. Schoedsack and Merian Cooper who made *Grass* (1926), which depicted the migration of Iranian nomads to find feed for their flocks. There is an arduous and impressive river crossing, filmed as it actually took place. They followed this with a fictionalised documentary made in the forest of Siam, *Chang* (1927). Cooper and Schoedsack achieved their greatest fame for the fictional and phenomenally successful *King Kong* (1933).

The Soviet Union provided exciting examples of this new style of non-fiction film. Apart from Dziga Vertov another important director was Esfir Shubb. She more or less developed the compilation documentary with a series of films using archive film. One of her major films is *Padenie dina stii Romanovykh* (*The Fall of the Romanoff Dynasty*, 1927). There were also examples by a number of Vertov's contemporaries and collaborators, including Victor Turin's *Turksib* (1929), which followed the building of the Trans-Siberian railway. This particular documentary was shown abroad and had a lot of influence on the British documentary film-makers.

The power of the new editing style was extremely influential among directors working in factual film. In particular there was a cycle of 'city films', which utilised camera and editing to provide a multi-faceted view of the city. Vertov's own *The Man with the Movie Camera* clearly falls in this cycle. Alberto Cavalcanti made a city film about Paris, *Rien que les Heures* (*Nothing But Time*, 1926). Cavalcanti portrays a series of episodes, of the people and of the city. More famous was Walter Ruttman's *Berlin: Die Sinfonie einer Grossstadt* (*Berlin: Symphony of a City*, 1927). Ruttman developed an almost abstract sense of buildings, architecture and landscape. Both Vertov and Cavalcanti's films have a much stronger sense of the city dwellers. A Dutch film-maker, Joris Ivens, made two films that fit in this pattern: *The Bridge* (1928), a portrait of the complete cycle of raising and lowering, and *Rain* (1929), a city poem that uses this common element to explore urban space.[9]

Both Cavalcanti and Ivens were to become key documentary film-makers in the sound era. Cavalcanti worked in the British Documentary Film Movement. This was founded by John Grierson, a Scot, who actually coined the term 'documentary'. In 1929 he filmed *Drifters*, a film about the herring industry which impressed the Film Society with its cinematography (it was shown in the same programme as Eisenstein's *Potemkin*). But Grierson's lasting contribution was to persuade the British Government (to be exact British civil servants) to support a cycle of factual films about Britain, which developed in the 1930s and founded an ongoing tradition of British documentary.

8. ANIMATION

A basic technique for animation, stop motion photography, was in use from earliest cinema. A New York Kinetoscope exhibitor in 1895 used stop motion to create the illusion of *Mary Queen of Scots* losing her head. Film-makers quickly grasped the combination of this technique with drawings and models to produce artificial movement. Émile Reynaud projected drawn images in his Praxinoscope to produce an illusion of movement prior to the development of film. One of the Vitagraph pioneers, Stuart Blackton, was a quick-draw artist in vaudeville and featured his skills in some early films. In the 1906 *Humorous Phases of Funny Faces*, Blackton animated drawn faces frame by frame ending with the rolling of the faces' eyes. In the same year a Spanish film-maker, Segundo de Chomón, used actual objects for a Pathé film about a toy box coming to life.

In the teens the US comic-strip artist Windsor McCay made a number of drawn animations based on his newspaper work. McCay used assistants to fill in the drawings, a sign of the increasing industrialisation of animation. At the same time in Russia, Ladislav Starevicz made a series of insect films. He achieved his effect by using plastic jointed puppets moved frame by frame. His films not only included striking effects, but were also graced by a sardonic humour. *The Dragonfly and the Ant* (Stekoza i muravei, 1913) remains comic even today.

In the teens animation developed with new techniques and an increasing replication of the way feature film production was organised. An important development was the introduction of cels. These were transparent sheets which could be layered, allowing successive frames to use the common cels and only change those where movement was needed. A similar efficiency was obtained by slashing drawings, where the moving parts of a body were redrawn on separate sheets for subsequent frames.

During this period some of the prominent names of animation started work. A pair of brothers, Max and Dave Fleischer, developed the rotoscope. This device was attached to a process camera and projected individual frames, which could then be drawn/copied for animation. Max Fleischer's famous cartoon character was *Koko the Clown*. This animated clown appeared in the films out of an inkwell, and interacted with the artist onscreen. The relationship was like that of the father / errant son, with Koko falling into endless scrapes. Gregory la Cava in the mid-teens developed a line in quite anarchic cartoons. He, like many animators, relied on children and animals for his characters. Two sterling characters were *Krazy Kat* and *Ingnatz Mouse*, constantly in conflict, like the later classic *Tom and Jerry*. In the UK a Welsh company developed a character in films that followed the model of the Fleischer cartoons. This was *Jerry the Tyke*. The term denotes a mongrel, but also a small cheeky child. And Jerry fitted this description, like Koko, ignoring his creator/father figure and falling into trouble.[10]

These animators owned or worked for independent production companies that relied on the major studios for distribution, but Walt Disney, who started in animation in 1919, was to eventually develop a major studio based on animation production. In 1927 he developed his first successful character, Oswald the Rabbit, but he lost control in a copyright dispute typical of the burgeoning industry. He then developed the Mickey Mouse character. It was with the addition of a musical soundtrack that Disney had his first big success, *Steamboat Willie*, in 1928.

In Europe, influenced by the avant-garde, film-makers developed more experimental animations. The Dada films by Clair and Leger used animation techniques. Ruttman, the director of *Berlin: A Symphony of a City*, painted oil on glass to produce abstract animation. At UFA Hans Richter produced scrolls of abstract designs aiming for a 'visual music'. His partner, Viking Eggeling, produced the longer *Diagonal Symphony* in 1924. The idea of a visual music was a particular preoccupation in this period, shared by the painter Wassily Kandinsky (and would also preoccupy Disney, for whom *Fantasia*, 1940, was a personal project).

Ruttman also assisted the film-maker Lotte Reiniger, who produced films using elaborate silhouettes. Her most famous work is *Die Abenteuer des Prinzen Achmed* (*The Adventures of Prince Achmed*, 1926), a sort of Arabian Nights story, with delicate and beautifully coloured silhouettes. And Oskar Fischinger, who was later to work for Disney on *Fantasia*, entered the field, as did Len Lye in England. Both produced distinctive animation films in the 1930s.

STUDY FILM: STRIKE / STACHKA

Goskino. USSR 1925. 6351 feet, running time of 95 minutes at 18 fps.

Directed by Sergei Eisenstein. Screenplay V. Pletnyov, G. Alexandrov and S. Eisenstein (called Prolekult Collective). Cinematography Edouard Tisse with V. Popov and V. Khuatov. Production Designer Vasili Rakhals. Assistant directors G. Alexandrov, A. Levshin and I. Kravchunovsky.

Strike is a film of incredible dynamism and excitement, surely a reflection of the political environment of the early 1920s in the newly born Soviet Union. It is also a reflection of the excitement felt by the young film-makers, especially Eisenstein, with their first fully-fledged intervention in cinema. Eisenstein had studied with the Soviet pioneer, Lev Kuleshov and practised editing with Esfir Shubb (on the Soviet release version of *Doctor Mabuse*, 1922, Fritz Lang's film that contains a bravura editing sequence of its own). He had also made a short film, *Glumov's Diary* (1923), which was used in a theatrical production, but *Strike* was a feature-length dramatic story with important political significance.

The film was part of a proposed 'Cycle of films on the Workers' Movement in Russia', *Towards Dictatorship*, which was to focus on important milestones in the struggle for the new socialist society. *Strike* generalises a story about the workers' struggle against capital, though much of the action is based on a series of strikes in 1903 at Rostov-on-the Don. The plot is presented over six reels, each one with its own title and topic (films were still frequently presented with a single projector and breaks between reels). The film's structure fits into and exploits this practice:

Part 1 – All is calm at the factory:

The action actually contradicts this title as it details the simmering discontent. It paints a picture of the opposition between the workers' organisation and the capitalist apparatus

Part 2 – A reason to strike:

In this episode management blame a worker for a theft and he commits suicide. This leads to a general walkout from the factory.

Part 3 – The plant stood stock-still:

The strike now impacts on both workers and owners, and they plan their responses. The capitalist apparatus includes the police and the secret police, with their network of spies and informers.

Part 4 – The strike drags on:

There is increasing hardship for the workers, whilst the management and police plan reprisals. They kidnap a worker and interrogate him.

Part 5 – The provocation to disaster:

The police provocateurs start a fire. When this fails to incite a riot the fire brigade turn their hoses on a workers' demonstration.

Part 6 – Liquidation:

Police and mounted Cossacks are turned loose on the workers; they invade their tenements and soldiers shoot fleeing workers.

The film ends 'REMEMBER PROLETARIANS!'

The film is intensely and overtly political. It spends an unusual amount of screen time on working people and their conditions. Unlike the contemporary mainstream film this is not achieved by focusing on a particular hero or heroine, but through the depiction of a whole class. In part, the film was intended as a 'production analysis', a series of lessons from history about the conduct of strikes and the struggle against capital and the Tsarist autocracy. However, it also functions as agitation, generating sympathy and solidarity with workers' struggles. And, to a degree, it works at an intellectual level, encouraging an understanding of such situations and their place in the broader social framework.

One aspect of the film's lessons for audiences is the documentary look and style of the film, as if recreating actual people, events and places. But other approaches are also used to develop the proletarian standpoint on the struggle. The main technique for depicting character in this struggle is typage, used extensively across Soviet film, dramatising through the use of types rather than psychologically drawn characters. The workers are predominantly presented in a heroic mode, 'monumental', though this does not exclude their foibles and weaknesses. The capitalist class and their hangers-on are comic caricatures in the manner of *Grand Guignol*.

Eisenstein reworked a number of influences from both cinema and the arts. He was influenced by D. W. Griffith, but also younger directors like Stroheim. And there seems to be some debt to Lang's *Doctor Mabuse*. Visually he was influenced by the Soviet constructivist movement, with its emphasis on machine type art. And the fragmenting approach also found in Cubism is also at work. Most importantly he brought his and other experiences from the avant-garde Moscow Theatre and especially the work of Vsevolod Meyerhold.

One important set of techniques was known as biomechanics. This was a stress on dynamic movement and gesture in acting. In *Strike*, there is constant movement within the frame, and action and emotions are capped by the distinctive gesture. One continually notices the workers' taut bodies and outstretched limbs. The emphatic sense of bodies reaches a peak in the sequence in which the workers' demonstration is attacked with the fire brigade's hoses. Among the enemy spies and informers there are more grotesque stances and gestures. The barrel sequence at the start of Part 5 is full of such performance. They are frequently reminiscent of circus clowns, whose techniques Eisenstein had exploited in his theatre work.

The other approach bought from theatre was the 'montage of attractions'. These were techniques which aimed to involve, stimulate and shock audiences: 'concentrating the audience's emotions in any direction dictated by the production's purpose'. The attractions in *Strike* work in a myriad of ways, from the impact of performance to the staging and the striking compositions. There are a large number of visual gestures and motifs that both emphasise particular shots and scenes, and combine across the whole film as a network of meanings. There are three especially noticeable sets of motifs across the film. There is water that flows and cascades in so many different settings. This reaches a climax when the workers' bodies are distorted and beaten by the gushing water from the firemen's hoses. Another frequent motif is the circle. These also tie into scripted meanings. At one point in Part 1 a title word transforms into 'HO', Russian for 'but…!'. The changing function of circles in the film parallels the changes in situations. In Part 2 a triptych of workers is framed against a wheel; it is a symbol of the power in unity as they confront the owners. But there is another circle (hole) that the workers' leader is forced into at the end of Part 5, when the jets of water have broken up the solidarity of the workers' demonstration. Thus, circles function symbolically within the film.

Another symbolic function is associated with the use of animals. The underground army of the police are all identified with and compared to animals. This animal motif returns when the savage 'liquidation' of the workers by troops is intercut with the slaughter of a bull. Symbolism was commonly used in silent films; one can see it in Griffith, but the dramatic contrast in Eisenstein's film is fairly unique.

The other aspect of 'montage of attractions' is the development of film editing. Montage, the use of film editing to set up discontinuities and counterpoint, was a key development of Soviet film. Eisenstein takes the techniques developed by film-makers like Griffith, and gives them dramatic new uses. Rather than the continuity of the Hollywood film Eisenstein produces discontinuities. One reason why the film's narrative can be difficult to follow is the constant cutting to new shots and scenes that do not seem to follow on from or connect with their predecessors. For example in Part 1, while it is clear that we are being shown a factory and a company, the film does not offer a discernible geography for this, rather a class divide made visible.

Eisenstein uses parallel cutting, again a technique practised by Griffith. But Eisenstein's cuts frequently take the viewer outside both continuity and the diegesis. At times it can be difficult to discern whether a particular shot is diegetic or extra-diegetic.[11] With the final images of the slaughter of the bull it becomes clear that only an extra-diegetic function can make sense of this scene. And Eisenstein's use of the camera is equally disconcerting. In fact, the film reads almost like a dictionary of camerawork. It is difficult to think of a technique that is not used at some point: the range of camera shots and positions, dissolves, superimpositions, double exposures, wipes, irises, travelling shots, etc., yet the individual shots are carefully constructed and full of visual meanings. Edouard Tissé was important in this respect. He was a gifted lighting cameraman, and subsequently worked on all of Eisenstein's films. The mainly in-camera techniques, such as the dissolve, produce striking images like the workers triptych against the wheel. The camera angles are unusual. Mainstream film tended to position cameras from a character point of view. Eisenstein's range of angles is omnipotent, and is determined by effect rather than viewpoint.

The lighting is also frequently set for effect rather than naturalism. The discovery of the theft of the micrometer in Part 2 uses effective side-lighting, and then lighting from below. The kidnapping of the worker in Part 4 looks as expressionist as a German film. Married to this is the frequent use of both a deep field of action and deep staging. During the workers' gathering in Part 3 important developments take place at the back of the screen. So the audience is constantly receiving fresh, and often unexpected, stimulation.

Strike premiered early in 1925. There was a positive critical response to what was seen as a political and stylistic step forward for Soviet film. Pravda praised 'the first revolutionary creation of our cinema', but it met with some resistance within the Soviet film industry. The film established Eisenstein's approach, which was radically different from some other pioneer film-makers. Kuleshov emphasised the importance of narrative for films aimed at the masses. From an opposite point of view Vertov criticised the fictionalising function of the film. His documentary Kino-Eye approach was some way from Eisenstein's Kino-fist.

Soviet audiences were, it seems, unenthusiastic. The film's lack of clear narrative and its box of stylistic tricks puzzled them. The most frequent screenings were actually in the cine clubs abroad, where Soviet film was admired and often enthusiastically copied. The film was also important because it set down a number of basic markers for Eisenstein's work. Work that was, especially with his next film *Battleship Potemkin*, to develop and refine his theories about revolutionary film form.[12]

STUDY FILM: WITHIN OUR GATES

Micheaux Book and Film Company. USA 1920. Written, directed and produced by Oscar Micheaux.

Existing print 5935 feet (six reels, originally seven or eight reels). Running time of 100 minutes at 16fps.

Cast: Evelyn Preer (Sylvia Landry), Charles D. Lucas (Dr Vivian), Jack Chenault (Larry Pritchard), William Stark (Jasper Landry), Flo Clements (Alma Pritchard), Ralph Johnson (Philip Girdlestone or Gridlestone), E. G. Tatum (Efrem).

Film-maker Oscar Micheaux, circa 1913

Within Our Gates is a riposte to the racism and white supremacy of D. W. Griffith's *The Birth of a Nation*. It is likely that Oscar Micheaux deliberately derived the title from a 1919 Griffith film, *A Romance of Happy Valley*, which contains the epigraph:

'Harm not the stranger

Within your gates

Lest you yourself be hurt'.

This point is made in an article by J. Ronald Green in *Griffithiana 60/61*, a publication that accompanied the Giornate Festival of 1997, which saw the screenings of both the Griffith classic and the less well-known Micheaux film. Seeing the two films in succession demonstrated Micheaux's success in confronting the pernicious dramatisation of the earlier film.

An important aspect of the rediscovery of Micheaux was a sense of the context for his film. *Within Our Gates* was produced for the US 'race' film market, and was therefore denied the resources and production values lavished on the Hollywood product, including Griffith's epics. The dominance of these values, even today, makes Micheaux's films appear inferior alongside those of Griffith. It is worth noting that at the 1997 Giornate, *The Birth of a Nation* received a full orchestral accompaniment, while Micheaux had to make do with a solo piano. But to appreciate Micheaux's work it needs to be approached in the way one responds to an independent film. The emphasis is not on grandiose spectacle but intelligent and meaningful narrative.

The surviving print is incomplete and, as previously noted, the film was frequently cut, sometimes by Micheaux himself, because the violence depicted in the lynching scenes sparked serious controversy. In Chicago the censors enforced cuts of 1200 feet, i.e. over an entire reel of the film. Moreover the source for the surviving print is a Spanish language version, so that the titles, translated into Spanish, have now been retranslated back to English. This apparently affects both the plotting and also the use of colloquial speech. One character's name, Girdlestone, has changed to Gridlestone. It is also possible that some shots are in the wrong position, either through poor copying or carelessness in post production. This makes the plot somewhat difficult to follow at first viewing. (As already noted, the contemporary terms for Afro-Americans citizens were Negro, or coloured, with more pejorative variations quite common. Negro was supposed to commence with a capital N; somewhat ironically, perhaps, not to do so was considered demeaning by black people.)

The protagonist of the film is Sylvia Landry, a southerner. At the film's opening Sylvia is in the north visiting her cousin, Alma. Alma, with the help of her other cousin, Larry, engineers the break-up of Sylvia's engagement to Conrad. (A shot shows Sylvia in a room with Armand, a character who will reappear in the penultimate reel of the film, see below.) Larry himself is involved in gambling and criminal activities. Sylvia now goes to work in a school for Negroes in the south, in the hamlet of Piney Wood. The school is clearly offering a path to betterment for poor Negro children, but it is almost bankrupt. Sylvia goes north again, to Boston, to raise money from wealthy benefactors. In Boston she meets a professional, modern minded Negro, Dr Vivian. Her rescue of a child from the path of an automobile brings her to the attention of wealthy Bostonian Elena Warwick. Though a southern acquaintance schemes to prevent her funding a Negro school, Mrs Warwick provides the much-needed funds for Piney Wood and Sylvia returns to the school. There she turns down a proposal from its head, Rev. Wilson Jacobs. Now

Larry reappears and tries to blackmail Sylvia. To avoid more trouble Sylvia again travels to the north.

Shortly afterwards Larry returns north and is shot in a robbery. Dr Vivian, now searching for Sylvia, treats the dying man. This leads to a meeting with Alma who, in a long flashback, tells him Sylvia's story. She reveals that the Landry family, poor Negro sharecroppers on the estate of Philip Girdlestone, adopted Sylvia. Girdlestone was 'feared by the Negroes, envied and hated by the whites'. Sylvia received an education and this enabled her to show the father, Jasper, that Girdlestone owed him money. When he tried to claim this Girdlestone turned nasty, pulling a gun on Jasper. At this moment he was shot by one of his white tenants – 'poor white trash' in Girdlestone's own words. Jasper was blamed and he and his family became the target of a lynch mob. After a week long manhunt they were caught. Their son Emil escaped but Jasper and his wife were lynched and their bodies burnt. Meanwhile Sylvia only narrowly escaped being raped at the hands of Girdlestone's brother, Armand. After hearing this tragic tale, Dr Vivian finally finds Sylvia and they marry. (A sub-plot involving the Landry's son Emil is completely missing in the surviving print.)

Some of the factors in engaging with the film are the conventions of the 'race' cinema. Whilst they follow the dominant Hollywood model in the main, the cultural opposition implicit in the films has an effect. Sylvia is introduced with a title card identifying 'the renowned Negro Artist Evelyn Preer'. The predominantly segregated black audiences would have enjoyed a familiarity with her career and performances probably completely unknown to equivalent white audiences.

A following title card then informs us that Sylvia is 'typical of the intelligent Negro of our time'. Micheaux immediately offers a contrasting characterisation to those of Griffith and his Hollywood contemporaries. Micheaux also taps into the debates within the Afro-American communities of the time about their social values. Like many other successful Negroes (relatively speaking) Micheaux embraced the bourgeois values of the dominant society. His male protagonists tend to be self-made men. In several films they are either a homesteader or prospector, seemingly utilising Micheaux's own earlier experiences. His arguments are for equality within the system. Dr Vivian clearly embraces the emerging imperial values of the USA. At the conclusion he proudly tells Sylvia of the Negroes' role in the US adventures in Cuba and Mexico.

But Micheaux is not just a dissident black voice. A remarkable aspect of the film is the centrality and action of the heroine. In Griffith's films women are idealised by men, saved by men and then married and protected by men. Sylvia travels, fundraises and fends off attacks on her own. She is an independent woman. Dr Vivian, a student of social affairs, persuades Sylvia to his point of view, but he does this through study and debate. Sylvia may be the victim of patriarchal violence, but she clearly confronts it.

It will be seen from the geographic plotting of the film that Micheaux also tackles the question of the South. Sylvia's travels between North and South expose the particularly vicious nature of white supremacy in the southern states. However, Micheaux is also clear about the limits of northern liberalism. A wry intertitle reads: 'At the opening of our drama, we find our characters in the North, where the prejudices and hatreds of the South do not exist – though this does not prevent the occasional lynching of a Negro.'

The performances and Micheaux's *mise-en-scène* are predominantly within the conventions of the mainstream. The film offers an equivalent melodrama to Griffith. His contemporary Negro society has a fairly clear split between reputable and disreputable. Larry and his criminal associates are defined in anti-social terms, and receive the appropriate melodramatic punishment. Another aspect of Negro society is the religious trend. When Mrs Stratton attempts to dissuade Mrs Warwick from supporting the Negro school she proposes instead that money be given to a minister and preacher, Old Ned. Old Ned preaches that Negroes should stay in their place and is clearly antithetical to the modern aspiring Negroes like Dr Vivian. He and his congregation are also characterised in the melodramatic performance similar to the Negroes in Griffith's epic.

Micheaux though adds complexity. After visiting his white patrons, who roundly abuse him, Ned confesses to himself: 'Again I've sold my birthright, all for a "mess of pottage". Negroes and whites – all are equal. As for me, miserable sinner, Hell is my destiny.' Another sycophantic black character is Efrem, Girdlestone's 'gossipy servant'. After the shooting he rushes to town to accuse Jasper. He follows the lynch mob round, acting like a cheerleader, 'da whi' folks love me', but frustrated by their failure to catch the Landrys they turn on Efrem and lynch him. Subservience is no protection from racism.

The plotting relies on melodramatic coincidences familiar from earlier film melodrama. Dr Vivian meets Sylvia when he sees her robbed in the street. She discovers her father when he recognises a scar on her shoulder. And Dr Vivian rediscovers Sylvia through treating the fatally wounded Larry. The innocent Jasper picks up Girdlestone's gun after the shooting and thus is seen standing over the body with the incriminating weapon in his hand. This last is an extremely familiar melodramatic trope. These characters are really melodramatic types rather than psychologically rounded individuals.

Visually the film shares the style of earlier film melodrama. The staging is straightforward, with characters placed within simple changing settings. The standard shot is the mid-shot, with the action played straight to camera. The lighting is mainly naturalistic, but clearly limited. Because of this, many scenes have a low-key look. Micheaux's choice of shots utilises a simple range and selection. He does use close-ups rather than the iris technique found in Griffith (iris shots tend to introduce or close sequences). He also follows the newly developed system of continuity, using shot, reverse shot and on- and offscreen actions matching.

His editing is the most distinctive use of technique. He parallels Griffith in his intercutting between characters and actions, both in order to generate drama and also to make comment. The manhunt and lynching of the Landry family is an incredibly powerful presentation. At the height of this sequence, Jasper, his wife and son, Emil, are captured and dragged to a gibbet. Emil escapes and rides off. Jasper and his wife are first lynched and then their bodies burnt. But at this point Micheaux intercuts with Sylvia. She is unaware of the lynching and is collecting things from the Landry cabin. Here the brother of Girdlestone, Armand, discovers her. He attempts to rape her. There follow a series of shots showing, alternatively, Armand's increasing menace towards Sylvia and the burning of the bodies of Jasper and his wife by the mob. At the climax we see Girdlestone's hand on Sylvia's breast and a close-up of a scar. A title card then tells us that Armand, seeing the scar, recognises Sylvia as his daughter through an interracial marriage. This flashback story ends with Alma as she finishes telling Dr Vivian of Sylvia's sufferings. There may be missing footage but it is as if Micheaux feels the audience cannot cope with the excess of emotion in the sequence. This arrangement of cuts also presents the reality of lynching and murders for southern Negroes, and the rape and incest that accompanied this. Griffith's inversion of the oppression of black people after the Civil War is here reinverted by Micheaux, and he uses Griffith's most notable technique to present his rebuttal.

Within Our Gates had a far more chequered career than *The Birth of a Nation*. Whereas the Griffith epic survives relatively unscathed, Micheaux's riposte is heavily mutilated. This would seem to be a direct outcome of the dominance of Hollywood, and the oppressed status of the 'race cinema'. Even so, it suggests a more complex audience experience in this period than might seem from the iconic status in which *The Birth of a Nation* is held.[13]

FOOTNOTES

1. This was known as the New Economic Policy, and allowed limited market activity.

2. According to Kuleshov's theory, the sense of a film sequence is determined by the consequence of juxtaposing different shots, rather than the sum of their meaning' (*Il Giornate del Cinema Muto*, 1996, catalogue notes).

3. *Potemkin* has suffered from the scissors of both censors and the authorities. The original film opened with a quotation from Trotsky. This was later replaced by a quotation by Lenin. And even Lenin's quote was later replaced by one that was less obviously political! Not only were shots and scenes cut by different censorship boards, in the 1950s a re-edited Soviet version changed the sequence of shots, bringing the opening of the Odessa Step section into line with continuity editing. In 2005 the Deutsche Kinemathek issued a restoration that is extremely close to the original, including reinstating the cuts and changes of previous decades.

4. The BFI DVD of this documentary has both a good transfer and also a commentary by Yurii Tsivian, which can be played over the film. The commentary is excellent, informative and accessible.

5. *More Treasures from the American Film Archives* includes an extract from a 'labor' film, the prologue from *The Passaic Textile Strike* (18 min., 1926), a docu-drama about a major textile strike in 1926. *Treasures III* has a section on 'Toil and Tyranny', which includes films in support of labour and counter-propaganda by capitalist films such as the Ford Motor Co.

6. The term Negro, with a capital N, was the common term used for African-Americans in this period, including by black people. 'Coloured' seems also to have been considered acceptable by African-Americans.

7. A Cinema Apart website is probably the best place to find copies of Micheaux's films and some of his contemporaries.

8. Germany and Italy also had avant-garde movements. In Germany this included work in the fields of animation and documentary – see pp. 127-130. And the US avant-garde film can be viewed and studied on the mammoth collection *Unseen Cinema: Early American Avant-Garde Film 1893-1941*, a seven-disc DVD set from the American Film Archives.

9. *More Treasures from the American Film Archives* features a Robert Florey 'city film' *Skyscraper Symphony* (9 min., 1929).

10. *More Treasures from the American Film Archives* includes examples of early animation, *The Breath of a Nation* (6 min., 1919, Gregory La Cava) and *Inklings* (6 min., 1925, by Dave Fleischer). *Treasures III* has examples of the use of animation in Ford Motor Co. propaganda.

11. *Diegesis* is a Greek word used in narrative studies, meaning 'the world of the story'. So, the musical accompaniment was not only not part of the film print in the silent era, it was outside the film's story as well – thus 'non-diegetic'. We assume that the bull is not being slaughtered as the same time as the workers, but symbolises their fate.

12. The Eureka DVD of *Strike* uses a fully restored print of the film. And there is a full-length musical score accompanying the film. The disc has the added option of a commentary by Yurii Tsivian. This has a very clear description of the film and important aspect of its style. It also fills in and explains many aspects of the narrative, and the political and social references built into the work.

13. *Within Our Gates* was available on NTSC VHS Video in 2001 and apparently now on DVD. The A Cinema Apart website is the best place to access.

6. THE WIDER CONTEXT

On the set of Blackmail

INTRODUCTION

The topics in this section are disparate but I would suggest that the common feature is that they are likely to be treated as parts of a wider study. This could be silent film, but also could be censorship, an aspect of world cinema and the development of cinematic technology.

Censorship is an often overlooked but vital topic. And the roots of all the major film censorship systems lie in the silent era. So it helps us to understand the peculiarities of the British system by explaining how the system emerged, and in particular the odd role of local authorities, which produces idiosyncratic exceptions to this day. Equally the US Hays Code, while its enforcement really dates from the sound era, was formed and moulded in the silent days.

The function of music in silent film does appear rather different from that of sound, but equally music's functions in sound film owe a lot to the silent age. The logic of music only being composed and added after principal photography has been completed follows from the silent logic of accompaniment. Equally, many of the motifs and generic elements of film music go back to silent roots. An interesting exercise would be for students to track down films that use Wagner's *Ride of the Valkyries*, just like Griffith's *The Birth of a Nation*.

The short items on the many national industries not given substantial treatment elsewhere is to ensure a sense of the widespread variety and diversity of silent world cinema. It is worth including these, even if only briefly, to reinforce this sense. One of the merits of 'The Great Escape' episode from the TV series, *The People's Century* is that it does include illustrations from a wide range of countries. The other source would be the *Century of Cinema* documentaries produced with the BFI for Channel 4. Not all deal with early cinema but they do cover some unusual terrain.

Sound remains the most dramatic and powerful disruption experienced in the film industry since its inception. It is possible that the ongoing digital revolution will equal it, but it is not yet certain that that is so. Sound transformed production, distribution and exhibition, reinforced the dominance of Hollywood, ensured the dominance of a narrative and realist cinema, and clinched the apparent superiority of Hollywood genres and representations. Classical Hollywood completed its formation in this transition. And the tendency to return to classical Hollywood for film plots and narratives in contemporary Hollywood exemplify its continuing influence. It clearly fits into a study of the development of film technology and language. And the impact on and response of audiences to this phenomena are interesting questions. *The People's Century* has some very good extracts from interviews on this topic.

I. CENSORSHIP

One of the key influences on early mainstream films, and one that affected what audiences could enjoy, was censorship. When film appeared, like any new medium, it fell outside the existing controls. There are several early examples of films being banned or censored, but on an ad hoc basic. Apparently the first film banned in Britain was *Cheese Mites* (1898). The crawling mites, filmed through a microscope, shocked the cheese distributors. Manufacturers thought it might shock audiences rather like the apocryphal train. Faced with their outrage the film-maker, Charles Urban, withdrew the film. In New York a film of a dancer, Fatima, had bars printed across her upper and lower anatomy. This, presumably, was the work of the civic watchdogs of morality. In 1910 the London County Council banned a film showing the black boxer Jack Johnson beating the white boxer James L. Jefferies.

In fact, Britain was one of the earliest examples of a systematic national film censorship policy being put into effect. By 1908 establishment figures were warning of the ill effects of cinema, especially in encouraging juvenile crime. In that year a crime melodrama, *The Black Hand*, provoked letters of outrage for depicting 'ruffians' placing a rope around the neck of a child and hoisting it in the air. In 1909 the government passed a Cinematograph Act regulating cinemas through licensing controlled by local councils. Aimed primarily at safety matters, councils quickly revised their practices to control content. Licences were the prerogative of the Watch Committees, who also supervised police forces.

The problem for the industry was less the direct banning of films than the variation produced by individual decisions by numerous authorities. The response was to set up an organ of self-censorship, the British Board of Film Censors (BBFC) in 1912. While it was an industry body there was close involvement by the Home Office. The Board charged distributors 30 Shillings a reel to vet films, issuing certificates of 'U' (Universal) or 'A' (for Adults). Films without certificates were considered unsuitable for general exhibition. However, in practice power still rested with the local authorities, and there was an extended period of uncertainty. The defining moment was in 1921 when the London County Council adopted a policy of following BBFC certification. Even so, there were occasional instances where the Councils did not follow the BBFC line, which has continued even relatively recently with cause célèbres such as *A Clockwork Orange* (1971) or *Crash* (1996).

The BBFC was a fiercely secretive body. It did not actually publish a code of practice and usually did not explain its decisions. However, its annual reports indicated the areas in which there were moral or ethical concerns. Early reports listed 'nudity', 'drug habits', 'the disparagement of public figures and institutions', 'outrages on women', 'cruelty to animals' and 'gruesome murders'. The figures of Christ and the British Royal Family were especially sacrosanct to the Board.

Among the notable films refused a certificate in its early years was *A Fool There Was* (1916). Theda Bara played a femme fatale who seduced a husband, wrecking his marriage and leading to his suicide. To this day the film has not received BBFC certification. Another, *The Martyrdom of Nurse Cavell* (1916) dealt with Edith Cavell, a British nurse executed by the German military in World War I. She was regarded as a martyr in Britain. When a film about the execution was proposed it was to be vetoed at the script stage on the grounds of exploiting the war. The film appeared with no actual reference to Cavell and retitled *Nurse and Martyr* (1915). In 1928 Herbert Wilcox made a film version of the story titled *Dawn*. Government pressure led to the BBFC refusing a certificate, but a number of local authorities, including the LCC, still allowed the film to be exhibited (Robertson, 1985:12; 14).

Increasingly, the Board intervened in the production stage of British films to advise the producers on content. Imported films, especially from the USA, were often trimmed before exhibition. Until the general acceptance by councils of the Board some distributors simply avoided certification, the most notable example being D. W. Griffith's *Intolerance*. The list of banned films is predominantly European in origin, and most frequently offer a rather more open or risqué depiction in sexual matters than was common in British cinema. For example, in 1913 twenty films failed to obtain certificates. Their offences included 'suggestive sexual situation', 'indecent dancing', 'the depiction of procuration, abductions and seduction' and 'impropriety in conduct and dress'.

In 1919 the Board rejected *Damaged Goods*, a dramatisation of a play concerning venereal decease. This was despite a happy ending and a strong moral tone, which condemned activities that spread such diseases. Another revealing case was *Masie's Marriage* (1923). This was a melodrama developed from Marie Stopes' book advocating birth control, *Married Love*. The film was only passed for exhibition on condition that no title containing either Marie Stopes' name or the title of her book appeared in the film. In the drama there is a scene which depicted birth control by a middle class housewife explaining matters to her working class maid. An inset sequence showed a gardener pruning rosebushes, and the flowers transformed into the faces of smiling babies. Despite the reticence of this portrayal the Watch Committee in Cheltenham were extremely concerned. They finally agreed to its exhibition on the condition that the national anthem was not played at any point in the programme, an ingenious protection of the establishment and royalty which apparently occurred in a number of instances in this period.

In the 1920s the Board extended its list of subjects to be 'eliminated' to include: 'passionate and unrestrained embraces', 'white slave traffic', and 'men and women in bed'. Among the important films that fell foul of the BBFC in this decade was *Nosferatu*, which was banned outright. Later in the decade Pabst's *Pandora's Box* was severely cut. One of the more memorable remarks by a film censor related to Germaine Dulac's surrealist film, *The Seashell and the Clergyman* (*La Coquelle et le clergyman*, 1928): 'This film is so cryptic as to be meaningless. If there is a meaning it is doubtless objectionable' (Robertson, 1989: 39).

A new area of concern in the 1920s was film that had a positive view of the new revolutionary Soviet society, classed as 'Bolshevik propaganda'. One victim of the ban was *Battleship Potemkin*. So vigorous was the pursuit of this material that even a poor distributor and his small staff who viewed the film in the privacy of their offices were visited and warned by the police. In fact, it was almost impossible to see any of the montage masterpieces in Britain at that time.

There was one exception. The Film Society was granted licences for films which were not publicly licensed. However, it would seem that the authorities thought that the bourgeois members of this Society were less susceptible to such propaganda. When the Workers' Stage and Film Guild attempted to arrange screenings of the same films they were turned down flat. Later other working class societies were able to arrange screenings in premises that did not require a licence. One rather odd aspect of the British system was that the 1909 Act only referred to nitrate or flammable film. In the 1930s 16mm safety stock was developed for the non-professional market which enabled film societies to avoid the Act's ruling. In 1952 a new act updated the legislation to cover safety film, just at the time that safety film was coming into general use in 35mm exhibition.

This rigorous control of what audiences could consume continued into the sound era. In fact, it was only when film was replaced by television as the most popular medium in the 1950s that the iron grip of the censors slackened. More than one critic blamed the Board's severe standards for the lack of contact with developments in international art cinema and the failure for the UK to develop such a cinema until the 1960s. Paul Rotha commented in 1930: 'Whereas a critic in Berlin may applaud the editing and cutting of a certain sequence of G. W. Pabst's new film, this sequence may have been re-edited or completely deleted in the copy of the same film seen by a critic in London' (Rotha, 1930: 85).

In the USA moral concerns also surfaced about the new medium. Local review boards appeared in many cities dedicated to 'cleaning up' film. The response of the exhibitors was to set up the National Board of Review in 1909. Its task was to vet content. In 1915 the US Supreme Court ruled that film censorship in the State of Ohio was legal, thus denying films the protection of the First Amendment to the Constitution, free speech (this stance was only reversed in the 1950s). In the same year the National Board of Review passed *The Birth of a Nation*. The protests and riots against that film's racism helped to undermine the standing of the Board.

In the 1920s a number of scandals about films and Hollywood fuelled criticism. The most infamous was the trial of Fatty Arbuckle on a charge of rape. Despite being acquitted, Arbuckle was deemed 'unsavoury' and his career became the victim of an unofficial 'listing' or ban by the studios. This was a tactic that reappeared in the 1950s with the activities of the House Committee on Un-American Activities. In the 1920s the producers were so frightened by the possible backlash that they formed the Motion Picture Producers and Distributors of America. To provide public legitimacy they invited the ex-Postmaster General of the USA, Will H. Hays, to become president. His task was to set up an effective system of vetting films.

In fact, he failed to impose standards that were acceptable to the public guardians of morality. In the late 1920s there was a fresh round of protests about film content. This was spearheaded by an organisation of Catholic fellow travellers, The League of Decency. This resulted in a Code of Content, known as the Hays Code, but more properly termed The Production Code. It was taken from a draft prepared by a Roman Catholic priest and it shared most of the taboos and limitations already followed by the BBFC. In fact, it was only in the 1930s that this Code was completely enforced for Hollywood films but it remained in place till the late 1960s.

Other major film countries also had their own systems of censorship, most dating from the teens or the 1920s. Certain national predilections could be found in each system, as with the protection of the Royal family in the British. In general there tended to be a firm control over the depiction of sexual matters, which varied according to the local mores. Most notably was the close eye kept on political expression and the protection of state institutions. And, as in Britain and the USA, censorship bodies tended to expand to control even those alternative facilities outside the mainstream system as soon as they involved the masses of working class people.

2. MUSIC

Sound is an under-researched area of silent cinema, partly due to the difficulties of such an investigation. There was a huge range of informal sound during screenings – the sound of the equipment, the sounds of the audience (including reading out titles), extraneous sound, which might include music in the foyer and other noises due to the poor soundproofing. There were more formal sound inputs, including in the early days the narrator or commentator, and later there were various effects including quite sophisticated sound machines. Both formal and informal acoustics could vary from screening to screening, even for the same film.

A more regular feature of silent films both when first exhibited and when recreated today, is the musical accompaniment. Such accompaniments were part of the predecessors of silent film, like the Magic Lantern. Whilst in the early period films also often enjoyed accompaniment from lecturers or showmen, music became the standard sound for an audience in a film theatre of the silent era. The most frequent accompanist was a pianist, but there were also organs, small ensembles and even sizeable orchestras.

In the 1920s several composers and arrangers who worked regularly on film produced books of generic music for different types of plots and sequences. A composer and arranger for German films, Giuseppe Becce, wrote a *Handbuch der Filmmusik*. He provided scores for *The Last Laugh* and some of the mountain films, including *Das blaue licht* (*The Blue Light*, 1932) directed by Leni Riefenstahl. For the standard exhibition programmes, an accompanist could often rely on recommended sheet music from the distributors. Certain films were associated with certain music. The 1927 *Seventh Heaven* had a soundtrack accompaniment using the popular song, 'Charmaine'. There were also generic musical sequences that musicians used repeatedly, for the danger, romance, the chase or comic sequences.

But there was also a long tradition of composers who would arrange and/or compose scores to accompany films. Apparently this occurred for the Bioscope presentations by the Skladanowsky brothers in 1895. In 1908 the successful composer Saint Saëns produced a score for the Film d'Art historical drama, *L'Assassinat du Duc de Guise*. An early German genre was the Tonbilder, where performers mimed whilst phonograph recordings were played. The most popular film-maker of these was Oskar Messter. In the early teens he also produced films focusing on music or a musician, as with *Richard Wagner* (1912), which had orchestral scores performed by well-known orchestras.

It was when feature films developed into six to eight reel presentations that arranging and composing developed. Griffith selected Joseph Carl Breil to arrange a score for *The Birth of a Nation*. Breil used a combination of composition and arrangement. The use of *Wagner's Ride of the Valkyries* for the Ku Klux Klan ride was apparently thunderous and exhilarating (for those unconcerned by its racism). Griffith used the musical score as part of the attractions for the roadshow screenings. As the studio system developed the producers became increasingly concerned with the accompaniment. It was an added attraction for audiences, but also tended towards a more uniform presentation. Sheet music and books of recommended variations appropriate to particular genres or generic scenes were increasingly provided for the musicians. Meanwhile the large-scale score became associated with the prestige film. And the employment of a particular composer was associated with the 1920s equivalent of today's 'event movie'.

An important composer in the late 1920s was Edward Meisel. He had theatrical experience and had worked with leftist organisations. When Eisenstein's *Battleship Potemkin* was released in Germany, Meisel was commissioned to write a special score. He was so successful that it has become the score for performance with the film. At the time it was considered so rousing that the German authorities tried to ban the score itself. It received Eisenstein's seal of approval when it was played to accompany the film at the screening at the London Film Society. Meisel bought modernist sensibilities and style to film scoring. He went on to write the score for Eisenstein's *October* (1928). He composed a number of other film scores, including for Ruttman's *Berlin: Symphony of a City*, but later became a refugee from the Nazis.

One of the other memorable film scores was Soviet. Dimitri Shostakovich, who had worked as a cinema pianist, was commissioned to compose the score for *The New Babylon* (1929). This occasion was not a success, partly because the music was so modern. But it also seems that the composition and transcription were done with such speed that mistakes were made on the sheet music which also crept into the performance. Today, as with Meisel's score for *Potemkin*, it is a major musical composition.

The coming of sound completely disrupted this musical world. In Britain something like 20,000 musicians lost employment at the end of the 1920s. Only some of them obtained new livelihoods in the fast growing entertainment world of the dance band and the dance hall. Meanwhile, a number of films, like *Sunrise*, had music on pre-recorded soundtracks.

3. SILENT FILM WORLD-WIDE

By the 1920s there was world-wide film production and exhibition. In most countries the films and stars of Hollywood dominated programmes of screenings. However, in a number of key countries distinctive and relatively successful film industries did emerge.

i. India

The first film show in India was in 1896, at the Watson Hotel in Bombay. French cameraman for the Lumière Company, Maurice Sestier, gave the exhibition. The audience included both the European and Indian elites of the city. The show then moved to the Novelty Theatre, where the lower classes, including women, could view the new wonder (although the women were seated separately).

n the early 1900s several indigenous films were produced, but the first important Indian ilm-maker was D. G. Phalke, who actually visited Cecil Hepworth in the UK to study he new craft. In 1913 he released a feature length fictional film, *Raja Harishchandra*. The tory was taken from the classic Indian epic, the *Mahabharata*. It told of a king whose love of truth is tested by a god. Indian audiences identified with this rendering of a familiar story from their own culture and the film was a resounding success. Phalke made a number of feature films based on traditional religious tales from Hindi culture. In 1919 he directed *Kaliya Mardan*. This portrayed the deity Krishna, using the sort of special effects that Méliès had pioneered in Europe. Phalke was able to build his own studio but his production methods befitted a cottage industry. He cast his own family members in the films, and he distributed and exhibited the films himself, using a bullock cart to take screenings to rural areas.

The 1920s saw the development of production, distribution and exhibition companies. The centre for Hindi film-making was the city of Bombay, but regional centres also developed, laying the basis for the regional cinemas of the sound era. H. J. F. Madan started as an exhibitor using a tent for Bioscope programmes. He expanded into both distribution and film production developing an early example of indigenous vertical integration. In 1923 his company controlled 50 film theatres, a third of the national total, but there were also touring showmen in the rural areas, such as Phalke.

In the 1920s film production passed the 100 mark annually. A series of film genres developed: the most common and popular being the mythological subject, following in the footsteps of Phalke. There were also social dramas, costume films, and stunt and swordplay action films, a genre shared with other Far Eastern industries.

Imported films, especially Hollywood products, were common on the cinema circuits. The prints often included titles in three or more languages, one of which was always English. As in other industries sound had a major impact on film-making. However, in India this produced an unexpected consequence. In the 1930s Hindi film developed the popular musical drama with numerous songs and dances. Whilst Hindi was not uniformly used across India, the music and dance provided a common cultural pleasure. From the 1930s onwards the Indian film market was one of the few in the world where Hollywood films did not reign supreme.

ii. Japan[1]

Japanese film archives have suffered from disasters, notably World War Two. A high proportion of early films have been lost. Sound arrived late in Japan and silent films were still made up until 1937. Japan also developed a film industry with a high degree of autonomy from Hollywood. The country enjoyed its first screening, by a Lumière cameraman, in 1896, attended by the Prince Royal. This assisted in the status of the new medium, which from its infancy enjoyed the interests of the wealthier and more educated classes. Japanese cinema was strongly influenced by the Kabuki Theatre. This was a nineteenth century variation on traditional Nô Theatre, but less formal and more popular. A crucial ingredient was a narrative figure, the Katsuben or Benshi. Their function was to explain the action, imitate dialogue and provide a commentary. A number of early films were versions of Kabuki plays, and the Benshi quickly became an established part of film screenings. One important formal consequence of this was that Japanese film rarely used title cards. The other aspect of Kabuki Theatre that was followed by films was the use of all male casts.

Two important film genres stemmed from Kabuki Theatre: jidai-geki was a historical film and gendai-geki was a film of contemporary life. The jidai-geki included the chambara (swordplay) and the samurai films. A fine and late example of the latter genre is *A Diary of Chuji's Travels* (*Chuji tabi nikki*, 1927). The film was released in three parts, running to approximately 20 reels. Chuji is a samurai superhero, with superb sword skills, craft and intelligence. However, in the final reels Chuji has become an old and frail warrior. The climax has the bedridden Chuji watching as his followers die fighting to protect him. He then is carried away, a living corpse. The film underlines the excitement of the swordplay scenes with a final sequence of extended hand-to-hand combat, but it also features conventions that will reappear in the samurai genre.

The early decades of the twentieth century were a period of modernisation in Japan. Both local production and exhibition prospered and Japan developed large, vertically integrated film companies. In the 1920s the two most powerful companies were Nikkatsu and Shochiku. By 1928 Japan produced between 600 to 800 films a year, the largest production total in the world. And Japan maintained this lead well beyond World War II. Also in the twenties the large companies profited from US imports and these had an effect on the indigenous film. Directors experimented with title cards. Women began playing female parts, and many directors adopted conventions from the continuity system, including shot, reverse shot editing.

In this period several directors emerged who were to become major figures in the industry right up until the 1950s. One was Kenji Mizoguchi. He developed a taste for powerful melodramas that highlighted the oppressive position of women. In a late silent, *The Water Magician* (*Taki no shiraito*, 1933), a music hall artist develops a relationship with a young student. She finances his law studies. Late in the film, in order to provide money for him, she is implicated in a murder. The student defends his lover in court, but she pleads guilty in order to uphold the law he practices. The film has a graceful style and splendid performances. And the combination of critical values and melodramatic moment is typical of Mizoguchi.

Another director was Yasujiro Ozu who worked predominately in the gendai-geki. Over the years he was one of the most popular Japanese film directors. Ozu's films featured accurate and sympathetic observations of lower professional or upper working class family life. In a late silent, *I Was Born, But* (*Otona no miro ehon - Umarete wa mita keredo*, 1932), an office worker moves with his family to the suburbs. This is in part an effort to improve his status and position at work. Much of the film is taken up with observing how the changes impact on his two sons. Ozu's film is a social comedy, rather in the sense found in Chekov's plays. There is one delightful scene where the father screens home movies for his boss. The interplay of class and family is simple, but powerfully represented.

The third popular and critically acclaimed director from this period is Mikio Naruse. Like Ozu he worked mainly in the gendai-geki. However many of his films treat the lowest stratum of the society, particularly women working as hostesses, geishas and actually involved in prostitution. A fine example of his work is *Apart from You* (*Kimi to Wakarete*, 1933). A widow, Kikue, works as a geisha to support her son. She loses patrons to younger geishas, and her son, ashamed of his mother drifts into delinquency. However, undaunted she struggles on: 'I would be so happy if I could die right now …but I'm going to live.' Such resilient women appear frequently in both Naruse's silent and subsequent sound films

Japan also had its own avant-garde films. Teinosuke Kinugasa directed two films that worked outside the conventions of popular feature films, *Crossways* (*Jujiro*, 1928) and *A Page of Madness* (*Kurutta ippêji*, 1926). In the latter an old man works in an asylum where his wife is incarcerated. Parts of the film appear to be the fantasies of these characters. The narrative is elliptical and there are frequent moments of intense subjectivity. Apparently Kinugasa had not seen the important European avant-garde films. However, the lighting reminds one of an expressionist film, the subjectivity of an impressionist film and the editing of Soviet montage. The whole film is a *tour de force* of style and imagination.

iii. Other Countries

Other early cinemas (not already described) that have left a distinct record include:

a. Argentina

The first feature film in Argentina was *El Fusilamento de Dorrego* (*The Execution of Dorrego*, 1908), a historical epic. Film production developed between 1915 and 1927, and several studios were established. By the late 1920s film production reached 12 films a year. One popular genre was the Gaucho film, based on Argentina's own ranching traditions.

b. Australasia

The first recorded film in Australia was made in 1899, *The Early Christian Martyrs*, a film sponsored by the Salvation Army. In 1906 it produced a very early four reel film, *The Story of the Kelly Gang*. By the 1920s Australia had a thriving film industry. The classic silent is *A Sentimental Bloke* (1919), directed for Southern Cross Feature Film Company by Raymond Longford. The film used a 'strine', or Australian slang, in the intertitles. Even so, it was a hit both in Australia and in Britain.

New Zealand, south of the great continent and another British colony, produced a range of early films. These included some relatively liberal records (for the period) of the Maori peoples. *Heeni tei Rei, Otaki* (*Rauparaha's Niece*, 1921) has intertitles in both English and the Pakeha language. It is filmed like a documentary but the plot is dramatised to produce a narrative. There is a rich portrait of Maori life in this period in the New Zealand Film Archive.

c. Brazil

There was an early period of successful film-making in this country. Between 1908 and 1911 there was an increase in film theatres and these screened a high proportion of local films. A particularly popular genre was *fitas cantatas*, singing films. These were operettas and musicals. They were silent but accompanied by live singers who stood behind the screens and lip-synched to the images. In 1911 Pathé led a sustained competition in the Brazilian film market, and local production declined. In the teens and the 1920s Luis Tomaz Reis filmed a series of expeditions exploring the unknown regions of the vast country. *Rituaes e festas Borôro* (*Rituals and Festivals of the Borôro*, 1916) captured indigenous and expiring rituals in a pure state.

d. Czechoslovakia

Film-making started in 1908, and the first studio was opened in 1921. An important film in the 1920s was *The Good Soldier Schweik* (1926), based on Jaroslav Hašek's novel. This satirical character turned up in a number of film versions in both the silent and sound eras, including one made in the Soviet Union. Another Czech version was *Schweik as Civilian* (1927) directed by Gustav Machaty. Machaty had started out as a cinema pianist, then actor, and finally film director. He both directed and co-produced *Erotikon* (*Seduction*) in 1929. This late silent depicted a short, intense sexual affair with great intensity and real style. In the 1930s Machaty filmed *Exstase* (*Ecstasy*, 1933), a sound film that was notably sensual and explicit.

e. Egypt

The production of short films began in Egypt in 1912. The first feature fiction films were joint Italian Egyptian productions in 1918. The two titles were *l'Honneur du bédouin*, a three-reel feature, and *les Fleurs mortelles* (listed in a French-language anthology). Apparently, neither film was a success and the company went bust. Really popular local films arrived in the late 1920s with films by a successful stage actress, Aziza Amir. She produced and starred in at least two silent melodramas, *Laila* (1927) and *Daughter of the Nile* (1929).

f. Hungary

Hungary produced its first newsreel in 1896. Feature production began in 1912. In 1919, under a brief Communist government, the film industry was nationalised and 30 films were produced by the state. There is a splendid one-reel dramatisation of a militant poem, *Jön Az Öcsém* (*My Brother is coming*, 1919) by the young Michael Curtiz (Mihály Kertész). However, the leftist regime was short-lived and soon replaced by a right-wing regime. In the 1920s Hungary's important contribution was the film-makers who fled this repressive regime, including Curtiz, Alexander Korda, and actor Peter Lorre.

g. Mexico

Early Mexican films were mainly actualities. After the end of World War I, feature film-making developed. A great success was *El automóvil gris* (*The Grey Car*, 1919). This was a serial in 12 parts following a gang who drove the eponymous vehicle, derived from real life events. In the 1920s there was also a rather specialised genre, anti-clerical pornographic films. These were stimulated by struggles against the church, a supporter of reaction.

h. Poland

An early film-maker, Kazimierz Proszynski, made short fiction films from 1902 with a camera he designed himself, a 'peographe'. The film industry developed its own star, Apollonia Chalupiec, in the teens. However, she was discovered and recruited by Hollywood as Pola Negri. Poland became independent in 1918 (after World War I) and then its first film studio was constructed.

i. Spain

Spain had an early pioneer in 'trick' or animation films, Segundo de Chomón. Other early Spanish films were adaptations from plays, produced by small unstable film companies. More stable film production developed in the 1920s. By 1928 indigenous production had reached 59 feature films.

4. THE ARRIVAL OF SOUND

The release of Warner Brothers' *The Jazz Singer* in 1927 was in many ways a parallel to the Lumière screening of 1895. It was not even Warner Brothers' first sound film, but it brought sound to the attention of the public. It provided a model which preserved many features of popular silent film, but also exploited the potential of the new technology. Edison had imagined a combination of sound and moving image, joining his inventions of the gramophone and the Kinematograph. Dickson produced the Kinetophonograph, but this again was a peep show machine which could only be enjoyed by one viewer at a time. It had limited success. Various inventors tried to marry the two technologies. A number of film-makers produced films with some accompanying sound.[2] There is an early short that features the opera singer Enrico Caruso. Many of these used a type of phonograph with a system for synchronising with film. In 1900 a patent was issued for the photoelectric cell which offered the possibility of recording directly onto film. However, these early systems lacked reliable amplification technology, essential for film exhibition in larger venues and theatres. This technology was developed in the early 1920s. Some of these developments took place in Europe. Ufa tried out the German Tri-Ergon system in 1925, unsuccessfully.

In 1926 Warner Brothers formed the Vitaphone Company with Western Electric. Warner Brothers were one of the smaller Hollywood studios, and sound offered a way of possibly establishing their position in the industry.[3] They relied heavily on new investment from Wall Street for this venture. Vitaphone used a sound on disc system; with each disc the length of a film reel. It depended on a synchronising link between disc and reels. This, in fact, frequently broke down. An example played comically of what then happened is depicted in *Singin' in the Rain* (1952), a film that also humorously shows the sort of problems confronted in film production with the new technology.

In 1926 Warner Brothers screened a number of sound shorts and a feature, *Don Juan*. Then *The Jazz Singer* was an enormous box office success when released in October 1927. Audiences reportedly cheered at the first spoken dialogue: 'It was a smash box office success for the mid-level studio, earning a total of $2.625 million in the U.S. and abroad, almost a million dollars more than the previous record for a Warners film' (Wikipedia page on Sound Film, a remarkably detailed source). The industry realised sound had arrived and was here to stay. Fox Films had also been working on a sound system, Phonofilm, which used the photoelectric cell. This was far more reliable than sound on disc and in a few years became the industry system. The competing struggles over patents in this period are an extremely complex saga and demonstrate that while Hollywood was a type of oligopoly, there was still intense competition at times.

The number of patents held by different individuals and companies complicated the market. The Tri-Ergon system was now owned by Tobis-Klangfilm. They were involved in legal cases in the USA and Europe. So, in 1930, a 'sound peace' conference was held in Paris (site of the earlier Versailles Peace Conference). There the market was divided up, with Tobis-Klangfilm taking continental Europe. Apparently the UK market was not included in the division, but it eventually adopted the US systems.

Contrary to expectations, when Hollywood films appeared with sound dialogue this did not undermine their international appeal. Despite the use of English, a foreign language in many countries, sound *increased* the popularity of Hollywood film. Other countries developed or attempted to develop sound systems. But the capital costs for both production and exhibition meant that once again the mammoth Hollywood studios enjoyed a clear advantage. The US exhibition market converted fairly rapidly to sound equipment. About two thirds of cinemas were converted by 1930. Abroad the changeover took longer. Britain and Europe changed over relatively fast, but both China and Japan were still producing silent films up until the mid-thirties. And this was also true of the documentary and independent film arenas.

Even in Hollywood there was a transitional period. *The Jazz Singer* actually combined title cards with recorded music and short sequences of recorded dialogue. A number of other films were released with music tracks to accompany title cards with dialogue and plot information. This was the case with the Academy Award Winners *Wings* and *Seventh Heaven*. Frequently, there were both sound and silent versions of the same movie – *All Quiet on the Western Front* (1930) was a successful sound film that also circulated as a silent.

In Britain the first talkie was Alfred Hitchcock's *Blackmail* (1929), released in both sound and silent versions. The two versions make interesting comparisons. In a number of scenes both the staging and the camerawork are different. The sound version required Annie Ondra, the star playing the heroine, to have her dialogue dubbed by an actress with an English accent. And the sound version shows the early and imaginative use of recorded sound to increase the drama. Another film that combined a soundtrack with title cards was Anthony Asquith's *Cottage on Dartmoor* (1929). The soundtrack is now lost. However, the film has a delightful sequence in a movie theatre with both silent and sound films in the programme which provides a revealing picture of the entertainment medium at that time.

Sound broke down the international production market. It therefore reinforced the idea of national cinemas. Only Hollywood circulated globally, though both Indian and Japanese sound films also had external markets. To a limited extent this was also true of Britain, France and Germany, but the instances of co-production, for example, a British film with European actors and director or cameraman, were rare, generally occurring only when refugees from oppression sought work in foreign territories.

Sound film was dominated by synchronisation, which fitted into the continuity values embodied in mainstream film. Some radical film-makers like the Soviet montage directors, advocated sound as a counterpoint. But this had little effect outside a limited area of cinema. The sound film, with dialogue and effects clearly linked to the visual, and either made in or modelled on the Hollywood conventions, thus became the norm for popular cinema.

STUDY FILM: A COTTAGE ON DARTMOOR

UK 1929 / 30. British Instructional Films. 7,183 feet, 90 minutes. Intertitles and sound (the soundtrack is now lost).

Directed and scripted by Anthony Asquith. Story Herbert C. Price. Cinematography Stanley Rodwell (Axel Lindblom un-credited). Continuity Ralph Smart. Design Ian Campbell-Gray.

Cast: Uno Henning (Joe), Norah Baring (Sally), Hans von Schlettow (Harry).

A *Cottage on Dartmoor* was produced by British Instructional Films and distributed by Pro Patria Films. The former had been founded in 1919, the latter in 1927. This, and a new studio at Welwyn, was the result of fresh investment following on from the 1927 Film Act. New companies and investment also increased with the prospects of the new sound technology. The film was originally planned using a UK disc system, but by the time of production this had become obsolete and the film used a German sound-on-film system, Tobis-Klangfilm.

A *Cottage on Dartmoor* was a joint Anglo-Swedish production, though there appears to be no record of the Swedish company involved (it was probably Svensk). The two male leads were both Swedish actors. Hans Adelbert Schlettow had worked in the German film industry, and had already appeared in another UK film (title not known) which was a co-production involving a German company. Norah Baring, a British actress, had appeared in both of Asquith's two preceding films for British Instructional. And there was a Swedish cameraman, Axel Lindblom, who had worked on a series of films at Svensk Filmindustri. It is possible that the British and Swedish version used different camera shots from the two cameramen.

The director, Anthony Asquith, represented a rather new type of industry craftsman. He came from a privileged background (his father was Liberal Prime Minister from 1908–16), and he was very familiar with the art cinemas of Europe, being a member of the London-based Film Society. This was his fourth film, and his earlier efforts had struck critics with their stylistic flair.

The plot is one of melodrama and revenge. Joe and Sally work in a hair salon, she as a manicurist. Joe's attempt to impress and date Sally fails. Then she catches the eye of a customer, Harry. He has just invested in a farm on Dartmoor and the couple becomes engaged. In a fit of jealous rage Joe attacks Harry. He is sent to jail for attempted murder. The actual setting of the film is on the night of Joe's escape from Dartmoor prison. The film opens on the bleak moor as Joe finds his way to the farm and confronts Sally. Then the events leading to the murder attempt are recounted in flashback. Back in the present, Sally is struck with pity for Joe and hides him from the searching warders. She then persuades Harry to help Joe escape. But rather than return to prison Joe allows himself to be seen and shot. He dies at the door of the cottage in Sally's arms.

The story is a fairly familiar and melodramatic one, but what is striking about the film is the style and the inventive way in which Asquith uses the new sound technology. There is a clear debt to some of the classics he must have seen at the Film Society, notably German Expressionism and Soviet Montage. Much of the atmosphere of the darker sequences in the film is due to low-key lighting, while both humour and shock are generated by fast, and sometimes disruptive, cutting.

The film's opening is dramatic, and is not dissimilar to David Lean's famous opening for *Great Expectations* (1946). Against a dark, stormy sky we see a tree, the moors, the skyline and then a man jumps over a wall into camera shot. We follow his progress across the moors to the cottage. Both the stormy moor and the partly darkened house are shown in low-key lighting, as is Sally's first sight of Joe as his face emerges from the shadows. With two title cards – 'Joe?' and 'Yes, Sally' – Asquith makes a surprising cut to the flashback and the hair salon where they work. The flashback is shot in fairly uniform high-key lighting, in clear contrast to the scenes on the moors. Asquith uses a range of mid-shots and close-ups, clearly organised in terms of continuity, as he sketches in Joe's infatuation for Sally and her lukewarm response. With the appearance of the affluent suitor, Harry, Asquith uses a series of parallel events to sharpen the contrast. Joe buys tickets for the cinema, but when Sally declines he throws them away and a colleague picks them up. When Harry successfully invites Sally to a talkie, he drops the tickets and Joe picks them up. Both men visit Sally at her lodging house, but Joe is unsuccessful in his efforts to kiss Sally. When Harry kisses her, after proposing, she flings her arms around and returns his kisses passionately.

Asquith breaks up the melodrama with sly visual humour. During one of Harry's early visits to the salon and Sally we see Joe dealing with other customers. In the first instance he tries to make conversation and a series of insert shots depict the subjects: cricket, speedway, Lloyd George. With a second customer Joe is distracted as he slyly observes Harry and Sally, whilst the customer now attempts to make conversation, also illustrated by insert shots: cricket, tennis, polo and a chicken! Meanwhile Harry studies the list of salon services, vainly trying to find one he has not already purchased in his pursuit of Sally.

The cinema visit (predominantly low key) is a particular delight and illustrates the young's Asquith willingness to reflect on the medium in which he works. The earlier *Shooting Stars* (1927) was set in a film studio. The cinema sequence in the original release version of *A Cottage on Dartmoor* had sound on the film track, but this is now lost. Even so, it works very well. Joe, having seen their tickets, has secretly bought a seat directly behind Sally and Harry. The opening film is a Harold Lloyd comedy, with a live orchestra in the cinema. The camera concentrates on the differing responses of the audience. This continues with the start of the talkie, *My Woman*. Now we not only watch the audience, but the actions of the unoccupied cinema orchestra. It is clear, from the audience response, that the fictional film offers mystery, shock and romance. In the later stages Joe becomes increasingly distraught. Fast cutting of images presents Joe's mental state as he imagines fighting and razoring Harry.

This is exactly what occurs on Harry's next visit to the salon, though now he and Sally are engaged. Once again Asquith uses a montage approach, with a sequence of short shots, acute camera angles and obtrusive cuts. The actual attack is not shown onscreen but the speed of the changing shots generates a real sense of shock. This continues as the staff reacts to the shocking deed. One shot shows the spreading contents of a spilt bottle, a shot that seems a direct borrowing from Eisenstein's *Strike*.

Asquith also uses parallel cutting to take forward the action and to comment upon it. Early in his escape attempt Joe stoops to drink water from a pool. A dissolve takes us to a tub of water as Sally bathes her infant son, introducing the heroine and the cottage. As is often the case in silent films, such cuts can be intentionally symbolic. As the distraught Joe fingers the razor insert shots show a snapping cord and a naval broadside. (Original prints may also have been coloured red at this point). At the end as Joe contemplates suicide there is an insert shot of waves crashing on a shore.

Soviet style cutting is matched by expressionist style lighting. Joe's face is frequently lit from underneath to intensify the sense of menace. In the cinema the pattern of light on the faces of Harry and Sally appears to be produced by the changing light intensity of the screen. And, as Joe dies on the cottage floor, the shadows of bars above his head reinforce his fate.

The history of the film's critical reception is unclear. However, Asquith, as with other British film-makers, endured an uneven response from critics. Writing in 1930, Paul Rotha, in his classic *The Film Till Now*, commented: 'That he possesses a feeling for cinema was proved by all these films, but that he is till groping and undecided in his mind as to how to find expression for his ideas is equally plain. He has learnt varied forms of treatment from abroad, but has not as yet fully understood the logical reason for using them' (Rotha, 1967: 320)

Viewing the film seven decades on this appears a grudging and unfair appraisal. Following techniques developed in the Soviet Union and Germany, as well as in France and Scandinavia, was common in late silent and early sound films. In fact, I would judge that Asquith's use of expressionist and montage techniques is closer to the originator's practice than many examples from Hollywood studios. And the combination of silent and sound technologies is as ingenious as in Hitchcock's *Blackmail*. Asquith's film has the advantage that it preserves the rhythms of silent film, whereas Hitchcock's suffers from the undeveloped pacing of early sound.

There is a frequent comment made that British film-makers failed to develop the sort of alternative art film approach that European film-makers offered as a cinema distinct from Hollywood. This may be true, but one factor would seem to be the oft-repeated disparagement of the British product by the critical and intellectual circles. Asquith's subsequent films, with the advent of sound, lack the style and innovation of his silents. It is only with the war years that we get films of the quality of *The Way to the Stars* (1945). There are probably a number of factors involved in this, including the low standard of British production in the 1930s. One thing missing from the British film discourse in the 1930s was the intelligent critical writing that graces French cinema culture.

FOOTNOTES

1.   The Japanese names are presented in the UK fashion, forename first then surname: in Japanese the reverse is the practice, surname and forename.

2.   *More Treasures from the American Film Archives* has examples of early experimental sound on film.

3.   Kevin Brownlow notes that Western Electric technicians checked projection speeds at the first-run Warnes Theatre and were told between 20-24fps. They settled on 24fps for sound technology (1968: 246).

EPILOGUE: DEATH AND RESURRECTION

After 1930 silent film was not only replaced by sound, it disappeared. Sadly, this was in many cases literally. The nitrate film stock used in the silent era contained valuable materials including silver. Old film stock was frequently pulped in order to extract these (a 1950 Italian newsreel showing this process caused an audible groan from the whole audience at a screening at the Cinema Ritrovato in 1995). It is reckoned that only about a third of silent films survive, though unevenly. India has just a few complete features. Japanese film is scarce; on the other hand, Hollywood star features are well represented.

In fact, at the same time as the old silent reels were being dumped and destroyed, people were also starting to save them. The two important groups in this process were collectors and professional archivists. The collectors were especially keen on comedies; hence the common sense people have of silent films as slapstick. This was an expensive and fraught hobby. The copyright issue was always confused. And the actual films were dangerous, being prone to both fire and explosion.

Archivists were often especially interested in particular blocks of films, like their own national output. Britain is fortunate in its National Film Archive, a long established repository for saving early film. The most famous and eccentric of the archivists was Henri Langlois. He started collecting both films and artefacts in 1930s France. A substantial slice of early film history survived due to his efforts. He was, however, also an obsessive and the Cinématheque Française, which he established, was apparently a ramshackle Aladdin's Cave of early cinema. (He enjoys an interesting footnote in non-cinematic history. Early actions in Paris during 1968's political upheavals were demonstrations to prevent his sacking by the French Bureaucracy.)

Another hero for the movement was the Library of Congress member who lay down in front of the lorries removing early paper prints for destruction. The paper prints were deposited between 1895 and 1912 in the USA to register early film copyright. In many cases they are the only versions of the films that survive.

Silent film also suffered from other abuses. My own memories of early screenings were comedies, in poor quality copies, projected too fast and with an inane commentary over the top. My dislike of the late British comedian Bob Monkhouse stems from these travesties, many of which he 'narrated'. However, there was a renaissance for early film in the late 1970s and 1980s. A key figure was the British film historian Kevin Brownlow. His restoration of Abel Gance's *Napoleon* was a major event and sparked great interest at a historic screening in November 1980. In Britain the subsequent Thames Silents and Channel 4 screenings were a marvellous opportunity for discovery.

In 1982 the first of what became the now-famous Il Giornate del Cinema Muto was held in Pordenone. The Festival grew out of the Cineteca de Friuli, developed by Paolo and Livio Jacob. They had started collecting and preserving 16mm copies of silent film and in

1981 they received a collection of Max Linder films (from Buenos Aires) which provided the basis for the first festival screening. Apparently, the first festival was so select that all the participants dined at one large restaurant table. Now the annual festival hosts hundreds of archivists, collectors, academics and enthusiasts. Italy is also blessed with Il Cinema Ritrovato, held each summer in Bologna. This festival features archive prints of both silent and sound films. One of its distinctive features is the open-air screenings held in the city's main square after dark. Watching *Faust*, or *New Babylon* or *The Man Who Laughs* on a 50 foot screen, with a full orchestra, and several thousand spectators, is cinema par excellence.[1]

There have followed a whole cycle of festivals, screenings and exhibitions in the wake of Il Giornate del Cinema Muto. A team of skilled musicians has developed to provide accompaniments. New archives have opened and new technologies have been developed. It is worth pointing out, though, that there is still great difficulty in reproducing the visual qualities of nitrate film and early colour systems. At the present there is a lot of experimentation with digital technology, but it still has some way to go. The different ratios and film speeds of silent film also present a problem. Both on 35mm and on digital versions one can be faced with prints that are cropped top and bottom or on the sides of the frames. Speed offers even more difficulties. With the advent of sound the varying frames per second (fps) facility was not always available. Some early films were re-issued with step-printing, i.e. inserting extra frames so that the print could be projected at 24fps. The ratio was usually about an additional frame in every three. A variation on this practice using computer technology frequently continues when films are transferred to digital – for DVD, Blu-Ray or High Definition theatrical projection – and there does not seem to be a standard system for this.[2]

It has to be admitted that in the silent era projection speeds varied widely. However, certain film-makers, such as Sergei Eisenstein, were very precise about their work and how their films should be exhibited. Ivor Montagu recounts how, at the London Film Society screening of *Battleship Potemkin*, Meisel's score was the accompaniment. However, Meisel's music was composed for the German censored version and the Film Society screening enjoyed a print acquired from Moscow. It seems that Meisel arranged for the film speed to be varied to accommodate the difference. Eisenstein was very angry about this – *Potemkin* is the sort of film, with its exceptionally short shot lengths, where such a technique becomes noticeable.

The silent era has figured as a setting and plot line in popular sound films. The most famous and successful would be *Singin' in the Rain*, a humorous picture of a fictional Hollywood studio facing the disruption of the new sound technology. The problems of the company, the stars and the craft people are played at a comic level, the technical problems of the new sound system (the sound-on-disc format) exaggerated to provide laughs galore, and the basic idea of using the musical genre, a sound form, for this comedy is extremely effective.

Almost equally famous is Billy Wilder's *Sunset Blvd.* (1950) in which forgotten star Norma Desmond recalls the lost glories of her silent career. The ironies are forceful. Norma Desmond is played by one of the greatest stars of the silent form, Gloria Swanson. In her decaying mansion she is served by a one-time silent director, now her butler. This is Erich von Stroheim, and in a powerful scene Norma Desmond screens a forgotten masterpiece for her gigolo, William Holden. The film is *Queen Kelly*, an actual silent production that starred Swanson and was directed by von Stroheim. And Cecil B. DeMille, another of Swanson's directors, also makes an appearance. *Sunset Blvd.* is part of the *film noir* genre. Here the silent film world is the antithesis of the contemporary and high-key world of Hollywood. It has also become irrelevant, a contrast emphasised in the plot as Holden, a would-be scriptwriter, and his girlfriend are working on a contemporary script that aims to capture real-life.

Irma Vep (1996, directed by Olivier Assayas) depicts a fictional French film-maker attempting to remake *Les Vampires*: it is as much about contemporary French cinema as the earlier silent era, but it is great to see Maggie Cheung in the outfits and character of Musidora. Possibly the most fascinating revisiting to this period is Theo Angelopoulos' *To Vlemma Tou Odyssea* (*Ulysses' Gaze*, 1995). In this story a film-maker from the USA (Harvey Keitel) returns to Greece to track down three missing reels of the first film ever shot in the Balkans. The film is based on the records of the Manakia brothers from Macedonia: an area disputed by Bulgaria, Greece, Serbia and related to Turkey through the defunct Ottoman Empire. The brothers made films between 1905 and 1911. In Angelopoulos' film the search becomes a political exploration of the recent turmoil and conflicts in the area. *Good Morning Babylon* (1987) by Paolo and Vittorio Taviani tells the story of two Italian brothers who create the marvellous giant elephants for a famous scene in D. W. Griffith's *Intolerance*. And slightly bizarre and definitely creepy is *Shadow of a Vampire* (2000) E. Elias Merhige's fictional account of the filming of F. W. Murnau's *Nosferatu*, in which the titular blood-sucker is played by a real vampire.

Great silent cinema moments influence later film-makers, who frequently include *homage* to their predecessors. In Jean-Luc Godard's *Vivre sa vie* (1962) the main protagonist, Anna Karina, goes to watch a screening of Dreyer's *The Passion of Joan of Arc*. Variations on the Odessa Steps sequence from Eisenstein's *Battleship Potemkin* turn up in numerous settings and guises: the most fantastic is in Brian De Palma's *The Untouchables* (1987), where a shoot out at New York's Grand Central Station takes place around a pram and baby rolling down the staircase. Not so much homage as pastiche.

Biographies and recreations continue. 2011 saw one of the most ambitious, *The Artist*, directed by Michel Hazanavicius, which utilises the form of the silent film in black and white, the old style aspect ratio (1.37:1 rather than 1.33:1) with title cards and a musical accompaniment on the soundtrack. *The Artist* tells the tale of a Hollywood star in the late 1920s whose career suffers with the arrival of sound, while that of his protégé soars. The plot is reminiscent of earlier Hollywood recreations like *What Price Hollywood*

(1932) or *A Star is Born* (1937 and 1954) and includes innumerable references to silent films, film-makers and film stars, including Rudolph Valentino, Greta Garbo, John Gilbert and Douglas Fairbanks: the last providing the only actual silent clip in the film, from *The Mask of Zorro* (1920). The film emerged as the 'feel good' hit from the 2011 Cannes Film Festival and was a worldwide popular and critical success, culminating in winning seven Academy Awards, including Best Picture – the first silent film to do so since *Wings* in 1927. Beautifully crafted, it is nonetheless something of a pastiche (which it has in common with other Hazanavicius films), inevitably suffering in comparison with the originals. It remains to be seen whether or not the popular interest in early and silent cinema which its success has undoubtedly sparked can be sustained.

CASE STUDY: METROPOLIS – RESTORED (2010)

Universum-Film-Aktiengesellschaft (Ufa) studios, Germany, 1927. Black and white, 35mm, silent: length 4189 metres originally, the cut version was only 3170 metres. Filmed 1925-26, in 310 days and 60 nights, in UFA Studios, Berlin.

Cost: Approximately 5 million Deutschmarks.

Screenplay: Fritz Lang and Thea von Harbou, from the novel by von Harbou; photography: Karl Freund and Günther Rittau; art directors: Otto Hunte, Erich Kettelhut, and Karl Vollbrecht; original accompanying music: Gottfried Huppertz; special effects: Eugene Schüfftan; costume designer: Anne Willkomm; sculptures: Walter Schultze-Mittendorff.

Main cast: Brigitte Helm (Maria/the Mechanical Maria), Alfred Abel (John/John Fredersen, Gustav Fröhlich (Freder), Rudolf Klein-Rogge (Rotwang), Fritz Rasp (Slim), Theodor Loos (Josaphat/Joseph), Heinrich George (Grot, the foreman), Olaf Storm (Jan), Hanns Leo Reich (Marinus), Heinrich Gotho (Master of Ceremonies).

2010 restoration runs 4070 metres, 148 minutes at 24fps. Restoration: Friedrich-Wilhelm-Murnau Stiftung (Wiesbaden), jointly with Deutsche Kinemathek – Museum für Film und Fernsehen (Berlin), in co-operation with the Museo del Cine Pablo C. Ducros Hicken (Buenos Aires). Musical score by Gottfried Huppertz, reconstructed and synchronised by Frank Strobel.

This restoration uses a 16mm dupe (duplicate) negative copied from a worn 35mm nitrate print that was discovered in the Museo del Cine in Buenos Aires, Argentina which came to light in 2008. This contained 30 minutes of previously missing footage. An earlier restoration had been accomplished in 2001 using new High Definition digital techniques and the newly found footage has been incorporated with this.[3] The new material is not only of relatively poor quality, but because it is taken from the 16mm print, the aspect ratio differs from that in the 35mm print. This makes the new inserts very noticeable, though it also has the advantage that it is easy to see what has been added.[4]

Restoring an old film is a task equivalent to restoring some great Quattrocento fresco. There is the detective work to find celluloid originals or copies. There is both study and comparison of existing versions, and the technical work of tackling the ravages of use and time. Deciding on which particular print or sequence is the best or most accurate also involves investigation in printed and written sources: of the production company and personnel: of the censorship authorities, distributors and exhibitors and of critics and audience records. In the case of *Metropolis* reference was also made to the original score composed by Gottfried Huppertz, which accompanied the premiere screening of the first version of the film.

The original *Metropolis* was premiered at the Ufa-Palast Cinema am Zoo in Berlin on January 10, 1927. This version was 4,189 metres in length, but Ufa had already prepared a version for the US market, which was considerably reduced for the distributor Paramount, to 3,100 metres. When the German release proved unsuccessful Ufa used the US version as the basis for a shorter print of 3,241 metres. This became the surviving and generally seen version of the film. During subsequent decades a full-length *Metropolis* became one of the Holy Grails of archives and restorers. There have been several releases on film and on video which offer a 'longer *Metropolis*': one of these actually appeared to run the film at a slower speed to make it last longer! Now, with the material found in Argentina, we have an almost complete length *Metropolis* (two short scenes are still missing and are described in titles) and one which offers a fairly complete narrative.

The basic story of *Metropolis* is well known. In a future city there is a clear division between a rich and idle dominant class and an exploited working class who only labour and reproduce. The division is structured into the film with an upper city where the rich enjoy the fruits of the workers' labour, whilst the actual producers work and dwell in a subterranean city. The key protagonists include John Fredersen, the super capitalist and his son, Freder. Freder becomes entranced by a young woman from the underworld city, Maria. He ventures down into the world of the workers where he is shocked by the exploitation and the appalling working conditions. Maria is in fact preaching to the workers a different way of life, but a message of change rather than violent rebellion. She recounts the story of the Tower of Babel as an example where failure in communication bought destruction (although even in the film other conclusions can be drawn from the tale). However, Fredersen is concerned that the impact of Maria's message will damage his empire and has his pet scientist, Rotwang, construct a robot copy of Maria in order to mislead the workers. For reasons that are obscure in the shorter versions, Rotwang uses the robot both to incite rebellion among the workers and to stir up the idle young men of the dominant class. At the film's climax the workers destroy the machinery but the consequent flooding threatens their own world, which lies beneath the factories. Freder and the real Maria lead the workers' children to safety. The robot is destroyed and Freder rescues Maria from the clutches of Rotwang, who has kidnapped her for a second time. At the film's resolution Maria brings together the workers and Fredersen, the heart (Freder) to mediate (in the German mediator is *mittler*) between the head and the hand. One of the illuminations in the restoration is that we discover that both Fredersen and Rotwang loved the same woman, Hel, who became Freder's mother and then died in childbirth. So the robot actually provides an opportunity for revenge by Rotwang on Fredersen.

The release of the restoration generated much interest, partly fuelled by the drama of the discovery of the missing sequences, an international news story. Theatrical audiences for the release in a digital version were noticeably large and a host of critical and illustrative material in film journals and on the Web followed. Critical approaches include the historical, generic, auteurist, allegorical, psychoanalytical and feminist. The film contains elements for which all of these are relevant, yet it seems to me that the central focus is the conflict between capital and labour. Science fiction generally is about the social order and *Metropolis* addresses the fundamental aspect, the reproduction of life and society.

This conflict would seem to be most influenced by the context in which Fritz Lang and Thea von Harbou came to write and direct the film. There are traces of the influence of early science fiction, especially the work of H. G. Wells. While overtly a vision of the future the film also displays a line in German Gothic evident in German Expressionist films, especially those by Lang himself. More contemporaneous is the influence of the look of the new modern city: Lang himself cited 1920s New York as an inspiration. There are the modern techniques of production and manufacture, and contemporary ideas about future inventions: Fredersen uses a two-way visual communication system with his factory. And there are the subterranean tenements of the workers, which look similar to contemporary tenements presented in German 'street' films. The stark contrast between the capitalist class and the proletariat in the film reflected the most significant and most obvious social issue of the decade. It fuelled the rebellions and revolutions, including the failed revolution in Germany in 1919, which are paralleled by the uprising in the film. This also explains one aspect of the film that puzzles many critics. As the workers storm the factories, Fredersen orders the opening of the gates to the Heart Machine, which results in catastrophe below ground and a breakdown above. Tom Gunning compares the film to von Harbou's novel and notes that in the latter: 'John Fredersen declares it is his will the city must be destroyed so that Freder can build it up again and redeem its inhabitants' (1997: 77). This fits with the context of the times, a period when (as Marx explained) capitalism launched a destruction of the means of production so that it could re-invest and redevelop, launching a new cycle of the accumulation of capital. Germany had already experienced this; the wider world was to follow. The film's use of melodrama provides the resolution, both individually between Freder and Maria, and socially between the workers and the capitalist. Some critics find this pat and certainly reformist. Some also attribute a critical strand to Lang and a more reactionary strand to von Harbou (a division this writer finds simplistic).

One of the really interesting writers on *Metropolis* is Siegfried Kracauer. He carefully discusses the style of the film, including the visual organisation of the workers:

> If in this [final] scene the heart really triumphed over tyrannical power, its triumph would dispose of the all-devouring decorative scheme that in the rest of *Metropolis* marks the industrialist's claim to omnipotence. Artist that he was, Lang could not possibly overlook the antagonisms between the breakthrough of intrinsic human emotions and his ornamental patterns. Nevertheless, he maintains these patterns up to the very end: the workers advance in the form of the wedge-shaped strictly symmetrical procession, which points towards the industrialist standing on the portal steps of the cathedral. The whole composition denotes that the industrialist acknowledges the heart for the purpose of manipulating it… (2004: 164)

In this last scene the workers are once again in the formation in which the viewer first sees them at the opening. The dynamic and vital behaviour that characterised the assault on the instruments of exploitation has been tamed.

The film's ending also reinforces the values of the dominant class. Capital is characterised as the head or the intellect by Maria, labour as the hand or manual action. In the course of the film the workers have been shown as easily manipulated: first by Maria with her Gandhian pacifism; then by the robot with the calls to violence; finally by the overseer Grot. This ending also undermines the characterisation in the film of Maria, who has been a resolute and courageous advocate. Yet now she is all emotion and must be rescued by Freder who, until now, has hardly acted heroically; earlier he had fainting fits and suffered what appeared to be a psychosomatic illness.

The robot Maria introduces a disturbing ambiguity into the equation. It is persuasive and powerfully active. It is also exceedingly erotic, arousing the young elite males almost to a frenzy. Kim Newman thought that 'Brigitte Helm's birdlike, lascivious movements remain astonishing – a combination of Salome, Rosa Luxembourg, Madame Defarge and the Terminator' (*Sight & Sound* October 2010; the reference to Luxembourg seems almost libellous, but one gets the point). He notes the visual references to the Whore of Babylon. One also senses the parallels to the erotic nightlife of contemporary Berlin, as well as the misogyny to be found in the rising fascist movement. In that sense *Metropolis* is very much a film of its time. However, problematically, there is one important contemporary movement that is absent from the film – the organisations of the proletariat. The discourses on offer in the film for the working class are a pallid reformism, unfocused destruction or continued exploitation. In reality both within Germany and further afield there was a titanic struggle between classes, though only explicitly political films like those of the Soviets or the avant-garde movement addressed this directly.

Generically *Metropolis* was a key film in the development of cinematic science fiction. And technically it was a film which pointed to a future of amazing and jaw-dropping special effects. The film opens on the upper city of *Metropolis* and harnesses all the skills and ingenuity of Ufa's production stars. Eugene Schüfftan had developed a method of combining set and miniatures through ingenious mirror techniques. The art, production design and costumes were of the highest standard anywhere in the world industry of that time. And Ufa's giant Neubabelsberg and Staaken studios provided the space and technical expertise to create the vast and impressive sets. This imaginative expertise is most visible in the climatic catastrophe that strikes the city. Gigantic sets are the site for an avalanche of special effects, while the dramas and traumas of the human actors caught within steadily rises to a crescendo (or indeed several). The German expertise in lighting also contributed. There are scenes of chiaroscuro in the catacombs where the workers meet secretly, and in the final night-time conflagration. There are frequent dissolves and superimpositions, again most notably so in the climax. The one technical development made in German film that is not extensively on show is the 'unchained' or moving camera, presumably partly because of the complexity of the many special effects. In many ways, including its imagination and hubris, *Metropolis* was the *2001* (1968) of its day and it continues to exert both a fascination and powerful influence in the twenty-first century.

FOOTNOTES

1. There is more detail on the history of Pordenone in Michael Walker's review of *Il Giornate* in *Movie*, available online.

2. In November 2012 the FIAF published *Digital Projection for Archival Cinemas* by Torkell SÆtervadet, which provides a guide through the emerging D-cinema. The volume includes specifications for frame rates between 16 and 22 fps. This will remove the need for step-printing DCP versions. It does require upgrading of projectors, either of the software or additional hardware depending on the model. It remains to be seen how quickly upgrades will occur, and how quickly films are transferred at the correct fps.

3. http://www.alpha-omega.de/doku.php?id=en:showroom:metropolis has an article describing the digital restoration for the 2001 version.

4. http://www.kino.com/metropolis/restoration.html includes a listing of the additional scenes.

BIBLIOGRAPHY AND RESOURCES

BIBLIOGRAPHY

Abel, Richard (1984). *French Cinema The First Wave 1915–1929*: Princeton University Press. Deals clearly and in detail with French film and the industry, 'a monumental work of scholarship' (Film Quarterly).

Altman, Rick (2004). *Silent Film Sound*: Columbia University Press.
A detailed study of the sounds that accompanied early films and an innovative study of how musical accompaniment developed.

Balio, Tino (1976). *The American Film Industry*: University of Wisconsin.
Parts 1 and 2 include an overview of developments in the USA film industry, and detailed academic articles and recollections like those of Norma Talmadge.

Barr, Charles (1999). *English Hitchcock*: Cameron & Hollis.
The book offers a detailed account of Hitchcock's career in the British industry, including all the surviving films. There are also comments on other important filmmakers such as Eliot Stannard.

Bergan, Ronald (1997). *Sergei Eisenstein A Life in Conflict*: Warner Books.
Well researched and readable biography.

Bondanella, Peter (ed.) (2014). *The Italian Cinema Book*: BFI/Palgrave.
Part One Deals with 'The Silent Era' and includes articles on genres and divas.

Bordwell, David (1993). *The Cinema of Eisenstein*: Havard University Press.
A detailed discussion of the career, the films and the theory of Eisenstein. Given some of the Inevitable complexities, this is fairly accessible.

Bordwell, David & Thompson, Kristin (1996). *Film Art An Introduction*: McGraw-Hill.
Probably the key book on film style. There are studies of a number of silent films, including *Our Hospitality*, *Ballet mécanique*, *Man With a Movie Camera* and numerous illustrations from other silent films. The selection of films changes with new editions, but the choice of silent examples has stayed fairly consistent.

Bowser, Pearl et al (2001). *Oscar Micheaux and His Circle*: Indiana University Press. Includes the Jane Gaines article 'Within Our Gates: From Race Melodrama to Opportunity Narrative'.

Brownlow, Kevin (1968). *The Parade's Gone By*: Abacus.
A pioneering book on early Hollywood, it includes extensive extracts from interviews made by Brownlow with Hollywood veterans of the silent era. There was also a BBC Radio 4 programme with the same title, including Brownlow and extracts from the interviews, broadcast in 2005.

Brownlow, Kevin (1990). *Behind the Mask of Innocence – Films of Social Conscience in the Silent Era*: Jonathan Cape.
Deals with sex, violence, prejudice, crime.

Buñuel, Luis (trans. Abigail Israel) (1983). *My Last Breath*: Flamingo.
Jean-Claude Carrière, who helped Buñuel write this autobiography, noted that the English edition has been edited from the French original, but did not specify what was missing.

Chabria, Suresh (ed.) (1994). *Light of Asia Indian Silent Cinema 1912–1934*: Le Giornate del Cinema Muto and National Film Archive of India.
Articles on, and a filmography of, Indian films from the silent era.

Chanan, Michael (1980). *The Dream that Kicks. The Prehistory and Early Years of Cinema in Britain*: Routledge, Kegan & Paul.
A materialist study of earthly cinema and its roots.

DeMille, Cecil (1960). *The Autobiography of Cecil B DeMille*: W H. Allen.

Dickinson, Margaret & Street, Sarah (1985). *Cinema and State The Film Industry and the British Government 1927–48*: BFI.
Despite the title the book has quite an amount of information on UK cinema before the 1927 Act.

Finler, Joel (1988). *The Hollywood Story*: Octopus Books.
Detailed study of Hollywood and the major studios, illustrated with a wealth of graphs and illustrations. Revised in 2003, published by Wallflower Press.

Finler, Joel (1992). *The Hollywood Story*: Mandarin.
A paperback version of *The Hollywood Story*, without illustrations.

Gevinson, Alan (ed.) (1997). *Within Our Gates: Ethnicity in American Feature Films, 1911–1960*: American Film Institute Catalog, University of Berkeley.
One in a series of catalogues by the AFI, this volume has very good production information and background information on films that deal with ethnicity and race.

Gifford, Denis (1991). *Books and Plays in Films 1896 to 1915*: Mansell.
Useful for checking out authors and titles. There does not appear to be an equivalent volume for later silents, however.

Grainge, Mark, Jancovich, Mark & Monteith, Sharon (eds) (2007). *Film Histories An Introduction and Reader*: Edinburgh University Press.
A compendium of mainly extracts from published articles, each section has an introduction detailing the context. The first 150 pages or so discuss the early and silent eras of cinema.

Grieveson, Lee & Krämer, Peter (eds) (2004). *The Silent Cinema Reader*: Routledge.
A compendium of mainly previously published articles on the silent era, it includes works by David Bordwell, Tom Gunning and Kristin Thompson among others. The book's prime

focus in the USA, with only the final section discussing European cinema.

Griffithiana 59 (1997). *Journal of Film History*.
There is a lengthy critique and a shot-by-shot description of *A Corner in Wheat* by Helmut Färber.

Griffithiana 60/61 (1997). *Journal of Film History*.
Extended articles on D. W. Griffith and Oscar Micheaux, plus an article on the UK director Maurice Elvey.

Gunning, Tom (1995). 'An Aesthetic of Astonishment: Early Film and the (In)Credulous Spectator', in *Viewing Positions*, edited by Linda Williams: Rutgers.

Hogenkamp, Bert (1986). *Deadly Parallels Film and the Left in Britain 1929–1939*: Oxford University Press.
Covers an under-researched area.

Kirby, Lynne (1997). *Parallel Tracks The Railroad and Silent Cinema*: University of Essex Press.
A fascinating study of how railways influenced silent cinema and became an important motif in early film.

Kremeier, Klaus (trans. Robert & Rita Kimber) (1999). *The UFA Story. A History of Germany's Greatest Film Company, 1918–1945*: University of California Press.
Covers the most successful and influential period of German silent cinema.

Low, Rachael (1948). *The History of the British Film*: George & Allen.
There are four volumes dealing with British silent film. The first volume was co-authored with Roger Manvell.

Lucia, Cynthia, Grundman, Roy, & Simon, Art (eds) (2012). *The Wiley-Blackwell History of American Film*: Wiley-Blackwell.
Volume 1 ('*Origins to 1928*') of this 4-volume work deals with the silent era. The best essays are informative and stimulating.

McKernan, Luke (1992). *Topical Budget*: BFI.
The history of this British newsreel company. There is an accompanying VHS video with extended extracts from newsreel issues.

Mahar, Karen Ward (2006). *Women Filmmakers in Early Hollywood*: John Hopkins University Press.
A study of the female film-makers and their declining presence in the film capital, including director Lois Weber and star/producer Mary Pickford.

Nelmes, Jill (ed.) (1996). *An Introduction to Film Studies*: Routledge.
A second edition in 1999 retained the sections on Documentary and Soviet Montage.

Popple, Simon & Kember, Joe (2004). *Early Cinema From Factory Gate to Dream Factory*: Wallflower.

Explores the period from 1895–1914 in both Europe and the USA.

Robertson, James C. (1989). *The Hidden Cinema British Film Censorship in Action, 1913–1975*: Routledge.

Robertson, James, C. (1985). *The British Board of Film Censors. Film Censorship in Britain, 1896–1950*: Croom Helm (out of print).

Robinson, David (1973). *Buster Keaton*: Secker and Warburg/BFI (Cinema One series). Robinson includes a brief biography but the bulk of the book is devoted to a discussion of all the Keaton shorts and feature films.

Robinson, David (1989). *Chaplin, His Life and Art*: Paladin.
The most extensive of the several books by David Robinson on Chaplin.

Ross, Stephen J. (1998). *Working-Class Hollywood*: Princeton University Press.
A study of labour films including those (often lost) produced by the US Labour movement.

Rotha, Paul (1967). *The Film Till Now, A Survey of World Cinema*: Spring Books.
Originally published in 1930 this is an impressive survey, though the terms of criticism have changed considerably since publication.

Salt, Barry (1983). *Film Style & Technology: History & Analysis*: Starword.
Detailed and systematic study of techniques and style in early film. It also has a theoretical chapter, which is much harder going.

Simon, Joan (ed.) (2010). *Alice Guy Blaché Cinema Pioneer.* Yale University Press.
A number of essays on this important pioneer.

Simmon, Scot (1993). *The Films of D. W. Griffith*: Cambridge Film Classics.
Simmon was a Curator at the Library of Congress and curated the *More Treasures of the American Film Archives* collections. He discusses a number of the one-reel films made at Biograph, including *A Corner in Wheat*, also *The Birth of a Nation* and *Intolerance*. The book's merits are detailed analyses of the films together with an intelligent grasp of their context.

Sklar, Robert (1993). *Film An International History*: Thames and Hudson.
Detailed and well illustrated.

Thompson, Kristin & Bordwell, David (1994). *Film History An Introduction*: McGraw-Hill.
Detailed, informative and impressively comprehensive.

Toulmin, Vanessa, Russell, Patrick, & Popple, Simon (eds) (2004). *The Lost World of Mitchell & Kenyon*: BFI.
A series of essays on an important collection of early British film only rediscovered in 1995.

Usai, Paolo Cherchi (as General Editor) (1996 to 2006). *The Griffith Project*: BFI.
Ten volumes covering all the films of D. W. Griffith. Published annually by the BFI to

accompany a complete retrospective of the Griffith films curated by the Pordenone Film Festival.

Vidor, King (1981). *A Tree is a Tree – An Autobiography*: Samuel French.
Vidor details his career and his films.

Withall, Keith (1999). *The Eisenstein Study Pack*: In the Picture.
Profile of Eisenstein's complete career and filmography.

Withall, Keith (2000). *The Battleship Potemkin*: York Film Notes.
A study guide.

RESOURCES – FEATURE FILMS

American Treasures from the New Zealand Archive 1914–1929
Includes John Ford's *Upstream* (1927) and the surviving parts of the British *White Shadows* (1924) on which Alfred Hitchcock worked with director Graham Cutts. National Film Preservation Foundation, NTSC Region 0.

Cinema Europe: The Other Hollywood
A six part series on European silent cinema by Photoplay Productions originally broadcast on BBC2. Available on a Region 1 DVD, NTSC format, from Image Entertainment.

Comic Actresses and Suffragettes 1910–1914
Edited by Marianne Lewinsky from a selection of films screened at Il Cinema Ritrovato. Includes English subtitles and a detailed bi-lingual booklet. Region 2 DVD, Cineteca Bologna.

European Cinema in 1909
Edited by Marina Lewinsky from the screenings at Il Cinema Ritrovato with English subtitles and a detailed bi-lingual booklet. Region 2 DVD, Cineteca Bologna. Intended subsequent DVDs cover will cover 1910–1914.

Hollywood
Photoplay Productions, 1980 for Thames Television. A pioneering series in 12 episodes by Kevin Brownlow and David Gill. There are many extracts from silent films, well restored and presented. There are also innumerable interviews with people from the silent film industry. An accompanying book, *Hollywood The Pioneers* (Collins 1979), was lavishly illustrated.

Holmfirth Hollywood
Sixty minutes, broadcast on BBC4 in June 2006. A profile of Bamforths of Holmfirth with a look at their films and their business between 1899 and 1915. The firm was a key family business in the early stages of the development of UK cinema. The programme includes complete short films and extracts from longer productions, expert opinion and

dramatised re-enactment of the period. The films are shown in good viewing copies, however, they are not that carefully presented – most are in a modern aspect ratio of 16:9 rather than the correct ratio of 1.33:1. The dramatisations are rather careless of the actual contemporary context. The expert opinions are informative, although there is a tendency for the commentary to over-hype the import of the firm.

Paul Merton's Silent Clowns

Four programmes, 60 minutes each, broadcast on BBC4 in June 2006. Merton offers profiles of the greatest Hollywood comics of the silent era: Charlie Chaplin, Buster Keaton, Harold Lloyd and Laurel and Hardy. The programmes include a road show by Merton with live audiences and screenings. The prints are restored, in good condition with correct aspect ratios and running times. Also, they have live musical accompaniment by Neil Brand. Merton interviews a series of experts and discusses stunt work, prints and restoration, and music both improvised and composed. Each programme features one complete title by the comic: Chaplin – *Easy Street* (1917); Keaton – *The Goat* (1921); Lloyd – *Never Weaken* (1921); Laurel and Hardy – *You're Darn Tootin'* (1928). An accompanying book, *Silent Comedy* (Merton, Random House) was published in 2007.

The People's Century

BBC2, 1995. The series reviewed the twentieth century through a combination of themes and chronology. *The Great Escape* episode dealt with cinema, from 1895 to the mid-1950s.

Screening the Poor 1888–1914

A two disc collection of European films dealing with the poor and working people. It includes examples of Magic Lantern slide sets and the same stories in early film. Bi-lingual booklet and subtitles for films from three German archives. Region 2, Doppel-DVD.

Silent Britain

Sixty minutes, broadcast on BBC4 in May 2006. An overview of UK silent cinema from pre-cinema until the arrival of sound. The early period, 1880s to World War I is well done. There are a variety of early short films, including the pioneer Louis Le Prince and the Brighton film-makers G. A. Smith and J. Williamson. The programme uses film historians to highlight the technical and innovatory aspect of their films and there is a brief but clear overview of the industry. The post-war scene is more generalised, focusing on key films and film stars, with less sense of the industry context. There is a clear intent to revise the often disparaging view of early UK film. However, there is a tendency to over emphasise some of those achievements, but the amount of illustrative material alone makes this an extremely useful resource. Now available on Region 2 DVD, BFI.

Treasures from American Film Archives

Three disc set from the National Film Preservation Foundation containing fifty films, both shorts and features from as early as 1894. Includes musical accompaniments to silent prints, and commentaries and contextual Information. NTSC format, available in Region 1 and 2 DVD. See also *More Treasures from American Film Archives 1894-193*, another three disc set containing fifty films plus six trailers, with musical accompaniments, commentaries and background information. NTSC format, available in Region 1 and 2 DVD.

Treasures of the West 1898–1938
Forty films, with accompaniments and a detailed booklet by Scott Simmon. The most famous feature is *Mantrap* (1926) starring Clara Bow. National Film Preservation Foundation, NTSC format, available in Region 1 and 2 DVD.

The Unknown Chaplin
Produced by Photoplay for Thames Television, 1983. Kevin Brownlow and David Gill use Chaplin's own archive to illustrate his work and practice. Chaplin shot scenes many times untill he was completely satisfied. He also retained all the outtakes, creating an impressive archive. Available on DVD and VHS Video, both NTSC.

Unseen Cinema: Early American Avant-Garde Film 1893-1941
It is rather difficult to give a clear impression of this vast collection. The discs include *The Mechanized Eye, American Surrealism, Light Rhythms, Inverting Narrative, Picturing a Metropolis, The Amateur as Auteur, Viva La Dance*. One key film in the collection is D. W. Griffith's *The House with Closed Shutters* (1912). Seven discs, NTSC format from Image Entertainment.

RESOURCES – FEATURE FILMS, INCLUDING ONE- AND TWO-REELERS

Alberta Capellani, A Cinema of Grandeur 1905–1911
Edited by Marina Lewinsky from the programme at Il Cinema Ritrovato. English sub-titles and a detailed bi-lingual booklet. Includes *L'Arlésienne* (1909). Region 2 DVD, Cineteca Bologna.

Asta Neilsen
Danish Film Institute, with subtitles. Includes *Afgrunden/The Abyss* (Denmark, 1910); *Balletdanserinden/The Ballet Dancer* (Denmark, 1911); *Den Sorte Dröm/The Black Dream* (Denmark, 1911); *Mod Lyset/Towards the Light* (Denmark, 1919). DVD Region 0.

The Birth of a Nation (Griffith, 1915)
Eureka Region 2 DVD. Eureka also have Griffith's *Intolerance* (1916) and *Way Down East* (1920). Image Video offers *Orphans of the Storm* (1921) Region 0 NTSC Video.

Cottage on Dartmoor (Asquith 1929)
Region 2 DVD, BFI. Asquith's next feature, *Underground* (1928) is also now available via BFI DVD.

The Crowd (Vidor, 1928)
Available on Warner Home Video NTSC VHS Video.

Dickens Before Sound
Two discs containing adaptations from Dickens made between 1880–1929 including
an example of a pre-cinematic Magic Lantern Show, extracts from a feature length UK
production of *David Copperfield* (1913), and a First National feature length *Oliver Twist*
starring Jackie Coogan and Lon Chaney. Region 2 DVD, BFI.

Faces of Children/Visages d'enfant (Feyder, 1925)
With English subtitles, Region 2 DVD, DCult.

Flesh and the Devil (Brown, 1926) Clarence Brown.
M-G-M Region 2 DVD.

The Kid (Chaplin, 1921)
The series of reissues also includes Chaplin's *Gold Rush*, *The Circus*, *City Lights* and *Modern
Times*. Region 2 DVD, Mk2. The BFI also has several DVDs that feature one and two reel
films by Chaplin.

The Last Laugh (Murnau, 1924)
English subtitles, Region 2 DVD, Eureka. There is also *Faust* (1926), which includes
both the domestic German and export versions; and *Nosferatu* (1922). The latter has
occasioned some debate about the version on offer.

Ma L'amor mio non muore/Love Everlasting (Italy, 1913)
A fine example of an early 'diva' film starring Lyda Borelli, With English subtitles, Region 2
DVD, Cineteca Bologna.

Mad Love – Three Films by Yevgeni Bauer (*Twilight of a Woman's Soul*, 1913; *After Death*,
1915; *The Dying Swan*, 1917)
English commentary, English subtitles, Region 2 DVD, BFI.

Our Hospitality (Keaton, 1923) and *Sherlock Jr.* (Keaton, 1924)
Region 0 NTSC DVD, Kino. Eureka also has *The General* (1927), *College* (1927) and
Steamboat Bill, Jr. (1928), all directed by Buster Keaton, on Region 2 DVDs.

Metropolis (Lang, 1926)
The new restoration, with English subtitles, accompanying material and a booklet of
background. Two discs, Region 2 DVD, Eureka / Masters of Cinema.

R W Paul – The collected films 1895–1908
The films of one of the most important British pioneers. There is a commentary by Ian
Christie, a noted historian of early film, and a musical accompaniment. Region 2 DVD, BFI.

Silent Shakespeare
With *King John* (1899), *The Tempest* (1908), *King Lear* (1909), *A Midsummer Night's Dream*
(1909), *Twelfth Night* (1908), *The Merchant of Venice* (1910) and *Richard III* (1911). Region
2 DVD, BFI.

Strike/Stacha (Eisenstein, 1925)
With English subtitles, Region 2 DVD, Eureka. Also available from Eureka are Eisenstein's *October* (1928), Pudovkin's *The End of St Petersburg* (1927) and *Storm over Asia* (1928).

USEFUL WEBSITES

A Cinema Apart: http://www.acinemaapart
Details on Afro-American or 'race' films.

Barry Salt at: www.cinemetrics.lv/salt.php.
This is an extract from his book that explains some of his working methods and gives an idea of his approach.

Bioscope Blog: http://thebioscope.net
An archive of articles and information on early cinema.

British Film Institute: www.bfi.org.uk.
Has a wide range of information. DVDs and videos are shown at http://www.bfi.org/uk/booksvideo/. The BFI Southbank in London offers film programmes, houses the Library and the new Mediateque, which features an extensive video archive of UK film, including silents.

Cinema Museum: http://www.cinemamuseum.org.uk
A London-based archive, with a collection of early materials and regular events including screenings.

Il Cinema Ritrovato: http://www.cinetecadibologna.it/cinemaritrovato2009/ev/intro
Material on the Festival, films, publications and their annual DVD awards.

Kino Video: http://www.kino.com
A number of early films on DVD NTSC but also Region 0, usually with musical accompaniment.

Le Giornate del Cinema Muto: http://www.cinetecadelfriuli.org/gcm/
Material on the Festival, films and publications.

Masters of Cinema: http://eurekavideo.co.uk/moc/
An extensive catalogue of DVDs and Blu-rays of early films with frequent new releases.

National Film Preservation Foundation: http://www.filmpreservation.org/
The source for the *Treasures* series and other resources.

National Media Museum: http://www.nationalmediamuseum.org.uk
Information on the Museum (based in Bradford, UK) collections, including archive material in the |Insight Collection, also pages explaining some of the key artefacts. The Museum now also has a viewing room for the BFI Mediateque.

Photoplay Productions: http://www.silentera.com/people/archivists/PhotoplayProd.html
Details of the numerous documentaries on early cinema. Also listings of key early films with links to sites where copies can be obtained.

Silent London: http://silentlondon.co.uk/
A metropolitan site with news, events and comment.

INDEX

#0007 - 180918 - C0 - 234/156/10 - PB - 9781906733698